# The Art of Access

# The Art of Access
## Strategies for Acquiring
## Public Records

David Cuillier
*University of Arizona*

Charles N. Davis
*University of Missouri–Columbia*

CQ PRESS

A Division of SAGE
Washington, D.C.

CQ Press
2300 N Street, NW, Suite 800
Washington, DC 20037

Phone: 202-729-1900; toll-free, 1-866-4CQ-PRESS (1-866-427-7737)

Web: www.cqpress.com

Cover design: Jeffrey Everett/El Jefe Design
Cover image: Getty Images
Typesetting: C&M Digitals (P) Ltd.

♾ The paper used in this publication exceeds the requirements of the American National Standard for Information Sciences—Permanence of Paper for Printed Library Materials, ANSI Z39.48-1992.

Printed and bound in the United States of America

14  13  12  11  10     1  2  3  4  5

**Library of Congress Cataloging-in-Publication Data**

Cuillier, David.
The Art of access : strategies for acquiring public records / David Cuillier, Charles N. Davis.
    p. cm.
  Includes bibliographical references and index.
  Includes a webliography.
  ISBN 978-1-60426-550-7 (pbk. : alk. paper) 1. Investigative reporting—Handbooks, manuals, etc. 2. Public records—United States—Handbooks, manuals, etc. I. Davis, Charles N. II. Title.

PN4781.C95 2011
070.4'3—dc22                                                2009050311

*This book is dedicated to the citizens, journalists and government officials who improve their communities by fighting the darkness of secrecy with the tools of transparency.*

# About the Authors

**David Cuillier,** Ph.D., is chairman of the Society of Professional Journalists' national Freedom of Information Committee and is a newsroom FOI trainer for the national SPJ on-the-go newsroom training program. He gathered public records as a government reporter and city editor for a dozen years at daily newspapers in the Pacific Northwest. He is an assistant professor of journalism at the University of Arizona, teaching computer-assisted reporting, public affairs reporting and access to information. He has earned national honors for his access teaching exercises and research in freedom of information, including the 2007 Nafziger-White Dissertation Award by the Association for Education in Journalism and Mass Communication for the top dissertation in the field.

**Charles N. Davis,** Ph.D., is executive director of the National Freedom of Information Coalition, former chairman of the Society of Professional Journalists' national Freedom of Information Committee and an SPJ newsroom trainer in FOI. A former newspaper reporter and national correspondent for Dublin-based Lafferty Publications, Davis currently teaches access to information and media law at the University of Missouri–Columbia. He has been honored by SPJ with a Sunshine Award for his work in FOI, and in 2009 he was named the Scripps Howard Foundation National Journalism Teacher of the Year. In 2009–2010 he was head of the Law and Policy Division of the Association for Education in Journalism and Mass Communication. He has been published extensively in academic and professional journals and is first author of the book *Access Denied: Freedom of Information in the Information Age.*

# Contents

# A Humble Foreword
## by Tom Blanton

Governments have created records and used them to run their citizens' lives for at least three or four millennia now, judging by the chicken scratches on the cuneiform clay tablets dug up by archaeologists at sites like Mari, on the border between modern Syria and Iraq. And over millennia, citizens have agitated for and ultimately won an extraordinary shift in the power over those records. No Babylonian except one selected by the king could see the tablets recording kingly actions. But every citizen of the modern world has a fundamental human right, according to the Universal Declaration of 1948, for the free exchange of information; and every citizen of the United States, according to the Freedom of Information Act of 1966 (amended multiple times since), has an ownership stake in all the information the government holds.

In the course of human events, this change is revolutionary. King Louis XIV said famously, "L'état, c'est moi" ("The state, it is I"). A modern physician would call this the bureaucratic disease; officials believe they own whatever information exists in government files. But freedom of information laws—first in Sweden and Finland in 1766 and since then sweeping the world—reverse the equation. The government is only the custodian; we the citizens own the information. The problem is: How do we take back what officialdom usurps? How do we fight the natural tendency of every bureaucracy to hoard its information, control its turf, set the frames of its policy debate and limit all access to its files?

This book answers those fundamental questions. The authors, David Cuillier and Charles N. Davis, are the dalai lamas of open government.

They bow before the reader, and with humor in their eyes explain in direct and exhortatory prose—written both for journalists and citizens—how to understand what information government creates and then how to go after it; how to get it; how to leverage the psychology of officials; and what to do with that information to make news, empower citizens and change the world. This is a tall order, fulfilled here to the max.

I filed my first Freedom of Information Act (FOIA) request in 1976, the bicentennial year, when I was a cub reporter for a weekly newspaper in Minnesota, and I really wish that I had had a copy of this book next to my typewriter before I let loose with that letter. Some bureaucrats may still be mad at me, in their retirement. I got a nice story out of that first request; it even ran in a New York–based national magazine, making a great clip for job interviews. But if I'd had all the expert advice that the authors walk us through in this lively and incisive text, I would have gotten a dozen stories, probably an award or two, and a much earlier appreciation of what has become my permanent condition: the Cuillier-Davis proverbial "document state of mind."

My little nonprofit center has filed about 40,000 FOIA requests in the years since 1985, and I can testify that this book would have added value to each and every one of those requests. Let me tell you about one for starters. Some years back, we heard that there was one particular document at the National Archives of the United States that more visitors asked for a copy of than any other. We thought: Sure, the Gettysburg Address?

No.

The original Declaration of Independence?

No.

How about a copy of the actual signed Constitution?

No.

OK, maybe more modern: JFK's inaugural, "Ask not what your country can do for you"?

Nope.

The one particular record that visitors asked for more than any other was the iconic photograph of Elvis Presley meeting with President Richard Nixon in the White House in December 1970. Remember, this was when Elvis was still alive, and before the *National*

*Enquirer* announced such sightings at every supermarket cash register. But after the barbiturate overdose, more visitors to the National Archives went away with copies of the Nixon-Elvis photo than any other artifact of our nation's history.

So, in our "document state of mind," we thought: If the president meets with anybody, there's a trail. Let's ask for all the records, in any media, related in whole or in part to the Nixon-Elvis meeting. Lo and behold, a few months later, a whole file emerged from the National Archives.

The most fun item was the handwritten letter from Elvis to Nixon on American Airlines stationery, citing his selection as an outstanding young man of America (Nixon had been one too) and asking for honorary credentials as a federal narc. (Seriously.)

Then there was the internal White House memo from the appointments secretary to the chief of staff, telling him that Elvis had showed up at the White House gate asking for a meeting with the president (let's you and me try that one) and arguing that if Nixon wanted to meet some bright young people, Elvis would be a good place to start. Out to the side, the chief, H. R. Haldeman of future Watergate fame, scribbled, "You must be kidding," but approved the drop-in!

The file had talking points for the president, encouraging Elvis to produce a TV special for the war on drugs (suggested theme: "Get high on life"); notes from the secretaries about what to do with the autographed Elvis photos he had left behind; and, best of all, the contact sheet from the White House photographer with all the shots of Nixon and shut-eyed, bleary-eyed, hung-over Elvis, with the final frame of Nixon admiring the King's rhinestone cufflinks.

After millions of downloads, this little package of documents has won us every Web award in the book, from Yahoo to CoolSiteoftheDay.com to the BBC to *Forbes* magazine's Best of the Web. The only challenger for most-downloaded document on our site is the transcript and video of Donald Rumsfeld chatting with Saddam Hussein in December 1983, telling him no problem with the chemical warfare as long as he whacks Iran. We got this one from FOIA requesting as well. And patience. And from following one of this book's core recommendations: learning to understand how officials think. Plus persistence, the most crucial element of that "document state of mind."

The bottom line is what Yosemite Sam pronounced in those ancient Warner Brothers cartoons: "There's gold in them thar hills!" This book is the ultimate prospector's kit. It will show you how to narrow down the targets, how to get your pan in the right stream, how to recognize gold flecks from mica and how to burrow right up into the main vein. You'll get richer, no doubt; but you'll also make our democracy richer, more robust and more righteous along the way. More power to you!

*Tom Blanton is director of the National Security Archive, an independent, nongovernmental research institute based at The George Washington University in Washington, D.C., that collects declassified government documents and posts them at www.nsarchive.org.*

# Preface

This is a book about freedom of information, yet it's about much more than that.

It's about gaining access to the records that good reporters need to break news and that citizens need to know what their government is doing. It's about how everyone, not just journalists, can find and use the information that will improve lives.

Public records, in addition to people sources and firsthand observation, are essential for good journalism. Documents provide the foundation for reporting that changes the world, and they keep government accountable.

But it isn't so easy getting public records sometimes, is it? It can seem impossible to get a simple police report or school budget, let alone an FBI record. That's why we wrote this book. We see the process of acquiring records like winding through a maze—turning corners, running into roadblocks, backing up and trying other avenues, until finally reaching the end and getting what you need. More than ever before, people need to be skilled in navigating that maze through the art of access.

Shrinking newsroom budgets are stretching journalists thin, making reporters more reliant on press releases and spoon-fed information. Government documents lend authority to stories, are verifiable and capture today's events for tomorrow's historians. Unlike officials, records don't spin.

Government secrecy has ballooned. Federal record request backlogs leave some people waiting nearly 20 years for their documents.[1]

Nationwide, police agencies, on average, illegally deny valid public records requests three-quarters of the time.[2] Requesters might think they have little recourse other than to sue. Or do they?

We believe that litigation is important, but we also understand that journalists and citizens don't have the time and often don't have the money to wait for a lawsuit to work its way through the courts. We believe requesters can overcome secrecy through a little ingenuity, strategy and understanding of human behavior.

This book is a user's guide to making freedom of information (FOI) work for you, to working cooperatively with government officials and using your reporting skills to pry records loose from officials who are uncooperative. To do that, journalists and citizens must rethink the information-gathering process and develop a document state of mind.

They must become students of the art of access.

## Our obsession with FOI

We too are students of the art of access.

Our journey in FOI began as high school journalism students, one in Washington state and the other in Georgia, and continued through college and then on the job as newspaper reporters, requesting records for covering city hall, schools, state government, federal agencies, businesses and other beats. When we got denied, we got mad. Sometimes too mad, sometimes not mad enough, but we learned along the way and we usually got the records.

Now, as journalism professors, we teach college courses on access to government information and on reporting and media law. Our teaching exercises are included in this book, as well as the best FOI teaching activities we could find in the field.

Our research focuses on freedom of information, including legal analysis of FOI laws, public opinion surveys, studies examining the state of access and experiments in psychological access strategies. Much of our own original research has been integrated into this book, such as experiments testing the effectiveness of differently worded request letters.

We also have pulled from our learning experiences as national advocates for FOI. Cuillier serves as chair of the Society of Professional Journalists' (SPJ) Freedom of Information Committee, and Davis is executive director of the National Freedom of Information Coalition (and a former SPJ FOI Committee chair). We are both FOI trainers for the SPJ newsroom training program, and we routinely speak to groups about access, sometimes on other continents.

We learn every day. We might get a call from a reporter trying to get a police report or a school superintendent contract. We hear new reasons for denials, and new ways of overcoming those denials. We watch students in our college courses fear the prospect of going to their city hall to ask for documents. We see citizens crying out for help when bureaucrats stonewall. These people are hungry for knowledge and skills.

After our training sessions we see the relief on their faces and the determination in their eyes. The word they consistently use to describe their feelings is "empowered." That is why we wrote this book. Knowledge is liberating. Requesters who practice the art of access and who develop a document state of mind feel empowered; and, ultimately, they get what they need.

## Who should buy this book?

We *know* this book will improve your career and life.

We know it because information is valuable for everyone: journalists, journalism students, bloggers, genealogists, private investigators, nonprofit managers and, for that matter, your parents, children and neighbors, and their parents and children.

*The Art of Access* will help journalism students taking classes in media writing, news reporting, investigative reporting, computer-assisted reporting and media law. This is the kind of nuts-and-bolts guide that works well in any skills course, or as a supplement to theory and legal analysis in a seminar or media law course.

We also think the chapters on psychological strategies and document ideas will be useful to seasoned professional journalists as a valuable desk guide in any newsroom cubicle. Newsroom trainers can schedule a year's worth of brown-bag lunches based on this book. Many of the tips and strategies we offer are the same lessons we incorporate in our professional newsroom training programs for SPJ. We have found that just about everyone walks away with something useful that they can apply to their jobs.

While the book was written primarily for journalists, including citizen journalists and bloggers interested in adding documents to their reports, we think nonjournalists also might benefit, such as private investigators, nonprofit directors, grant writers, business data analysts and contractors. And we hope citizens active in their communities will use the book to acquire documents about their neighborhoods. Everyone can use these skills for their personal lives.

## Organization

The chapters in *The Art of Access* walk the requester through the process of accessing records, step by step, from getting into the right document state of mind to the final step of publishing a newspaper story, newscast or Webcast.

We first focus on why accessing records is important, including the benefits that come from documents and their importance to society.

Then we get to the nitty-gritty of the request process, starting with how to teach yourself the law, how to find records, how to effectively request them and then how to overcome denials. This is the heart of the book, as it focuses on practical strategies and techniques proven through personal experience, interviews with experts and our own research.

Because so much government information is now computerized and kept in databases, we provided a chapter focusing on the specific issues of finding, acquiring and transferring government data. Cuillier obtained and analyzed government databases as a journalist and now teaches computer-assisted reporting.

We made sure to include a chapter focusing on how public officials see the access process. We believe it is crucial that requesters understand the attitudes and culture of records custodians, as well as the barriers they face in providing documents.

We end the book with a chapter that pulls the process together, including organizing records, writing the document-based story, thinking about "FOI ethics" and understanding how people view access issues, especially in light of identity theft and terrorism.

Check out The Record Album in the back of the book for a list of document ideas, as well as the FOI resources grouped by topic. We think both appendices will be useful for quick reference.

## Key features

You will find several key features that we hope will help you get the most out of this book.

First, we want to provide you with so many ideas for document-based stories that you could produce 10 years' worth of projects from this one book. Throughout the chapters we provide examples of different kinds of documents that led to great reporting. We provide Web sites in the endnotes so you can look up the stories yourself. And at the end of the book, in The Record Album, we offer a list of dozens and dozens of records and how you can use them.

Second, we tried to pack as many practical tips and strategies into the chapters as possible, and highlighted some of the most interesting ones in quick "Pro tip" boxes that feature professionals from a variety of fields speaking in their own words. We interviewed more than 100 experts from throughout the world. You'll see revered print journalism icons Bob Woodward and Carl Bernstein. You'll learn from media lawyers, television reporters, nonprofits such as the American Civil Liberties Union and veterans groups, the U.S. FOIA ombudsman, a college newspaper editor, a Pulitzer Prize–winning reporter from a weekly newspaper, a private investigator, the owner of a "competitive intelligence" company and a database negotiator for the Web site Everyblock.com.

Third, we tried to provide the most complete guide to practical FOI resources that you will find anywhere. We include references to Web sites and other resources throughout the chapters and then highlight at the end of each chapter a list of suggested links. In Appendix B, we compiled all of the resources into one place, grouped by topic as a quick desk reference when you are on deadline looking for that online request letter generator or free media legal hotline number.

You'll be able to get even more information on our blog, at www .theartofaccess.com, including more records ideas, more resources and the ability to contact us and ask questions if you run into problems.

Finally, at the end of every chapter we have provided five or six "Try it!" activities that can be used by newsrooms, classrooms or individual citizens. Some of these activities are award-winning exercises that we believe will help you improve your FOI skills and lead to great reporting.

## Acknowledgments

We would like to thank the outstanding people at CQ Press for making this book possible, including Charisse Kiino and Aron Keesbury for valuing the importance of the topic, Jane Harrigan and Talia Greenberg for their astute editing and suggestions, and Christina Mueller and Gwenda Larsen for putting it all together so well. We are proud to be affiliated with an organization that is dedicated to furthering journalism and other disciplines that positively influence society.

We could not write this book without the support of our universities. We thank Jacqueline Sharkey, founding director of the University of Arizona School of Journalism and a passionate advocate for watchdog journalism. We also thank Dean Mills, dean of the School of Journalism at the Missouri School of Journalism at the University of Missouri, for his support, as well as that of the staff of the National Freedom of Information Coalition.

We also appreciate the support and dedication to freedom of information by the Society of Professional Journalists, including fellow FOI trainer Joel Campbell of Brigham Young University, and the John S. and James L. Knight Foundation for its continued support of FOI initiatives. We thank everyone who provided thoughts, tips and insights for this book, as well as the FOI warriors who have personally influenced and inspired us to write this book—Bill Chamberlin, Lucy Dalglish, Frank Garred, Jane Kirtley, Ian Marquand, Paul McMasters, Susan Dente Ross and too many others to fit in this book. We thank those who reviewed this project—both at the proposal and the manuscript stages—and provided us with many helpful suggestions: Cory Armstrong, University of Florida; David Bulla, Iowa State University; Ira Chinoy, University of Maryland; Martin Halstuk, Pennsylvania State University; Carol Polsgrove, Indiana University; Kenneth Pybus, Abilene Christian University; Joey Senat, Oklahoma State University; Sig Splichal, University of Miami; and Derek Willis, The George Washington University. We also thank Tom Blanton, an incredibly prolific records requester, who provided a masterfully written foreword.

Finally, we are eternally grateful to our families for their patience and loving support in these crazy projects—the clacking on the laptop at night, phone calls interrupting dinner and fretting over that extra-needed fact. While we are fortunate to have incredibly rewarding jobs fostering FOI, we are even luckier to have wonderful families who share our passion for making the world a little better.

David Cuillier
Charles N. Davis

# Records that matter
## Improve your community, career and life

When news broke that the FBI was listening to recordings of telephone calls made by a University of Missouri basketball player, every newsroom and basketball fan in the state wondered, "What's going on?"

The basketball player, Ricky Clemons, was serving a jail sentence for domestic assault. The jail in Boone County, like most jails, records all inmate phone calls. The Associated Press (AP) had sought Clemons' recordings but the jail denied the request, saying that the FBI was investigating.

After writing the breaking news stories, Nate Carlisle, then a reporter for the *Columbia Daily Tribune,* couldn't get the tape recordings out of his mind. So he went straight to the sheriff, sending him a records request. That request was promptly denied, on the same grounds as the AP's request: The tapes were part of an ongoing criminal investigation.

Rather than take the denial at face value, Carlisle puzzled over the answer and asked the sheriff a few follow-up questions, always keeping it polite and friendly but signaling his intensity.

"I asked him why that exemption was applicable. Did the FBI say it was investigating, or did it just ask for the recordings? *What* was it investigating? How long will the investigation take, and will the sheriff's department apply some deadline to the FBI or federal government to make a case? The sheriff could not answer many of my questions," Carlisle said.

But Carlisle didn't sit around complaining. He started preparing for what he'd do when the exemption was lifted. The sheriff wanted hundreds of dollars for sorting Clemons' calls from all the other inmate calls and copying them onto CDs; he said the department would have to pay overtime to the only lieutenant who knew how to work the equipment. Carlisle started asking whether the cost could be reduced if he listened to the recordings at the jail. After several weeks of discussion, the sheriff and Carlisle agreed on the cost and format for the records. So "he at least knew how badly I wanted them," Carlisle said.

Then one day in December 2003, when Carlisle arrived in the newsroom his editor called him over and opened a desk drawer. Inside were CDs in cases labeled "Ricky Clemons." In the 40 hours worth of calls, Clemons discussed his relationships with coaches and the politics of college athletics. He received calls from the wife of the university's president at the time, from associate athletic directors and assorted hangers-on. It dominated the news agenda of the city for weeks.

Carlisle got the story because he spent time developing what we call a "document state of mind." He was thinking about a story in a records-first way, exploring all of the possibilities and, most importantly, never giving up. He was interested enough to persevere, and curious enough to ask for the records in the first place.

You too can be a records whiz.

In this chapter we'll start by describing the benefits of documents to your career and your life, providing dozens of examples to inspire and motivate. When you finish reading and then skim The Record Album at the back of this book, we hope you walk away with dozens of ideas for documents that will produce award-winning stories, better your community and improve your life.

Years of working with requesters has convinced us that (1) anyone can do this, and (2) it has benefits for anyone willing to invest the time.

So let's get started.

## Find great stories

Records can be used to initiate stories, confirm hunches, produce more meaningful questions for interviews and confront recalcitrant officials bent on secrecy. One way to look at records is as agency "footprints": they tell us what an agency is and perhaps more importantly is not doing.

Pete Weitzel, a reporter and editor at *The Miami Herald* for nearly four decades, covered city and county government before Florida adopted its open meeting and open records laws, also called sunshine laws. "We often had to cajole, and work the system, and call in favors to get official records," Weitzel says. "It was much more difficult to get access to information, but we were very much aware of how powerful those records could be."

Weitzel recalls urging young reporters at the *Herald* to "find the anomalies."

"It's in the cracks, in the things that just don't line up, that records turn up gold," he says. "I remember going through a Dade County financial report on the public hospital and seeing numbers that just didn't add up. It turned out the hospital was operating at a huge deficit taxpayers would have to cover. It was a big story, just huge, and it was sitting there for anyone who took the time and initiative to go look at the records and then ask a few questions."

### Identify the 'performance gap'

Charles Lewis, a former "60 Minutes" producer who founded the Center for Public Integrity and the Investigative Reporting Workshop at American University in Washington, D.C., can trace his fascination with records back to his days as a student at the University of Delaware working for the *Wilmington News Journal* as a part-time sportswriter. He noticed that many of the student-athletes were taking far longer to graduate than the school wanted anyone to know.

Realizing that he couldn't get his hands on the athletes' transcripts, he sat down and began pondering the records he *could* get.

"I was learning all about public and nonpublic information," Lewis said. "So I sorted them in my head and realized that I had access to rosters and commencement programs. So I laid the commencement programs beside the team rosters, and just like that I had my story: nongraduates, six-year kids, the whole deal.

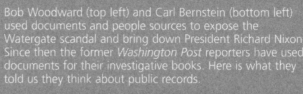

## Pro tip

**Be like Woodward and Bernstein: Bolster stories through public records**

Bob Woodward (top left) and Carl Bernstein (bottom left) used documents and people sources to expose the Watergate scandal and bring down President Richard Nixon. Since then the former *Washington Post* reporters have used documents for their investigative books. Here is what they told us they think about public records.

**Woodward:** There has never been a news story I know of that could not be improved or buttressed by a document of some sort. Many, many times these documents are public records, or the reporter can find a source who will decide to add some documents to the public record. Liberating such records for the public good is part of the job of those in government. Documents establish in time, person and authority what has happened or might have happened. They have been and I hope will always be part of the record.

**Bernstein:** Journalists need to make more use of public records. They are there for the taking, usually, and with a little extra effort can be located and perused even when they're difficult to take.

"I was a 19-year-old kid looking at the stark difference between what people said and reality, and it hit me that this is what I wanted to explore," he said.

Documents help journalists find great stories by identifying the "performance gap." For example, U.S. immigration officials claimed to be working hard to combat terrorism by deporting 814,073 people from 2004 through 2006. The AP relied on records-driven analysis of the Transactional Records Access Clearinghouse to show that only 12 deportations actually involved terrorism-related charges.[1]

The government claimed one thing; its own records showed another. That gap between what an agency says it is doing and what it actually does—the performance gap—is a critical engine of accountability for reporters and citizens intent on monitoring government performance. Suppose your local police force says that it is stepping up enforcement of speeding violations. That's an invitation for you to measure the performance a few months later.

Remember how federal officials assured us that they were getting serious about air safety following the Sept. 11, 2001, attacks? The government spent tens of millions of dollars establishing the Transportation Security Administration (TSA), whose indignities all air travelers have suffered. Take a minute to develop your document state of mind. What records-driven performance measures can you think of that would allow you to check up on this relatively new and extremely expensive government agency?

Reporters at *The Washington Post* thought about it and informed readers that Los Angeles International Airport officials had uncovered 12 airport screeners with felonies or other criminal backgrounds just weeks after the federal government said it had "rescrubbed" the backgrounds of its work force there.[2] Several of the 12 screeners working for TSA had criminal records related to "unlawful use, sale, distribution or manufacture of an explosive or weapon" and held security badges that provide access to secure areas of the airport for more than 200 days.[3]

OK, but surely TSA and U.S. airports are getting much more serious about security violations, aren't they? Another impressive use of FOIA-generated documents examined air security fines at airports across the country, finding wide disparities in TSA's penalties for carrying banned items. *The Wall Street Journal*'s 2005 story examined data on fines from across the nation, concluding that while passengers carrying banned items face the potential for heavy fines, the reality depended a great deal on the airport in question:

> At the airport in Manchester, N.H., last year, for instance, nearly 700 people were fined for carrying prohibited items, while at Seattle-Tacoma International Airport—which had nearly 12 million more people passing through security during that time—just 35 penalties were issued. At New York's La Guardia, 286 passengers were fined last year. But just a few miles away, at John F. Kennedy International Airport, only 83 people were penalized. . . . [4]

Over all, the story showed that the vast majority of people who try to bring prohibited items through airport security aren't fined at all. In 2004 TSA collected more than seven million prohibited items from passengers, of which 81,600 were firearms, explosives, box cutters and knives with blades over three inches long. But it levied fewer than 14,000 fines, the story said.

Sometimes the documents reveal stories as obvious as the composition of an agency's staff. The *Denver Post* found that of the 19 senior executives of the Federal Emergency Management Agency (FEMA) in 2005, only one was a person of color.[5] The story used the records to foster a broader discussion of the cultural issues facing people displaced by the storm, mixing the records-driven reporting with interviews.

Records also help you follow the money. In 2008 U.S. Immigration and Customs Enforcement raided a meatpacking plant in Iowa and arrested almost 400 workers. It was the largest worksite operation ever— and the *Cedar Rapids Gazette* found that it cost U.S. taxpayers at least $6.1 million. It was a huge local and regional story, and the document-driven price tag story was a strong addition to coverage of the aftermath of the raid.

### Help society

These great document-driven stories aren't just fascinating to read. They help society, and they help government improve its performance.

First, the mere knowledge that records are being kept, and that some day they will be reviewed, serves to remind stewards of the public till to mind the store.

## Pro tip | Request records about yourself

Request documents pertaining to you to find out what the government thinks about you and your coverage, or how it is even trying to manipulate your reporting. We got records that showed how a public relations firm contracted by the military was analyzing reporters' stories and rating them as positive, negative or neutral. The Pentagon was making decisions on who could be embedded with troops based on the ratings.[6] After we exposed the profiling system the military fired the PR firm and journalists FOIA'd their own rating records. Request to see your FBI file, or e-mails or memos at City Hall pertaining to you and your coverage.

—Kevin Baron, Washington, D.C.,
bureau reporter, *Stars and Stripes*

"Publicity is justly commended as a remedy for social and industrial diseases. Sunlight is said to be the best of disinfectants; electric light the most efficient policeman," U.S. Supreme Court Justice Louis Brandeis wrote in *Other People's Money, and How the Bankers Use It* in 1933.

Second, document-based stories can lead to new laws that can help save lives. In 2005, for example, Joe Adams, an editorial writer at *The Florida Times-Union,* read a press release from the governor saying the latest state statistics showed crime had declined statewide to the lowest level in decades. He was curious about Duval County, home to the consolidated city-county government of Jacksonville, and he noticed the numbers of murders had sharply increased in one year while most other categories had fallen slightly. Using per capita calculations used by the FBI but not for the state statistics, Adams discovered that Duval County had been the murder capital of the state, even more so than Miami-Dade County, for six years running. The distinction had been overlooked because local officials compared Jacksonville—at more than double the population of the second-largest city—with other cities rather than with counties, a more apples-to-apples comparison. An *editorial writer* breaking news, thanks to public records.

The day Adams' editorial hit the streets, the mayor responded by vowing to create a task force. The eventual result? A chain of events that led to a landmark $31 million anticrime program, The Jacksonville Journey, approved by the Jacksonville City Council in 2008.

"The real picture and its severity were right there in the public record," Adams said. "Somebody just had to uncover it."

Adams is a document zealot, authoring *The Florida Public Records Handbook,* a university course on using public records, and a Web site that underscores the value of public records society (www.idiganswers. com). He said that once a person gets hooked on the power of documents and the good they can do for people, the rest gets easier.

"It's always a renewable opportunity," he said. "You keep driving and seeking information, even though you're going to find a lot of minutiae. It's the excitement of the revelation."

Adams is constantly studying public records for stories to help his community. In 2007 he gathered more than 4,000 pages of city council meeting notices, minutes and calendars over an 18-month period to find widespread noncompliance with the state open meetings law. Work by

Adams and staff writer Beth Kormanik led to a grand jury investigation and the emergency crafting of Florida's first local government sunshine law.

None of these stories could have been done without access to government information—made possible because freedom of information (FOI) laws exist, but also *because someone thought to ask*. That's the secret: putting yourself in a records-driven mindset, so you constantly think about what records might be available in any given situation.

If you do, you will soon see the benefits—in your career and life.

## Advance your reporting and career

It's not selfish to think about how documents can benefit your reporting and career. You'll get more front-page stories and better performance reviews, and maybe you'll win awards—all because you'll be writing better stories that will help more people.

### Improve your stories

Records don't stonewall or spin. They seek neither power nor favor. They don't whine, chisel or avoid your phone calls. They might contain inaccuracies, but they are incapable of lying.

Instead, records document the deeds and misdeeds of officials great and small, chronicling the byways of government and memorializing our collective history. This will strengthen your stories, making them more valued by editors and readers. Stories that include authoritative sources are better liked, and readers perceive them to be of higher quality.[7]

Documents are that important. If you don't take our word for it, then next time you stand in a bookstore look at the history aisle or the nonfiction section and ask yourself where all those books came from.

### Regain power of verification

Some journalists, particularly those starting out, rely heavily on official sources for their information. They base their reporting on press releases and news conferences, relying on agencies to voluntarily tell the public when something is going wrong. They try not to anger their sources, for fear those people won't talk to them in the future.

That's not journalism; that's stenography.

Documents place the power of verification back in the people's hands. With records, journalists don't need to talk to officials, except for context or response. Once journalists realize that documents give them power, then a whole new world opens to them.

Mike McGraw, a legendary investigative reporter at *The Kansas City Star* and a public records addict, thinks the first time he used the federal Freedom of Information Act (FOIA) was in the early to mid-1970s, while covering the Teamsters union in Kansas City and the Chicago-based Central States Pension Fund.

"I used FOIA to get some government documents on the fund's investments, to go along with what I was finding in court documents," he said. "Here's what it taught me: I no longer had to depend on Teamsters officials to tell me what they were doing with their members' pension money. Instead, I could now go to them and ask: 'Why did you spend your members' pension funds on a casino you have a personal interest in?'"

## Put editors at ease

Documents can save your bacon in court. In many cases, the law considers public records, such as police reports and court documents, to be privileged. As long as you quote the documents correctly, even if what you quote makes someone look bad, you have more protection if you're sued for libel.

McGraw found that carefully using and citing public documents made his bosses and lawyers feel a lot better.

"I didn't have to give my editor a story based on unnamed sources or named sources who were probably lying to me; and I could show actual documents backing up my stories to the newspaper's nervous lawyers."

## Win awards

Take a look at Pulitzer Prize–winning stories (www.pulitzer.org) and you'll see the depth of reporting through the use of documents and government databases.

Remember Adams' great document-based reporting about the Jacksonville City Council violating sunshine laws? The work that he and

BOX 1.1 **Enter sunshine contests**

A number of state and national organizations sponsor contests for outstanding work in acquiring public records and shedding light on government. Here are a few you can enter:

- **Society of Professional Journalists Sunshine Award**, given to individuals and groups for making important contributions in open government. SPJ also gives out First Amendment Awards and the Eugene Pulliam First Amendment Award, often for FOI work. Journalism students who enter the Mark of Excellence competition do well with record-based stories (www.spj.org/a-sunshine.asp).

- **Joseph L. Brechner Freedom of Information Award**, which comes with a $3,000 prize for excellence in reporting and writing about FOI issues (http://brechner.org/award.asp).

- **Investigative Reporters and Editors FOI Award**, offered as one category in its annual reporting awards (www.ire.org/resourcecenter/contest/index.html).

- **National Freedom of Information Coalition and SPJ's Heroes of the 50 States Open Government Hall of Fame**, a prestigious honor for those who have a long record of fighting for open government (www.nfoic.org).

- **State press associations and FOI coalitions**, many of whom honor individuals within their state each year for fostering open government through their reporting.

Kormanik did on that issue led to 17 awards in 2008, including a National Headliner Award for Adams in editorial writing.

His previous work with FOI garnered him such national honors as the Society of Professional Journalists (SPJ) Sunshine Award and the Eugene Pulliam First Amendment Award, which comes with a $10,000 cash prize. Record-based reporting can pay off!

But those awards have a deeper meaning: Good document-based reporting is honored because it improves lives and makes the world a better place. Documents are the historical record of the democracy. They provide proof, refute spurious allegations and discredit lies. They level the playing field for citizens seeking redress of grievances against their government.

## Improve your life

Public records can help your life in ways that go far beyond work. They can help you buy a house, find the best schools for your children, reveal the criminal history of a potential babysitter, become a more informed consumer and even see what information the government collects about you.

As you learn what documents can make your life better, you will bolster your reporting skills because you'll feel motivated and become more adept at searching and finding records. Also, you'll be able to pass along your knowledge to readers, friends and relatives, who will be amazed and grateful.

### Buy a house

When looking for a house or checking out a neighborhood, request police incident reports for crimes in the area. Look for sex offenders nearby through your state sex offender registry online. At the county assessor's office, look up assessed values of neighboring homes, and the zoning for neighboring vacant land to make sure a warehouse or mall can't be built next door. Check municipal plans for future development, roads, parks and fire stations. Stop by the airport or check online to see noise maps and flight path maps. Toxic release records indicate big polluters nearby; environmental records indicate polluted groundwater or soil. Acquire copies of neighborhood newsletters that are kept by a city neighborhood department to find out problems and issues in the area. Other records that can assess an area are dog bites, nuisance complaints and graffiti reports. For dozens of other ideas for house-buying documents, see The Record Album at the back of the book.

### Check out schools

Thanks to a host of federal and state laws mandating all sorts of reporting, schools are a data goldmine. Examine school test scores on your state education department's Web site, criminal incidents at schools, suspension rates, Title IX compliance, school lunch nutrition reports and drop-out rates. Also request employee tenure and salary information to find schools with low turnover and seasoned teachers. Be sure to check teacher certification for your school of choice, also available from some states' education department Web sites.

### Background people

You can check out the criminal background of people who have access to your possessions or children, such as a housekeeper, babysitter, teacher, coach, bus driver or someone you or a loved one are dating. Go to your county courthouse and look them up, or see if your county or state court system allows you to search online—many do nowadays. Don't just stop at criminal records. You can find out if someone (a potential date, perhaps?) is bankrupt, married or divorced. You can also find out if someone is being held in jail or prison (check out links to state inmate locators at www.publicrecordfinder.com/criminal.html).

### Buy smart

Armed with nothing more than a company name, you can log onto a court Web site or walk into a clerk's office and see whether the company has had previous problems. State attorneys general often maintain complaints against companies, as do many state insurance commissions. Many health departments post their restaurant inspection data online.

Before contributing to a charity or nonprofit, check out its IRS-990 forms to see what it does with its money and who is running the organization. Many of the forms are posted online and available for free through www.guidestar.org.

Find out if your doctor, chiropractor, dentist, lawyer, hairdresser or other licensed professional is in good standing. State bar associations often post lawyer suspensions and disciplinary decisions online. Request official university student evaluations of professors to find individuals who stand out as particularly good or bad—many universities provide them for students to check, and if so, they are a public record.

### Find your FBI file

Find out what's in your own FBI file, or check information in the files of relatives who have died. A fun reporting hobby: Note the passage of each famous or infamous news figure in your market by sending in an FOI request for their FBI files. You'll be surprised: *The Columbus Dispatch* sent a request after legendary coach Woody Hayes died, and ended up with an entertaining story noting that Hayes had an FBI file. Hayes once recruited the son of an agent in the Cleveland office to play for the Buckeyes, prompting a letter to FBI headquarters. J. Edgar Hoover and Woody Hayes were pals—great stuff!

**Pro tip** | **Make yourself marketable**

There are lots of applications of public records in and out of journalism. Even if you don't plan to go into journalism, or if you ever leave the field, the ability to access government records is an extremely marketable skill. Companies are finding that not only are they not good communicators but they also are not good at research. For example, there's a huge demand for people who can access information for "competitive intelligence." Corporations are very aggressive users of FOIA, but they also want proxies. They want to look at public records, but they don't want everyone and their mom to know they are looking at public records. The proxies will get the records and analyze them. I also see grant writers who are adept at searching public records are smarter about capturing grant money. Those are opportunities for people who know how to gather information.

—Christine Tatum, chief executive officer, Media Salad, Inc.,
a market intelligence company, and former Colorado
newspaper reporter and SPJ president

## Develop a new way of thinking

Think about how you drove to work or class this morning. What route did you take, and what did you see? Odds are you take the same route every day. You've calculated the shortest route, or the fastest; but we are guessing you didn't choose the most colorful or interesting way to get to work, for that would be less efficient.

What do you remember about the commute today? Probably very little. When we get caught up in the routines of everyday life, we pay less and less attention to the world around us.

Just as varying your route to work or school would prompt you to notice different things, we suggest you vary your information-gathering routines by asking yourself these questions:

- "Who says?"
- "Can they prove that?"
- "How much did that cost?"

- "Are they doing what they said they'd do to fix that?"
- "How can we check that?"

And so on and so forth—you get the idea. The result is an inside-out way of looking at government, in which the FOI requester anticipates the questions that should be asked and predicts the paper trails created by bureaucrats.

Here is what we mean. In 2004 KBCI-TV, a Boise CBS affiliate, won award after award for a series entitled "Shake-Up at City Hall," in which the station's reporters uncovered a trail of financial corruption by the mayor of Boise and his chief of staff that led to the resignation and indictment of both officials.

Records played a prominent role in the stories, as the reporters methodically documented city credit card expenses for items such as junkets to conferences, a side trip to a Broadway show, an ornamental fireplace and other goodies that could not be located at City Hall.

The stories grabbed attention, but the coup de grace came when one of the reporters found himself in the mayor's office, scratching his head and trying to figure out the "smoking gun" that would link the mayor to the city-purchased luxury goods.

The "Eureka!" moment came when the reporter looked up and saw the video surveillance system on the ceiling. The reporter then filed a public records request for the surveillance video itself—and that was the capstone of the series, as the videotape showed city employees, including the mayor, hauling the merchandise into City Hall before transferring it to their homes.

The grainy surveillance tapes say everything there is to say about the power of records to provide the unassailable truth, of the benefits of thinking strategically about FOI and of the boundless potential for storytelling that records promise to those with the motivation to find and use them.

It is time to develop a new way of thinking, a document-driven state of mind.

Try it!

**Exercises and ideas for journalists, newsrooms and classrooms to improve your skills and foster FOI in your community.**

### 1. Analyze awards

This exercise shows how records lead to award-winning stories and generate ideas for future stories and documents to acquire. Go to the following three Web sites and scan some of the award-winning investigative or public service stories from the past year:

☑ Pulitzer Prizes (www.pulitzer.org)
☑ Investigative Reporters and Editors annual awards (www.ire.org/resourcecenter/contest)
☑ SPJ Sigma Delta Chi awards (www.spj.org/a-sdx.asp)

Choose the one story you find most interesting. Print out the story, and with a highlighter mark all the parts that were attributed to government records. Think about how the reporters might have obtained those documents. Next, look for any sidebars or "nerd boxes" that explain the background of the projects, including the data and documents used for the story. See if the news organization posted any of the original documents online with the story. Explain what the story would have been like without the records. Now request those records in your community for a similar story.

### 2. Find your dream house

This exercise can be done for personal uses or a class activity, and is a lot of fun. Identify a house—either your own or one for sale in the community (see www.zillow.com). Then collect as much information solely through public records as you can about the house, property and surrounding neighborhood. Here is a list of potential records you can tap:

- ☑ Property tax records including assessed value, owner's name, taxes paid and square footage
- ☑ Police reports of nearby crimes and sex offender registries
- ☑ Development plans, including road plans, proposed commercial development and zoning for future development
- ☑ Parks plans
- ☑ Airport flight-pattern maps that show sound levels
- ☑ School test scores to compare schools
- ☑ Environmental Protection Agency records regarding hazardous chemicals and polluted sites
- ☑ Nuisance complaints reported to the city

Write a summary for your class or family about whether you should buy this house (or keep living in your current one!), citing and attaching the document sources.

## 3. Get Grandpa's FBI file

Impress your family (or get ostracized from the next reunion) by requesting Grandpa's FBI file, or your own. Anyone is allowed to request to see their own FBI file, if they have one. Also, you are allowed to request the files on anyone who is deceased. Check out the Web site "Get Grandpa's FBI File" at www.getgrandpasfbifile.com. To request your own file, see the companion Web site, "Get My FBI File," at www.getmyfbifile.com.

## 4. Create a communal document pool

On your newsroom Intranet or university online course system, or perhaps through Google Docs, create a place where reporters can post documents they have received that might be of help to other beats. Post the document and location, or the actual document or data. Create a running index of great documents in the community. Look at The

Record Album at the back of the book and see the authors' blog (at www
.theartofaccess.com) for ideas.

## 5. Get connected

Keep up on FOI news and then spread it around the newsroom or for
your classmates via e-mail. Subscribe to listservs, including the FOI-L
listserv (http://listserv.syr.edu/archives/foi-l.html) and the FOI Advocate
e-mail newsletter (http://foiadvocate.blogspot.com). If you work for a
news organization, designate a records conduit who gleans FOI news,
tips and document ideas and shares them with everyone else. Here are
some other sites to stay in the loop (sign up for the sites' RSS feeds to get
notifications for when the pages are updated):

- ☑ **SPJ's Open Doors** publication guide to access, which includes an A
  to Z list of useful records for stories (www.spj.org/opendoors.asp).
- ☑ **The FOIA Files,** with hundreds of document-driven stories
  provided online at the Sunshine in Government Initiative Web site
  (www.sunshineingovernment.org/index.php?cat=33).
- ☑ **Investigative Reporters and Editors** has an Extra! Extra! Web
  site posting great stories often based on documents (www.ire.org/
  extraextra).
- ☑ **Society of Environmental Journalists** provides a story archive of
  great stories, often based on records (www.sej.org).
- ☑ **Center for Investigative Reporting** provides a story
  blog of good ideas and investigative stories (http://
  centerforinvestigativereporting.org).
- ☑ **Joe Adams,** a Florida journalist and SPJ FOI Committee member,
  provides great record ideas at his iDig Answers Web site under the
  title "Joe's Hit Records" (www.idiganswers.com).
- ☑ **Google News Alerts** allow you to have Google search the Internet
  for news and Web sites based on keywords you specify (such as
  "freedom of information" or "public records"). Click on "News
  Alerts," then set up an alert with keywords you choose (http://
  news.google.com).

**Suggested links**

**Extra! Extra!**   www.ire.org/extraextra
Investigative Reporters and Editors provides daily synopses of
outstanding investigative reporting, with links to the actual stories.
Often the stories are based on documents.

**FOI Advocate blog**   http://foiadvocate.blogspot.com
Probably the most comprehensive updates of daily FOI news, by the
National Freedom of Information Coalition.

**FOIA Files: Stories That FOIA Made Possible**   www.sunshineingovern
ment.org/index.php?cat=33
Hundreds of document-driven stories are provided online at the
Sunshine in Government Initiative Web site.

**FOI FYI blog**   http://blogs.spjnetwork.org/foi
FOI news posted by SPJ's Freedom of Information Committee,
often including tips for record-based story ideas and FOI strategies.

**Idiganswers**   www.idiganswers.com
Provides examples of how documents can benefit your reporting
and life. You'll find document-based story ideas and even advice
on how to background your date through government documents.
Created by Joe Adams, an editorial writer from Florida.

**News Media Update**   www.rcfp.org
Daily news posted by the Reporters Committee for Freedom of the
Press on a variety of press issues, often regarding FOI.

**Open Doors: FOI ideas, A to Z**   www.spj.org/opendoors.asp
SPJ's Open Doors publication guide to access, including an A to Z
list of useful records for stories.

# Develop a document state of mind

ACCESS ACTION AGENDA

☑ Be The Donald
☑ Exercise your document muscles
☑ Find inspiration and support

You have more power than your city's mayor. More power than your state's governor or senators. More power than your nation's president.

After all, they work for you. You're the boss. You are entitled to see most of the records they produce for you.

Know it.

Believe it.

Most important of all, use it.

Robert Faturechi wasn't so sure at first. A college journalist for *The Daily Bruin* at the University of California, Los Angeles, he didn't know anything about requesting public records. One day in 2007 he got an e-mail tip from an alumnus alleging that the university's School of Dentistry was admitting students whose parents provided big donations to the program. He didn't know where to start, so he started with everything.

On the Web site of the Student Press Law Center, Faturechi filled out a public records request letter, asking the university for all internal memos, investigation reports, donations, e-mails and other documents related to admissions into the orthodontics program. In response, a university official put in a public records request for Faturechi's own notes and attempted to have him censured for unethical behavior, efforts that ultimately went nowhere. Months later, after haggling with uncooperative university officials and making persistent calls to the public records officer, Faturechi got a packet in the mail. "It was a thrilling experience for me," he said. "I ripped it open and flew through the documents all day."

The documents told tales the university never would. For example, a real estate developer pledged $1 million to the university, and soon after the donation his niece was admitted to the school of dentistry. A doctor pledged $500,000 and his son was admitted the following year. One applicant was told by the admissions board that a $60,000 gift could greatly improve his chances of getting into the program. Faturechi exposed a problem, won several awards, landed an internship at *The Seattle Times* and eventually a job at *The Sacramento Bee,* and then a fellowship at the *Los Angeles Times.*

Like Faturechi, even many experienced journalists start out feeling intimidated about requesting documents from a bureaucracy or asking questions when documents are denied. They're forgetting the basics of U.S. Government 101: We're the boss.

No way, our students say. The president is far more powerful than any journalist. The president is *the* boss. Well, yes, most of the time. But who got Richard M. Nixon fired? Bob Woodward and Carl Bernstein, two reporters from *The Washington Post* who effectively used people sources and government documents. Instead of feeling like you're begging when you ask for records, you should feel like Donald Trump, confident and in charge of your own corporation we call the U.S. of A.

This chapter will help you develop a "document state of mind" by getting you to think like The Donald of Documents. We will highlight the principles of open government that support you in your search for information, and then you'll be ready for tips and specific workout exercises that will help make FOI requests part of your daily reporting routine. Developing a document state of mind means constantly wondering what documents are out there and laying the groundwork to get them.

Reporters who can start seeing the world this way empower themselves and open a whole new universe of possibilities.

## Be The Donald

Donald Trump is in charge of his domain, and he knows it. As chief executive officer of the Trump Organization, with properties around the world and a net worth in the billions, he has the confidence and responsibility to do whatever it takes to make sure his companies prosper. "I like thinking big," he says in his book *The Art of the Deal.* "To me it's very simple: If you're going to be thinking anything, you might as well think big."

If that means buying a $40 million house or building a Las Vegas casino, he'll do it. If it means walking into his office, slipping behind the counter and checking the books to make sure no employees are stealing, he'll do it. He scans memos and reports to keep himself apprised of his employees' actions. He does his homework before every major deal. And if someone screws up, they hear the words, "You're fired."

Just as Trump is in charge of his private company, we the citizens are quite literally in charge of our public companies—federal, state and local agencies. Government employees work for us. We pay their salaries. As their bosses, we have not just the authority but the duty to make sure our employees are doing what we pay them to do. If they aren't, we point them to the door. That's democracy. Thomas Jefferson said our country is based on government "deriving their just powers from the consent of the governed."

Government employees work on our behalf. Eric Nalder reminds himself of that truth every time he walks into a government office to get public records. Nalder, a two-time Pulitzer Prize winner who is a senior enterprise reporter for Hearst Newspapers, uses visualization to rehearse in his mind what he will say. "It's not so much *asking* people things, but *telling* them what to do," he says. Nalder is not rude about it. His puppy-dog eyes and mild demeanor belie his confidence and aggressiveness. He simply remembers who is really in charge—just like The Donald.

### Remember all-American values

Freedom of information is an all-American value. When Harold L. Cross wrote the FOI movement's bible, *The People's Right to Know*, in 1953, he

boiled access down to one opening statement: "Public business is the public's business."[2] The "right to know" is not just some overused catch-phrase. It's part of America, part of our government and part of our history.

Our founding fathers firmly opposed tyranny and wanted to make sure that the people stayed in control of their government by staying informed—through a good education system, libraries and open access to information. John Adams said, "Liberty cannot be preserved without a general knowledge among the people, who have a right . . . and a desire to know."[3]

Open government provides tangible benefits for society. It limits misinformation and promotes trust in officials. It encourages efficiency by allowing agencies to share information and learn lessons. Public records help citizens arm themselves with knowledge for defending their neighborhoods from criminals or intrusive development. Transparency discourages corruption and mismanagement.

Open government also keeps our capitalist economy running smoothly, allowing investors to make informed business decisions. In fact, studies show that more than two-thirds of FOIA requests are submitted by businesses; only about 5 percent to 10 percent are submitted by journalists.[4] If all those business people can think like The Donald, why can't more journalists?

Throughout our history we've seen examples of these principles integrated into our laws and policies. In 1813 Congress created the Federal Depository Library Program to get federal records out to the people. Since 1816 the salaries of federal employees have been public information. Wisconsin was the first state to adopt laws protecting open records and open meetings, in 1849. Since Congress passed the federal Freedom of Information Act in 1966, it has been improved several times, most recently in 2007 through the OPEN Government Act.

Now, let's be honest. Government has always been secretive, right from the start. And to be fair, there is a legitimate need for secrecy. Keeping certain records secret, such as troop movements, medical records and city labor negotiations, serves a public interest. The U.S. Constitution was drafted behind closed doors, and it mentions nothing of a "right to know." During the Civil War, Abraham Lincoln not only worked in secrecy, but he suppressed 21 newspapers from publication.[5] Some political leaders couldn't see why commoners would need access to government information. Important decisions were made by the educated elite and handed out on a need-to-know basis.

The United States wasn't even the first nation to adopt a national freedom of information law. In 1766 Sweden, which included Finland at the time, passed a national FOI law, exactly 200 years before the United States. Anders Chydenius of Finland could be considered the father of FOI and press rights for pushing through parliament the Freedom-of-Press and the Right-of-Access to Public Records Act.[6] The law required government to provide official documents immediately and at no charge, and also created the world's first ombudsman (something the United States didn't put into place until 2009). The second nation to create a federal FOI law? Colombia, in 1888.

Australian researcher and computer-assisted reporting teacher Stephen Lamble found that Chydenius credits not himself for the idea of FOI, but a Chinese emperor from A.D. 627 named T'ai-tsung. The emperor established an Imperial Censorate ombudsman's office, making available

## Father of FOI

"No proof should be necessary that a modicum of freedom for writing and printing is one of the strongest pillars of support for free government, for in the absence of such, the Estates would not dispose of sufficient knowledge to make good laws, nor practitioners of law have control in their vocation, nor subjects knowledge of the requirements laid down in law, the limits of authority and their own duties. Learning and good manners would be suppressed, coarseness in thought, speech and customs would flourish, and a sinister gloom would within a few years darken our entire sky of freedom."

—Anders Chydenius, the "father of FOI," in his "Memorandum on the Freedom of the Press," 1775

public records and allowing anyone who had a grievance with the government, or anyone who wanted information from the government, to

simply walk to the palace steps and beat a drum until satisfied. T'ai-tsung, following Confucian philosophy, said emperors were expected to "admit their own imperfection as a proof for their love of the truth and in fear of ignorance and darkness."[7]

Despite taking a few centuries to catch up, the United States has done a pretty good job of serving as a role model for accountable government. More than 70 countries have freedom of information laws patterned after the U.S. Freedom of Information Act, and dozens more are considering adopting similar legislation.[8] Open government reduces corruption, helps citizens make informed decisions and exposes wrongdoing. Requesting public records is not just a part of being an American; it is universal.

Emperor T'ai-tsung

### Presume it's open

OK, great. The law says government information should be open. Now what? Remember, you're The Donald. He'd never let the lack of a law degree scare him. Sure, it's useful to learn the details of the particular state or federal law you want to use. But to get started, all you really need to know is one thing: Government documents are open unless there's a law that says otherwise. In other words, it's not your job to prove that a record should be made public. It is the government's job to prove that it should be made secret. Once you understand that, you're empowered to get moving.

Sometimes when reporters request public records, they approach government agencies as if they must genuflect at the altar of bureaucracy and apologize for asking. They get butterflies in their stomachs and fret over how they are going to persuade officials to hand over the records. Flip that thinking around. The burden of proof is not on you. "I never, ever apologize for asking for public records," said Ken Armstrong, an award-winning investigative reporter at *The Seattle Times.*

Just look at the law itself. Most state laws have a "preamble" that provides context and purpose for the law. For example, check out the Washington state public records law preamble:

> The people of this state do not yield their sovereignty to the agencies that serve them. The people, in delegating authority, do not give their public servants the right to decide what is good for the people to know and what is not good for them to know. The people insist on remaining informed so that they may maintain control over the instruments that they have created. This chapter shall be liberally construed and its exemptions narrowly construed to promote this public policy.

Openness should be "liberally" construed and secrecy "narrowly" construed. That's what the law says. Transparency is the presumption.

So let's say you go to City Hall and ask to see copies of the mayor's expense reports for the past year. The clerk cocks an eyebrow and says, "Tell me where it says in the law that I have to give those to you." At that point, a lot of people panic, trying to think of an answer. Actually, you can't show the clerk a law saying those records must be provided, because no law says that. But remember, government records are public unless a statute says otherwise.

A good reporter turns it around on the clerk: "Well, gee, you might want to confer with the city attorney on this, but it's my understanding that the state public records law (which you're pulling out of your bag as you talk) says everything is public unless there is a state statute that says otherwise. Can you show me the statute that makes that record secret?" Now the clerk is on the spot. Once he or she confers briefly with a supervisor and is told that you are correct, you'll get the records.

The law does let some records stay secret, and for good reason. Medical records, students' grades and records of active law enforcement investigations are typically exempt from disclosure. We need to balance the public interest in the records being open against the harm that disclosure could cause to individuals or society. But still, in most cases the same principle holds: It's the government's responsibility to prove that the harm outweighs the benefits, not your responsibility to prove the opposite.

If an official provides you a citation showing that a particular record is not public, simply read it, confer with experts and go from there. But the key is to make the government do the work by proving the information is secret. It's not your responsibility to prove it is public. If you remember that, then requesting records becomes a lot less stressful and a lot more effective.

## Exercise your document muscles

Sometimes it seems impossible to make time for public records requests, especially when the pressures of daily deadline journalism or constant Web updating cut into reporting time. But everyone, including those working in small newsrooms, college newspapers and television newsrooms, not to mention average citizens, can gather public records if they get into the habit and develop a document state of mind.

A document state of mind requires a new way of thinking, training your brain to react instinctively so that in every journalistic situation— on deadline or on longer projects—you'll be thinking about how to

BOX 2.1 **Four justifications to push hard for public records**

Sometimes journalists are afraid to push too hard for public records, nervous that if they do their official sources won't talk to them anymore. If you feel that way sometimes, here are four points to remind yourself to request records without hesitation, getting the goods while building the beat:

1. **You're doing your job.** Public officials generally don't resent a journalist for exercising his or her legal right to examine government records. Most bureaucrats expect it, and many even support that right. From their perspective, you're doing your job. And if you are polite, accurate and fair your doggedness will be rewarded. If an official is petty and paranoid, then it's likely he or she will throw tantrums whether you request documents or not.

2. **It's the records, not you.** Documents provide an intermediary between you and your sources. You can be the good cop and the records can be the bad cop. It's not *you* alleging that the mayor is spending public funds improperly. It's the mayor's credit card receipts that show purchases at an escort service and parasailing excursions in the Bahamas.

3. **Decrease reliance on officials.** Document-driven reporting decreases your reliance on press releases and official spin. Instead of trusting the school finance director to explain the budget and highlight the most newsworthy parts (unlikely), just look at the budget yourself and find the news. Instead of relying on the parking department manager to tell you about cronies getting their tickets waived (unlikely), look at the parking ticket database yourself.

4. **Generate better tips, sources and stories.** Once citizens and frontline government workers start seeing aggressive reporting that looks out for them, not for high-ranking government officials, they'll start calling and e-mailing with more tips and more information. With document-based reporting, the only time you'll need an official to talk to you is when you are asking for a response to or an explanation of what you find in the records.

identify and acquire public records. Just like a professional athlete, you can condition your thinking and reflexes to maximize efficiency and performance, even without steroids.

The rest of this chapter outlines a training regimen that will condition your journalistic muscles to think about documents in new ways. These techniques, tested and used regularly by some of journalism's best, will help you identify and acquire public records with more confidence and efficiency. While we can't be in your cubicle to bark at you like a drill sergeant, we can encourage you to develop a workout program and condition your document state of mind.

### Sketch a 'circle of light'

Documents can help you assemble a picture not just of an agency but also of individual people. So when it comes to backgrounding a person or a policy through public records, sometimes it helps to think in circles.

Duff Wilson, an investigative reporter at *The New York Times,* and Deborah Nelson, a former investigative editor for the *Los Angeles Times* and current journalism professor at the University of Maryland, have developed a technique they call "circling" to systematically and creatively think about documents when embarking upon an investigation, particularly when it involves profiling a person. Here's how it works.

Duff Wilson         Deborah Nelson

Write the name of the subject of an investigation in the middle of a sheet of paper or a whiteboard. Then, circling around the name, write labels that represent the different identities and roles the person has in life: property owner, student, husband, parent, driver, elected official, criminal, business owner, pet owner, etc. Then, around that circle, write all the documents you can think of related to those different identities. "Imagine all the records in your life that you have left behind," Wilson says. Before you know it, you'll have dozens of documents that you can tap to find out about the person (see Figure 2.1).

Politicians leave massive paper trails, but even private citizens touch government in ways that leave document prints. For example, Wilson said, a marriage license will provide the date and location of marriage, which then may lead to a newspaper marriage announcement that provides attendants and family members or identifies social, business or political connections. Get in the habit of "circling" every person you profile, and you'll be in a document state of mind.

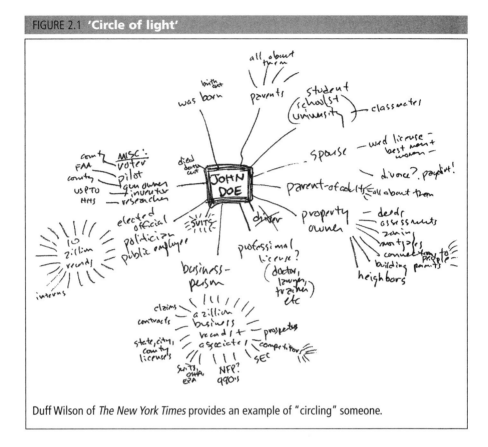

**FIGURE 2.1 'Circle of light'**

Duff Wilson of *The New York Times* provides an example of "circling" someone.

## Make FOI first on Fridays

Now that you've identified documents held by an agency, or records that would help you background an individual, it's time to develop a routine for requesting records. Think of a story you could write with the help of documents, or a record that might yield stories (see Chapter 3 for more document ideas and where to get them). On a Post-it note, write "FOI First!" in big letters and then write the name of the document you'd most like to obtain. Stick it to your computer monitor.

Then, on Friday morning (or whatever day works for your schedule) as you sit down at your computer, before opening your e-mail or checking phone messages, grab the sticky note and do the following:

1. If you don't already know where to get the document, think about what agencies would keep such records. Check their Web sites. Make some calls.

2. Ask for the record verbally, or write a public records request (see Chapter 5) and send it out. You can do this by e-mail in most states now.

3. In a notebook, create a page for the record and write the date, agency and what you requested so you can track your request, or track your requests using a computer program, such as Microsoft Excel. Leave space to write in who responded, their contact information, what they said, when they responded and how you responded. You may need this information months or years from now if the request is delayed.

There's nothing magical about Friday, or any other day. The point is to request a document on the same day every week without fail. Before long you'll have acquired dozens of public records leading to dozens of good stories—and you'll have developed a document state of mind.

Developing a routine works. Take, for example, John O'Connor, an Associated Press political statehouse reporter in Illinois. Since 2001 he has submitted an average of two public records requests a week, tracking each request in a Microsoft Excel file. Some weeks he may go without filing one, but in other weeks he might file a dozen requests, depending on what he is working on.

O'Connor said requests send a strong message to officials that you know what is going on. He once heard that two public information officers, one experienced and one new, had been talking about him. "The veteran said to the young PIO: 'Keep in mind that when he [O'Connor] asks a question, he already knows the answer.' That's far from the truth, but I'll take that reputation. When you submit FOI requests, they automatically think you know more than you do."

Mike McGraw, an FOI warrior at *The Kansas City Star*, said he sends out FOI requests even when he isn't at all sure there is a story at the end of the request, just to stay in the habit of making requests and "let the agencies know I am watching."

Submitting a request one week might lead to a package in the mail four months later. "I love the feeling when I go to my mailbox and see a big fat envelope with stuffing in it," McGraw said. "It's like Christmas morning to me. I get a document high."

That's what we're talking about!

## Find inspiration and support

Nicholas Wilbur felt beaten down and out of steam. In early 2007 he was just a year out of the University of Oregon and working at *The Kingman Daily Miner,* a small daily newspaper in an Arizona city that's a waystop for truckers and Vegas-bound SUVs. Wilbur covered City Hall, but every time he requested information officials gave him guff and complained he was being "too negative" and "making a mountain out of a molehill."

"For a buck reporter with only a year's experience, it's tough to be the source of so much criticism," he said. That spring Wilbur decided to drive across the state to an FOI workshop sponsored by the Freedom of Information Coalition of Arizona and the Society of Professional Journalists (SPJ). "I went to the conference questioning myself, my duties and stories published, my general bulldoggish style and the criticisms I'd been receiving from certain officials," he recalled later. But in a room full of compatriots, Wilbur discovered other journalists in the trenches who shared his values and determination. It made him feel good about himself and his profession again. He drove back home invigorated and wrote a column for the paper.

"This conference reminded me that I am doing my job, even if a couple of officials don't like it," he wrote. "It's my job to report to residents what's happening with their money. It's that simple."

Wilbur's story is all too common. Research shows that the No. 1 reason journalists voluntarily leave the profession is not the low pay and long hours (although those things hurt morale); it's the feeling that nobody really cares about good journalism anymore and that their bosses don't support quality work.[9] Without a sense of purpose, why put up with it all?

Couple that with shrinking staffs, increasing workload and online demands, and it's no wonder burnout among journalists is high. Therefore, it's important to develop strategies for staying motivated and enthusiastic, especially for going beyond the daily work to request documents. Document-driven reporting helps you find fresh new ideas and break out of the assignment-driven, reactive reporting all too common in journalism these days. If you find your own stories, you'll be deeply invested in their outcome. Or you can sit around and wait for whatever your editors need done.

It's your choice.

### Build strength through sharing

One way to stay motivated and fired up is to build excitement in your own organization, whether it's a newsroom, television station, campus newspaper or classroom. Track records requests and share that information among your colleagues. Create an Intranet to share the ideas, sources and even the records themselves. Or simply create a bulletin board for people to post their record requests or schedule brown-bag lunches to share ideas.

*The Seattle Times,* for example, created a simple database that tracks all FOI requests in the newsroom, including the agency, date of request and outcome. The database serves as a gathering place for reporters throughout the newsroom—and it triggers alerts via e-mail to remind reporters to follow up on outstanding requests.

Sharing information can spur others around you to request documents on their own beats, and provide a critical mass of FOI requesters to boost expertise and story possibilities. For example, say the court reporter acquires criminal conviction data and lets everyone in the newsroom know. Then the education reporter snags a database of school bus drivers. The two work together to link the databases and find school bus drivers who have been convicted of assault, child molestation and drunken driving.

That's powerful reporting.

### Attend a conference

Professional conferences and workshops can do wonders for inspiration and ideas. Unfortunately, not everyone can afford to make the national

> ## Pro tip | Ask for more than what's open by law
>
>  Just because a record is legally exempt from disclosure doesn't mean you are prohibited from getting it or publishing its contents. Working on the Chauncey Bailey Project Web site (www. chaunceybaileyproject.org), dedicated to finding the killer of Bailey, an editor at the *Oakland* (Calif.) *Post,* a coalition of journalists acquired documents usually kept secret during open murder investigations, including the detective's full file with notes, evidence obtained through subpoenas and phone records. It's all about source development. You need to be very familiar with laws at the state level to promise confidentiality. Learn your state shield law and explain it to sources. Also understand the limits of shield laws, and situations where confidentiality cannot be promised. It establishes your credibility and it helps assure people that there is some level of protection.
>
> —Thomas Peele, investigative reporter, Bay Area News Group, Oakland, Calif., and a lead reporter for www.chaunceybaileyproject.org

conferences across the country, but many opportunities are available in your own backyard. The workshop that Wilbur attended was a half-day meeting in his own state. Chances are, similar opportunities will arise near you. Check these out:

- **Society of Professional Journalists newsroom training.** SPJ's newsroom training includes a module specifically focused on freedom of information. Contact SPJ for more information and to ask for trainers to come to your newsroom or community (www.spj .org/bbtraining.asp).
- **Investigative Reporters and Editors better watchdog training.** For years, IRE has provided regional workshops that focus on investigative reporting, including accessing public records. Find a workshop near you (www.ire.org/training/watchdogjournalism/ index.php).
- **State press associations.** Most newspaper groups put on annual conferences that include training, including in freedom of information.

- **Access conferences.** Several groups sponsor workshops and conferences focused exclusively on access to information. Check out the opportunities by the National Freedom of Information Coalition (www.nfoic.org) and the American Society of Access Professionals (www.accesspro.org).

## Get e-inspired

The Web is a great place for finding inspiration in the great work being done by document-minded citizens and journalists. Check out these sites:

- **FOI blogs and Web updates.** Some of the main blogs and Web updates dedicated to freedom of information include SPJ's FOI FYI (http://blogs.spjnetwork.org/foi), the National Freedom of Information Coalition's FOI Advocate (www.nfoic.org/issues), Reporters Committee for Freedom of the Press (www.rcfp.org) and the FOI-L listserv (www.nfoic.org/foil).
- **IdigAnswers.** Joe Adams is a journalist in Florida and an FOI trainer for the Society of Professional Journalists. He created his own Web site dedicated to helping Floridians locate and use public records. Check out his "Joe's Hit Records" list of great documents for journalists (www.idiganswers.com).
- **Investigative Reporters and Editors Extra! Extra!** This Web site highlights links to great investigative reporting, much of it document-driven. Also, become a member and get access to the IRE online morgue of more than 20,000 stories, keyword searchable, along with online archives to IRE Journal and Uplink stories. The Web site also has more than 3,000 tip sheets from conferences that can be searched by keyword (keyword "documents" yields more than 230 tip sheets) (www.ire.org).
- **Sunshine Troublemaker of the Week.** This award, handed out through WikiFOIA, a project of the Lucy Burns Institute, profiles a citizen who fought for public records to make his or her community better (http://wikifoia.pbwiki.com). You'll find some great examples and inspiration!

### Find an FOI friend

Some journalists, including seasoned investigators, find that it helps to develop a relationship with another like-minded journalist, near or far, to share tips and, more important, vent and get a renewed sense of purpose.

It's helpful if you find a buddy in the same state because then you both will get to know your state open record and meeting laws well. But the most important thing is that he or she shares your passion for open government. Here are some places to find an FOI friend:

- **State Society of Professional Journalists sunshine chairs.** Nearly every state has a "sunshine chair" who is knowledgeable and passionate about open government. Check out the sunshine network at the SPJ Web site (www.spj.org/foi.asp) to find the sunshine chair in your state.
- **State coalitions for open government.** Just about every state has an active coalition for open government, coordinated by the National Coalition for Open Government. Find the coalition in your state (www.nfoic.org/nfoicmembers) and contact board members.
- **Press associations.** State press associations are paid by their members to keep an eye on access legislation and answer questions from members. Some have FOI hotlines for member organizations.
- **Other reporters on the same beat.** Find a journalist at a similarly sized noncompeting news organization in your state who shares the same beat, and develop a collegial working relationship for sharing story ideas and suggestions for document requests. Also, if you are seeking a document from a reluctant state agency, you might go in on the request together, to apply more leverage and work out a publication agreement with your newfound colleague.
- **State experts.** Develop relationships with FOI experts in your state. These might include a media law attorney, a college professor or an assistant attorney general who believes in government transparency.

Jennifer LaFleur, director of computer-assisted reporting for the nonprofit investigative reporting organization ProPublica, is an expert at acquiring government databases and fighting for open government. But every now and then even her colleagues question her determination, so at times she consults with her FOI friend. Like the time when proposed legislation in Texas would have made dates of birth secret in government records, preventing the accurate matching of databases to find important stories, such as identifying guards at youth prisons who had abusive pasts. LaFleur testified at a legislative hearing to advocate for openness. "I got a little bit of flak from some colleagues, that this is inside baseball and that I shouldn't be doing this," she said. She called up a colleague, and "he said if we ignore the issue, then we'll lose the records. He gave me a pep talk."

That chat gave LaFleur the boost she needed to keep on fighting, and to maintain her document state of mind.

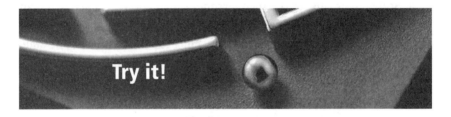

**Try it!**

**Here are some exercises and ideas for journalists, newsrooms and class-rooms to improve your skills and foster FOI in your community.**

### 1. Circle yourself

Grab a piece of paper and put your name in the middle. Then around your name write all the different roles and identities you represent (e.g., student, taxpayer, homeowner, driver, parent, pet owner). Then, around those roles, write all the public records that might contain information about those roles. Be amazed at the paper trail you will leave behind in this world. Now do the same thing for a prominent person in your community or someone you cover on a beat. Go examine those records to see if you find anything surprising or newsworthy.

## 2. Make an "FOI First" sticky note

Create an "FOI First" sticky note with a document you would like to get and post it on your computer monitor. Then select a day and once a week, first thing, submit a public records request for that document. Request a new document each week.

## 3. Find an FOI friend

Go to the "FOI friend" ideas listed on page 35 and find someone who can be your document buddy. Contact that person with an e-mail or phone call. Arrange to have coffee and talk about records you have and plan to request. Try to get three tips or records ideas from the person.

## 4. Get inspired by others

Troll the inspiration list on page 34 or do a quick Google search for "freedom of information" or "public records" with a date delimiter and read news stories driven by use of public records. If it worked in one city, it will likely work in yours. Jot down records that people are tapping, for future use.

## 5. Post FOI editorial cartoons

A great way to foster FOI and a document state of mind is to post editorial cartoons on the subject on bulletin boards and cubicle walls. Check out a plush archive of cartoons regarding access to public meetings and records provided for 2007 Sunshine Week (www.sunshineweek.org/sun shineweek/aaec07) or for 2009 (www.sunshineweek.org/sunshineweek/editorial_cartoons_09).

**Suggested links**

**Allies in your state**   www.nfoic.org/nfoicmembers
Check the National Freedom of Information Coalition Web site's
members listing to find coalitions in your state for allies and
inspiration.

**International FOI**   www.freedominfo.org
A great run-down of right to know laws throughout the world.
Pick a country and compare it to the United States. Some are better,
some are worse.

**Newsroom FOI training**   www.spj.org/bbtraining.asp
Find information about how to have the Society of Professional
Journalists send an FOI trainer to your newsroom or for your area
SPJ chapter.

**Pulitzer Prizes**   www.pulitzer.org
Get inspired to think about records by perusing Pulitzer Prize–
winning work.

**Watchdog training**   www.ire.org/training/watchdogjournalism/index.php
Check the Investigative Reporters and Editors Web site to find out if
a watchdog training session is being held in your area soon.

# Become an access law expert

- ☑ Master the law in five steps
- ☑ Dip into alphabet laws
- ☑ Access public meetings
- ☑ Tap into legal resources

Semester after semester, students in media law courses look at the syllabus and gasp. There in front of them is that first chapter of their textbook—the one with the writs of certiorari, the courts of original jurisdiction and the *stare decisis*—just in the first five pages! Welcome to the law.

Fifteen minutes into the first class, you can see the thought bubbles over the students' heads: "Hey man, I am not a lawyer. I am *so* outta here."

But don't bail on us yet—we promise not to get too legalistic. In fact, this chapter is designed to walk you back from the precipice and help you get up to speed on public records law fast—so you can put this book's advice into action right away and get your hands on the documents you need.

First, let's revisit an important caveat: This book is a how-to guide, not a legal reference tome. You will need to read your state public records laws, for starters, and if we listed every state's laws here we'd have a dictionary-length document on our hands. Instead, we've directed you to a variety of resources that cover the legal nuances of federal FOIA and state public records laws.

We aim to help you become an expert in the areas that matter most for scrutinizing government. Becoming familiar with the law gives you the confidence you need to approach officials and the backbone not to bolt if they start spouting legal mumbo-jumbo.

To put it another way: If we gave you a lecture detailing all the laws, its usefulness would last a year; if we teach you how to fish through the laws yourself, the benefits will last a lifetime. This chapter will teach you how to fish by explaining the basics of FOI laws, state public records laws, the odd little "alphabet" laws, open meeting laws and how to get started with legal research.

Ask a lawyer friend, and he or she will tell you it really doesn't take a law degree to understand and use FOIA. It takes a bit of initiative, a healthy dose of skepticism—and, more than anything, a deep and abiding refusal to be intimidated.

## Master the law in five steps

You can teach yourself the ins and outs of any public records law through five basic steps:

1. Learn the lingo
2. Identify what records are covered
3. Identify what agencies are covered
4. Identify exemptions that allow secrecy
5. Identify your rights to appeal

Let's look at each step.

### Learn the lingo

It's critical to get a general lay of the legal land and terminology, including terms we use throughout this book:

**Exemption:** A part of the law that allows an agency to keep something secret. For example, one exemption under FOIA is "oil and gas well data," so parts of records that would divulge the locations of oil wells can legally be kept secret, or exempt from disclosure.

**FOI:** When we talk about "FOI" we mean freedom of information in general. To most journalists this catch-all term is synonymous with "access to records" or "government transparency." We pronounce it by sounding out the letters: F-O-I.

**FOIA:** The federal Freedom of Information Act, passed in 1966, covers federal agencies. It's better known as "FOIA," pronounced FOY-uh. In this book, and in the general world of public records access, when we talk about "FOIA" we mean the actual federal Freedom of Information Act (Title 5 of the United States Code, section 552), not state public records laws or freedom of information in general.

**Permissive:** Access laws are generally written to be "permissive," which means agencies can make something secret if the law says they can, but *they don't have to.* With the exception of some school and health records, agencies can provide it to you if they want, even if there is an exemption. It's important to remember that the law represents the minimal standard for disclosure, not the maximum. Governments large and small release information far beyond the requirements of the FOI law all the time.

**Redaction:** Rarely are whole records exempt, or allowed to be kept secret in their entirety. Usually it's just a part, such as a Social Security number, the location of military weapons or the physical location of an oil well. The government "redacts," or blots out, the secret stuff but leaves the rest for you to see.

**State law names:** The 50 states and the District of Columbia have their own laws, which typically apply to state executive agencies and local governments, such as cities and school districts. It's important to learn which names your state uses so you don't make a rookie mistake like saying you want to make a sunshine law request in Minnesota, which calls its law the Data Practices Act.

### Identify what records are covered

Freedom of information laws are very broad in what they cover. The federal FOIA covers all "records" in the possession or control of a federal executive agency, and most state laws contain similar language. The term "records" is defined expansively to include all types of recorded information, such as papers, reports, letters, films, computer data, photographs and sound recordings.

BOX 3.1   **Not your father's documents**

Here are examples of the diversity of records covered by state access laws:

- E-mails, in some states even those from officials' personal accounts
- Text messages and Twitter communications
- Photographs of crime scenes
- Audio and video recordings of public hearings
- Video surveillance camera recordings at government buildings
- Databases in Excel files or other software
- Notes jotted down in a mayor's calendar book

It's important to remember that these laws do not require an agency to verbally tell a citizen anything—they simply give citizens the right to inspect recorded materials. So if a mayor doesn't return your phone calls or says "no" to an interview, that's his or her prerogative. There is no law requiring any official to talk to you. These laws require only that the government let you see recorded materials in its possession.

### Identify what agencies are covered

Know who is covered by the law. The federal Freedom of Information Act states that it covers every "agency," "department," "regulatory commission," "government controlled corporation" and "other establishment" in the executive branch of the federal government. Public records laws do not typically cover private entities, such as local businesses, private schools, churches or nonprofits. While those entities might file records with government agencies that are public (e.g., IRS 990 forms for nonprofits), typically their internal records are not for public viewing unless the private group wants them to be.

The federal FOIA covers Cabinet offices, such as the Departments of Defense, State, Treasury, Interior and Justice; independent regulatory agencies and commissions, such as the Federal Trade Commission; "government controlled corporations," such as the Postal Service and Amtrak; and presidential commissions. FOIA also applies to the Executive Office of the President and the Office of Management and Budget, but not to the president or immediate staff.

FOIA does not apply to Congress, the federal courts, private corporations or federally funded state agencies. Congress passed the federal FOIA law in 1966 to force openness upon the president's agencies, but made itself exempt from openness. Convenient, eh? However, documents generated by Congress and filed with executive branch agencies of the federal government become subject to disclosure under the act, just as if they were documents created by the agencies.

At the state and local level, the state public records law typically will apply to executive agencies (the state transportation department, the health department, state police, etc.) and local governments, such as cities, counties, school districts and even mosquito control districts— anything that is established by statute, funded primarily through taxes and empowered to make decisions that affect people. Yes, that means public universities as well.

In some states, the public records laws also apply to the legislatures and courts, but usually just the executive branch. The key: Assume that the agency is covered until you find out otherwise.

### Identify exemptions that allow secrecy

As you know by now, persistence is the cornerstone of any access request. So if you make a request and an agency says "no," ask the officials to show you the exemptions—to show you what provision of the law allows them to refuse. To do that, you'll need to understand the exemptions yourself.

The federal FOIA has just nine exemptions, but over the years court rulings on them have generated a nine-inch-thick digest called "Litigation under the Federal Freedom of Information Act"[1] and hundreds of exemptions are spread through other federal statutes. Check out the U.S. Department of Justice's "Freedom of Information Act Guide," which encompasses 1,135 pages to explain all the ways to use exemptions for keeping federal records secret.[2]

But we're more interested in *using* FOIA, so we'll apply the simple "show me" rule to FOI law, as in "show me the exemption." If the agency denies your request and cites a specific exemption, kindly ask someone

## Pro tip | Fight phantom exemptions

Michael Reitz

Jason Mercier

With talks of tax increases swirling across the Washington state capitol in 2009, newspaper reporters grew curious. Several sent records requests to the Department of Revenue to see what work it had done for lawmakers on the issue of tax increases. The response? DOR would have to check if the records were subject to "legislative privilege"—an exemption that doesn't exist in the public records statutes. We politely called them on it, and months later the records were finally released after intense media pressure—though the Legislature "reserved the right" to claim the nonexistent privilege in the future.

Then, a few months later, we requested documents related to the drafting and implementation of an executive order issued by the governor. The governor provided hundreds of pages, but withheld several dozen records on the basis of "executive privilege." We again pointed out there is no "executive privilege" exemption found in the Public Records Act and asked the governor to reconsider. We advised the governor we would consider legal action if denied again. Within a week the governor's office responded and provided the records. Agencies will often rely on stretched interpretation of exemptions—and even phantom exemptions—that may dissuade most requesters. Individuals who demonstrate a willingness to sue, as well as a familiarity with the law, are more likely to convince an agency to reverse its decision to withhold records.

—Michael Reitz and Jason Mercier,
Evergreen Freedom Foundation, Washington state

to show you where in the law the exemption exists—and then read it yourself, carefully.

Denials come on impressive letterhead, full of legal citations and signed by titled lawyers. But here is the news: Agencies make exemption claims unsupported by the law all the time. They bend and twist exemptions to suit their needs, and they bet the house you'll take the denial, sigh and walk away. By now, you know that's never the best way. Just politely ask, "Can you show me where in the law it says that this record is not public?"

Let's look at an example. A public school district denied access to a report that teachers, parents and reporters were after: The school had been closed temporarily, then reopened, following a black mold out-break. If you know anything about black mold, you understand the con-cern. It's a dangerous situation for kids and teachers with respiratory illnesses, and so, when the district hired an air quality consultant who came in, then declared the air quality fit for school again, everyone wanted a copy of his report.

The district denied access to the report. When asked why, it said that the report was exempted from disclosure because it was "legal work product," exempt under state law.

So we took a look at the exemption in question, which states: "Legal actions, causes of action or litigation involving a public governmental body and any confidential or privileged communications between a pub-lic governmental body and its attorneys. . . ."

Would a report produced by an environmental consultant for a school district—not in response to any litigation at all, but in response to a school closure—meet that definition? You don't have to be a lawyer to figure that one out. It was a public record, and after a lot of back and forth, it was released.

The breaking point came when one of the parents demanded that the school district show them in writing how the exemption fit the report. The district couldn't.

### Identify your rights to appeal

For the sake of argument, what if the air quality report really had fit the exemption? Is that the end of the discussion?

No!

There is no need to know your state's exemptions by heart. If you did, well, that would be scary. Instead, know them well enough so that when someone says no, you have a clue whether it's worth arguing about. Do you have a leg to stand on?

We've seen countless cases in which records custodians claim exemp-tions that simply do not exist—or at least do not exist as the custodian is interpreting them. So we listen carefully, we ask for specific citations and we check them out afterward. If your request is denied, and the exemp-tion is not an absolute slam dunk, always, always appeal.

To appeal a denial under the federal FOIA and most state FOI laws, all it takes is a letter to the agency—nothing fancy, just a letter making your arguments. The letter should always argue that release of the information is in the public interest and should always remind officials that the FOI law is the minimum level of disclosure.

Appeals often work, so never walk away without trying. Wendell Cochran, an American University professor who has studied the results of FOIA appeals, found that only about 3 percent of the 240,000 FOIA requests that were denied in 2006 were appealed. Of those few people who did appeal and got an agency ruling, about a third received something in the end, if not everything they asked for.[3] So clearly, it doesn't hurt to appeal!

## Dip into alphabet laws

In addition to public records laws requiring agencies to provide government documents to the public, specialized laws require agencies to keep certain kinds of records secret. From time to time, depending on what you are covering, you'll be presented with a dizzying array of acronyms. Again, no need to be a legal scholar: Just know what you are dealing with. We call them "alphabet laws."

### Health information: HIPAA

Interested in medical topics? Covering an accident or following up on a car crash? No doubt you'll encounter the Health Insurance Portability and Accountability Act (HIPAA). It's the same law that requires you to sign that privacy statement when you visit the doctor, guaranteeing that the office won't release information without your consent.

In 2001 HIPAA created new privacy rules regarding personal health information. An amendment clarifying the rules of HIPAA was adopted a year later. The rules are so confusing that the "simplification regulation" is 367 pages long!

Since the Privacy Rule went into effect in April 2003, it has become more difficult for reporters to get information about individuals' health care. For example, hospitals will no longer give out the names and conditions of accident victims unless the reporters know each victim's name, and then only general information will be provided. But other HIPAA obstacles are unnecessary. Fearful of HIPAA's civil and criminal penalties, some health care providers have overreacted, while others may simply use HIPAA as an excuse not to cooperate with reporters.

Reporters can work more effectively if they understand what HIPAA does and does not do. Essentially, HIPAA requires "covered entities" to keep "protected health information" private.

"Covered entities" include health plans, health care clearinghouses and most health care providers that reimburse insurance charges. Examples include hospitals, college health clinics, ambulances/emergency medical technicians (EMTs), private physicians and social workers.

The following are *not* covered entities that can keep things private under HIPAA: police and fire departments (except EMTs), patients and their relatives, clubs and associations (which are not health care providers) and religious organizations.

Additionally, the following are *not* examples of protected health information: police and fire incident reports, and court records. Also, birth records and autopsy records are not protected health information, to the extent that they are maintained by state agencies. In addition, if a state FOIA law designates death records and/or autopsy reports as public information that must be disclosed, covered entities may disclose that protected health information without an authorization, effectively trumping HIPAA.

The key lesson with regard to medical information is that you are less likely to obtain information from hospitals—so go straight to the source! To release additional information to a reporter, a hospital must obtain written authorization from the patient (or the patient's parent or guardian in the case of minors). Many patients—especially those upset with their care—will happily sign documents over to a reporter working on their behalf.

### Education records: FERPA

The ivory tower can be as secretive a place as you ever cover, and if you are covering a college campus, you'll have the Family Educational Rights and Privacy Act (FERPA) thrown in your face the first day you are on the beat. FERPA covers students from kindergarten on, but most student reporters run into it on the college level.

The foundation of FERPA is that a student, upon notification, is given the right to inspect and review his or her own records while, generally, everyone other than the student is prohibited from access to student information.

Note that another federal law, the Clery Act, sometimes conflicts with FERPA. This law, named for a college freshman murdered in her dorm, was passed to require universities to make crime information public. If a university fails to make available daily crime logs, an annual statistical report and basic police reports for serious crimes, then it can face federal fines. It's important for student journalists to be aware of the Clery Act, and to exercise their rights to access campus police records under the law. Campus police can't tell you that crime information is private under FERPA.

## BOX 3.2 Open even under FERPA

A lot of people assume everything at all levels of schools is secret under FERPA, and many colleges and universities are happy to let that misconception stand. The law, however, allows the release of law enforcement records and "directory information." Typically, the following is considered directory information:

- Name
- Address
- Telephone listing
- University-provided e-mail address
- Date and place of birth
- Major field of study
- Dates of attendance
- Student level
- Degrees and awards received
- Weight and height of members of athletic teams
- The most recent education agency or institution attended
- Participation in officially recognized activities and sports

If a school balks, just send it to the Web site of the U.S. Department of Education, which enforces FERPA (www.ed.gov/policy/gen/guid/fpco/ferpa/index.html).

If you need more help with FERPA issues, the Student Press Law Center is the place to go (www.splc.org).

### Driver's licenses: DPPA

The Driver's Privacy Protection Act of 1994 (DPPA) prohibits Department of Motor Vehicles offices nationwide from releasing personal information from driving records unless it falls under one of 14 exemptions, including use by a government agency or insurance company. The person can also opt out to allow records to be released. In 1999 Congress amended the act to require opt-in consent before information can be released for marketing or solicitation purposes.

The DPPA forbids states from distributing personal information to direct marketers but allows personal information to be shared with law enforcement officials, courts, government agencies, private investigators, insurance underwriters and similar businesses.

The bottom line: You aren't getting drivers' license records with identifying information anymore, so think creatively. Can you do the reporting with data that doesn't include identifying information?

## Access public meetings

Freedom of information is not only about records; the law requires that most government meetings be open to the press and public too. The purpose of open meetings laws, often called sunshine laws, is to eliminate much of the secrecy surrounding the deliberations and decisions on which public policy is based. If the whole democratic process depends on we the people knowing how and why governments are making decisions, then open meetings are a pretty important part of the equation.

### Exercise your right to watch

Open meetings laws give anyone, including any member of the public as well as members of the traditional and nontraditional press, the ability to scrutinize and report first-hand on government meetings. Most federal, state and local government bodies are covered by open meetings laws, which also require the government agency to provide reasonable notice of meetings. In many instances, they also allow you to record what happens at meetings and to get copies of minutes, transcripts or recordings at low cost.

These days, "meetings" is being redefined to include e-mail discussions that involve a majority of board members and other high-tech variations on a theme. Not everything is public, though. It's crucial to understand what government bodies are covered and what kinds of gatherings qualify as a "meeting" for purposes of the law.

Then there are the exemptions: Federal and state open meetings laws allow government bodies to close meetings or portions of meetings to the public when they deal with certain subject matters, like pending litigation, the purchase of real estate and personnel matters like disciplinary measures. The exemptions vary widely from state to state, in number and in detail, so it's important to know your state's law and its exemptions, much like the case with public records.

In fact, the same rules apply for meetings exemptions—if the government agency moves to exclude you from a meeting, kindly ask them to explain why. They need to be able to cite a specific exemption—and even if they do, make sure it squares with your understanding of the exemption's meaning. Many state open meetings laws state that minutes of closed sessions must be kept and must be released within a number of days.

Knowing the basics can come in handy. An example: A few years ago, a public hospital announced that it was going to hold a staff meeting with all employees of the hospital—more than 1,300 people—to discuss ongoing financial problems, including the possibility of layoffs. When a student reporter showed up to cover the meeting, she was asked to leave. The exemption cited? Personnel matters.

The student reporter gave up and left the meeting, unaware of what the sunshine law's personnel exemption actually said. It states that meetings should be closed when discussing "[the] hiring, firing, disciplining or promoting of particular employees by a public governmental body when personal information about the employee is discussed or recorded. . . ."

Problem was, no one was discussing any specific personnel cuts, or even personnel, at all! It was a broad, name-free discussion of future scenarios—and it was all closed by an exemption that didn't fit the meeting. Had the student known the exemption—or even had it handy—she could have politely challenged the secrecy, and won.

### Question meeting red flags

Joel Campbell, a former reporter who teaches journalism at Brigham Young University in Utah and served as the Society of Professional

Journalists' Freedom of Information Committee chair, said government agencies frequently violate their state open meeting laws. "Most of our local governments don't understand the law," he said.

He suggests journalists watch for a few red flags to alert them to possible meeting shenanigans:

1. **Retreats.** Just because a public body wants to meet at the beach or mountains for a retreat doesn't mean the open meetings law doesn't apply. It's still a quorum, and so it should still be public.
2. **Attorney-client privilege.** Some public bodies try to get around their open meetings law by claiming attorney-client privilege, thinking they can talk about anything in secret as long as their attorney is in the room. Question the use of such ploys.
3. **Stealth agendas.** If the agenda says only "minutes," "old business" and "new business," begin challenging the public body for more information. Some state laws demand "reasonable specificity" on the agenda.
4. **Boilerplate closures.** In some states, cities include an "executive session" on their agenda as a matter or practice whether they really need it or not. Such a practice may encourage more closed meetings and violates the spirit of most open meetings laws.
5. **Electronic meetings.** Some states allow meetings to be conducted over the telephone or via video or audio conference. However, such meetings usually require that journalists and the public can listen or watch. Also be aware of the emerging trend to conduct public business via e-mail. Make sure the public bodies you cover aren't engaged in e-mail conversations about public business.
6. **No votes for executive sessions.** Some state laws require that a majority vote be taken to go into closed session.
7. **Work meetings.** In some places, public bodies hold regular "work sessions," "committee of the whole meetings" or "work meetings" before their regular meetings. In most cases, these are meetings to discuss matters informally and line up votes. These are still public meetings, no matter what they are called.

BOX 3.3   **Handy-dandy objection card**

Many journalists carry in their wallets or purses a laminated meeting closure "objection card." On the card they include a statement they can read to the governing body if they think a meeting is being wrongly closed. Do not argue or be disruptive (they can arrest you for disturbing the peace), but you can certainly object and then consult an attorney and pursue legal action later. Adjust the template text below to create your own card and use it if you think a meeting is being closed illegally:

*Pursuant to the state open meetings act [insert the legal citation here], I formally object to the closure of this meeting. I ask the body to reconsider and I ask that my objection be noted in the meeting minutes.*

Find a good description of your state's open meeting law and the full text at www.rcfp. org/ogg.

## Tap into legal resources

With FOI requests come legal questions—and to answer those questions you'll often need to get the law in your own hands, rather than relying on some bureaucrat's take.

In the course of making hundreds of FOI requests, we've found that many of the questions that arise can be answered by checking one of three sources: the FOI statutes themselves, the case law and opinions from the state's attorney general. If you follow a few basic procedures, you can quickly become more knowledgeable.

### Find shortcuts

The first step to understanding the statutes is to look at summaries, usually provided by expert attorneys and access organizations. Fortunately, there are some great sources available for this:

- **The Reporters Committee for Freedom of the Press.** This organization provides several wonderful resources that explain public records laws in plain English. The first is the Federal Open Government Guide (www.rcfp.org/fogg), which covers federal FOIA, including an explanation of exemptions and sample request letters. The second resource is the one that you will likely use most often: the online Open Government Guide (www.rcfp.org/ogg), which is a complete compendium of information on every state's open records and open meetings laws. Each state's section is arranged according to a standard outline, making it easy to compare laws in various states, and there is a keyword search tool as well. The guide also has an explanation of each part of the law, provided in plain English by an expert attorney in each state.

- **State access organizations.** Just about every state has some sort of a public records guide put out by a coalition for open government, the attorney general or a press association. You should be able to quickly get your hands on the state's FOI law in question through a number of avenues, but the easiest way usually is by going through the state's FOI coalition (www.nfoic.org/nfoicmembers)—they all have the state's law prominently linked from their home pages. Also, the Society of Professional Journalists (SPJ) provides a state-by-state list of FOI resources that includes links to guides (www.spj .org/foi.asp). The National Freedom of Information Coalition also has a state-by-state listing (www.nfoic.org/state-foi-laws).
- **Guides and studies.** A wealth of studies and guides are available online that explain the nuances of access laws:
  - o WikiFOIA (http://wikifoia.pbworks.com) continues to grow, and includes information about the laws and tips for requesting records.
  - o The Freedom of Information Center, now housed by the National Freedom of Information Coalition, has a wealth of guides and reports at http://www.nfoic.org/foi-center.
  - o Check out the authors' blog for *The Art of Access*, at www.theart ofaccess.com, for a list of research studies conducted about access laws, such as studies examining agency delays, effectiveness of laws, and enforcement provisions.

## Read the statutes

After getting a sense of the law from the summaries, *actually read* the statutes. Some statutes are clearly written, and you can easily understand exactly what the legislature intended and what "the law" is on a particular subject. Unfortunately, many statutes are difficult to understand. But the more you read, the more the language begins to make sense. Here are some other tips:

- Read the statute twice—slowly—then read it again.
- Pay close attention to all the "ands" and "ors." The use of "and" to end a series means that all elements of the series are included, or necessary, but an "or" at the end of a series means that only one of the elements needs to be included.
- Assume all words and punctuation in the statute have meaning. For example, if a statute says you "may" do something, that means you are allowed to do it. But if it says you "shall" do something, it means you are required to do it. This can be hugely important, particularly in the FOI context.
- It's tempting to skip words you don't quite understand. Don't do it. If you're confused about what a word means and can't understand from the context, look the word up. A great legal dictionary is available at http://dictionary.law.com.

Still confused? Turn to a friend, an editor or a lawyer and get a second opinion. Many lawyers are happy to coach you behind the scenes, to ensure that coverage is done right.

---

## Pro tip | Compare state laws

Use the "compare" function of the online Open Government Guide (www.rcfp.org/ogg), which gets millions of hits a year. Choose a part of the law and then click on "Select All States" and then "Compare." For example, a public university might deny a public records requester an Excel computer file of the student directory, requiring instead that the requester pay for photocopies of hundreds of printed pages. To help persuade the university to provide the records electronically, the requester could use the comparison function on the Reporters Committee Web site to learn that more than 35 states allow the requester to choose the format of the record. Sharing such information with the people who control the records sometimes provides fodder for pressuring them to provide records in searchable electronic format.

—Lucy Dalglish, executive director of the Reporters Committee for Freedom of the Press (www.rcfp.org)

### Identify key court cases

The statutes can help you with the slam-dunk easy issues, like whether the law allows autopsy reports to remain secret. But sometimes the statutes don't address a particular record or are vague, especially when it comes to emerging issues regarding e-mail and text messages. If the statute is unclear, then turn to case law—rulings that clarify statutes by showing how a court applied the law in a specific case. Being able to cite case law—meaning, showing what a court decided in an earlier case similar to yours—will make your requests much stronger. Some of the law summary resources mentioned above (e.g., Reporters Committee Open Government Guide) mention key court cases that you can cite.

Court decisions are published chronologically in volumes called case reporters. Different levels and types of courts have their opinions published in different sets of case reporters. A case reporter is just a bound set of opinions. And everything found in just about every case reporter is now available online, so while it helps to have a citation to search for, it is by no means the only way anymore.

A citation for a court case looks like this:

U.S. DEPT. OF JUSTICE v. REPORTERS COMMITTEE, 489 U.S. 749 (1989).

The "489" is the volume number of U.S. Reports to which you go. If you pull Volume 489 from the shelf and turn to page 749—voila!—there is your case, U.S. Department of Justice v. Reporters Committee.

***Federal courts.*** Where the U.S. Supreme Court is concerned, two private publishers emerged over the years to better serve lawyers with much quicker turnaround and detailed annotation. West Publishing Company publishes Supreme Court Reporter (S. Ct.) and Lawyers Cooperative publishes United States Supreme Court Reports, Lawyer's Edition (L. Ed. and L. Ed.2d).

So each Supreme Court opinion has at least three different "cites"— one to the U.S. Reports, one to Supreme Court Reporter and one to the Lawyers' Edition. Confused? Don't be! All you need is one cite, and off to the Internet you go.

Lower federal appellate decisions (United States Circuit Court) since 1880 are in West volumes known as Federal Reporter (F., F.2d, F.3d).

U.S. District Court decisions since 1932 are in West volumes known as the Federal Supplement (F. Supp., F. Supp. 2d). There are very few of these federal trial court opinions published, though, so don't get your hopes up.

**State courts.** Each state has at least one official reporter for the decisions of its highest court, and some states also have reporters for their intermediate appellate courts and, in a few instances, trial courts.

State appellate court decisions can also be found in West's seven regional reporters, each of which publishes decisions from the courts in specific geographical regions: South Eastern, Atlantic, North Eastern, North Western, Pacific, South Western and Southern.

**Media Law Reporter.** Another fine source for access cases is the Media Law Reporter, which combs through all published decisions from every level of court and handpicks the media law decisions.

You can find Media Law Reporter in any law library and in a lot of public libraries, particularly college libraries. The front of each volume of Media Law Reporter contains an index digest organized by subject. Under each subject heading you will find one-paragraph summaries of the cases within the volume addressing that issue.

**West Digests.** The West reporters provide a huge shortcut: digests that summarize court decisions by subject matter. The digests use what is known as the key number system. Each major category of law is further subdivided into subtopics. Each subtopic is assigned a key number.

So if you were interested in doing a study of the constitutional right of access to judicial proceedings and records, you would look under the digest topic Constitutional Law and find that key number 90.1(3) deals with First Amendment access rights. One-paragraph summaries or blurbs of cases addressing that issue would then be provided in the digest under the appropriate key number. Ask any friendly law librarian to walk you through the process, and in five minutes you'll be homing in on just what you need.

**LexisNexis and Westlaw.** If you took most of the contents of a modern law library and the key holdings of every news library in the country into one database, you'd have built LexisNexis and Westlaw. You can choose to search databases covering cases from all federal and state courts, a particular level of court (for instance, the U.S. Courts of Appeal) or a particular court (such as the U.S. Supreme Court). Everything is keyword search-enabled, and if you have a citation in hand, you'll have your case in seconds.

The cases are hyperlinked to all the other, older cases cited within the opinion you're reading, so you can easily bounce to the earlier cases on the subject. You can e-mail the results to yourself, save them to your desktop or print them out.

The downside to these databases: Unless you are a student with access to an educational account, they cost quite a bit to use. The good news is that for most of the FOI work you need to do, the case law is available online through a variety of sources for no cost. Our favorite quick-and-free online site is FindLaw (www.findlaw.com)—an online cornucopia of legal resources. You'll find an array of resources, such as law journals, mailing lists and bulletin boards where you can post questions. FindLaw also has a handy legal dictionary, which you'll need to translate all that Latin (http://dictionary.lp.findlaw.com).

## Pro tip | Don't be a jerk

View the process of seeking public information under an FOI law as a continuum. Start with sweetness and light, and escalate accordingly. Do not underestimate the value of trying to establish some personal rapport with a public official before or at the same time as making a written request. The law is not a blunt instrument. Using it to bludgeon a recalcitrant public official rarely leads to the release of information. Working with them one-on-one with a degree of courtesy and respect is more likely to produce results than legalistic demands. If the nice-guy routine does not work, be firm in insisting on your rights. Explain your position calmly and clearly. Know what your rights are. When it is time to involve a lawyer in your case, he or she will appreciate that you have made the effort to get public information released in a professional manner. A lawyer always likes representing the guy wearing the white hat. Judges and juries don't like ruling in favor of jerks. Make sure the jerk in the case is not you.

—Paul Watler, media law attorney at
Jackson Walker L.L.P., Dallas, Texas

*How to read a case.* When reading case law, the first thing to recognize is where the opinion of the court actually begins. If you are reading a case in a reporter published by a private company, the actual opinion of the court will be preceded by material written by the editorial staff of that company, not the court. Most of the time, there will first be a brief summary or synopsis of the case written by the editorial staff of whatever company publishes the volume you are using. This usually is followed by "headnotes." Headnotes are one-paragraph summaries of the key points of law covered by the case. They are tied to the particular publisher's digest or indexing system and are the same descriptions you will find about the case in the digests or indexes.

After the headnotes, the names of the attorneys who participated in the litigation usually are listed. Then, generally labeled "Opinion of the Court" or "Full Text of Opinion," will begin the actual words of the court.

When you first begin reading judicial opinions it can be difficult to separate the holding and essential reasoning from superfluous material (known as dicta or dictum). You will also need to learn how to summarize pages and pages of words into some useful format.

A handy shortcut we often use is called the FIRAC system—which stands for Facts, Issue, Resolution, Analysis and Conclusion. If you take notes as you go based on the FIRAC system, you'll find that you can easily compare and contrast cases, which is the key to making sense of the law.

## Ask the attorney general

In addition to statutes and case law, attorney general opinions can help you understand FOI law better. Typically when a question arises over whether a record should be public or not, and the statutes and court rulings don't address the question, then the state government's highest attorneys will sometimes issue an opinion explaining their take on the issue.

Often opinions are requested by agencies that want advice on whether to give out a document. Sometimes a requester asks for a formal opinion to convince an agency the document should be public. The opinions usually are not binding, but they often provide a good overview of the law and relevant issues.

Most states provide their attorney general opinions online at their state Web sites, indexed by topic or keyword searchable.

Now you're up to speed on the law and have a good sense of what is public and what isn't—or at least know where to find out when you run into a question. Now it's time to go find documents!

Try it!

**Exercises and ideas for journalists, newsrooms and classrooms to improve your skills and foster FOI in your community.**

### 1. Look next door

Identify strengths and weaknesses in your state public records laws by comparing the FOI law to other states. Find an area of your state public records law that interests you by scanning the Open Government Guide at the Reporters Committee for Freedom of the press (www.rcfp.org/ogg). For example, look at the category "How is e-mail treated?" or whether "gun permits" are secret. Then use the "Compare" function to get a list of how every state handles that particular issue. Get out a piece of paper and divide it into three categories: Open, Secret, Unclear. Write down where each state fits and then tally what percentage of states make that information public or secret. Once you've identified the weaknesses in the law compared to other states, contact your press association and state coalition for open government (www.nfoic.org/nfoicmembers) to see if something can be done about it. Also, check out four studies that have ranked states on various aspects of transparency, to see how your state shakes out:

☑ **Freedom of Information in the USA** (2002). Investigative Reporters and Editors and the Better Government Association rank states according to a survey of investigative journalists (www.ire.org/foi/bga).

☑ **States failing FOI responsiveness** (2007). National Freedom of Information Coalition and the Better Government Association rated the effectiveness of state laws regarding penalties for noncompliance and timeliness of response (www.nfoic.org/bga).

☑ **State of State Disclosure** (2007). Good Jobs First evaluates the quantity and quality of state government Web-based disclosure on economic development subsidies, contracts, and state lobbying activities; finds lack of disclosure (www.goodjobsfirst.org/pdf/state disclosure.pdf).

☑ **States of Disclosure** (2007). Center for Public Integrity ranks states by their openness in providing information about the financial interests of governors (http://projects.publicintegrity.org/ StateDisclosure/Default.aspx?act=executive).

## 2. Hidden, in plain sight

This exercise will help you get familiar with the law and highlight the number of secrecy exemptions enacted for special interests. In many states, exemptions are scattered throughout statutes, not just within the actual public records law. Go to your state government Web site and find the portion that provides state statutes online and keyword searchable. Search for such keywords as "records," "disclose," "disclosable," "secret" and "confidential." Note the hundreds of records that are kept secret by hidden exemptions. Copy and paste the list to a Word file and e-mail it to your state press association and legislators to highlight the extent of secrecy through hidden exemptions.

## 3. Befriend a media lawyer

It's important to develop relationships with media law experts. Every state has at least one or two expert media law attorneys—usually more—who are extremely knowledgeable about access law and are often willing to provide suggestions or thoughts about a records issue. Find a lawyer, invite the attorney to coffee or lunch and get to know the person. Here are some ways to find a media lawyer:

☑ Look at who wrote the state public records guide at the Reporters Committee for Freedom of the Press Open Government Guide (www.rcfp.org/ogg) for your state. It's almost always a premier access law attorney in the state.

☑ Ask your state press association. Often your press association will provide information about media law attorneys on their Web site.

☑ Find out which attorney or law firm represents the major daily newspapers in your state by asking an editor at the newspapers. Usually a few attorneys handle most of the media work in each state, and they have to be expert in access law.

☑ Look up recent public records case law and see which attorneys handled the lawsuits on behalf of requesters.

## 4. Visit your local law library

The best way to become adept at legal research is to dive in, with a little help from the people trained to help: law librarians. Visit the closest law library to get a primer on the legal resources available. Even if you don't have a law school nearby, a general university library or public library will have some resources you can try out. Ask a law librarian to show you the resources and databases. Find three resources that will help you understand the law.

## 5. Organize FOI training

Coordinate a training session for your fellow students or area colleagues. Invite your state's leading media lawyer to a session to discuss access law. The Society of Professional Journalists provides FOI training for SPJ chapters or newsrooms, provided enough people are likely to show up. An FOI trainer (possibly one of the two authors of this book) will come to your newsroom or community and provide a two-hour presentation on great documents and strategies for requesting records. For more information, check out the SPJ newsroom training page (www.spj.org/bbtraining.asp). Or coordinate a brown-bag lunch session with FOI PowerPoint presentations provided by SPJ online (www.spj.org/foiddnr.asp). Download one and tweak it to suit your needs and specific state.

**Suggested links**

**FOIA-able agencies**   www.usdoj.gov/oip/foiacontacts.htm
The U.S. Department of Justice provides the full list of federal
agencies that are subject to the Freedom of Information Act.

**FOIA guide**   www.rcfp.org/fogg
A helpful description of the federal Freedom of Information Act,
produced by the Reporters Committee for Freedom of the Press.

**Guide to educational records**   www.splc.org/legalresearch.asp?maincat=2
The Student Press Law Center provides a wealth of information
about FERPA and access to campus crime information. It can also
go to bat for students, providing free legal advice and counsel.

**Guide to HIPAA**   www.rcfp.org/hipaa/index.html
The Reporters Committee for Freedom of the Press published this
helpful guide to working with HIPAA to cover accidents and other
incidents involving medical records.

**HIPAA authorization form**   www.aha.org
Provides a checklist of what should be included in an authorization
form, along with other guidance on HIPAA, put out by the
American Hospital Association.

**Legal Information Institute**   www.law.cornell.edu
Provides free access to statutes and court opinions that you might
want to look at before jumping into some of the more complicated
legal search tools.

**Open Government Guide**   www.rcfp.org/ogg
The most helpful quick online resource to every state public records
law and open meeting law, produced by the Reporters Committee

for Freedom of the Press. Includes a comparison function to compare different aspects of state laws.

**State FOI Coalitions**    www.nfoic.org

A complete list of state FOI groups can be found at the National Freedom of Information Coalition.

Chapter

# 4

## The hunt
### Find records in the dark

---

**ACCESS ACTION AGENDA**

- ☑ Explore document habitats
- ☑ Find records in records
- ☑ Build on others' successes

---

Before requesting records, it's good to know what they are, where they're kept and what they're called. Otherwise, you're aiming for something you can't see. And that won't do.

This chapter walks you through strategies for finding documents. We will cover how to go into a record's world to understand where and how it lives, how to find records within other records and how to locate information alone or with others' help.

This is one of the most overlooked steps in records access. Too many people just sling out a request letter asking for a broad array of records without really knowing what is out there. As a result, most of the time the agency doesn't know what they want and denies the request, or the records it provides are unhelpful. Do your homework to know exactly what you need.

### Explore document habitats

When hunting for records, it's important to get to know your prey's habitat. You can do this by mapping out the lay of the land, trekking through the forest of documents and understanding the life and death of an agency's records.

### Map the government

Most public documents are generated by, well, public agencies. So understanding an agency is crucial to knowing what documents might be available and might yield newsworthy stories. Mapping the government is the first step in developing a document mindset. No GPS required.

Go online to the main Web page of a local government agency, such as the city, university or school district. Then start burrowing through the Web site. On a piece of paper, literally sketch out and map the agency based on what you find. This is an effective technique for large agencies that encompass a variety of programs, such as a state health department or an entire city Web site. You will be amazed at what functions an agency covers, and the documents recording such functions.

Ask yourself the following questions:

1. **What does the agency do?** Look at all the departments and subunits in the agency, through an A–Z index or list on the site. Think about all the tasks they must carry out and the resulting documents they produce.
2. **How does the agency spend its money?** Look at the budget online. What is being spent? Where is money coming from? What records would provide details? If the budget is not online, you have your first records request. Ask for three years' worth, so you can compare over time.
3. **What is the agency required to accomplish?** Check out the regulations, missions and goals. Chances are there are reports and documents assessing whether the agency meets the regulations, such as audits or accreditation reports. Often these highlight strengths and weaknesses of an agency, and allude to other documents. Every time you see a report named or listed, jot it down; you'll be building a "records inventory."
4. **What does the agency regulate or inspect?** If an agency is in charge of safety or regulation, then it keeps track of what is safe and what is unsafe. Make notes as you go of the proper names of the inspection reports generated by the agency.

5. **Who works for the agency?** Find employee lists and directories. Request copies if they aren't provided online. Even better, request old directories to find people who have left the agency as well. Good reporters know that "formers" make great sources.

6. **What statistics are provided online by the agency?** Those stats were created by analyzing individual records or data. Request those records to do your own analysis.

7. **What files and data are generated by the agency?** Look at the report footnotes and appendices to find references to other records that are more telling. Add them your inventory as you go.

8. **To whom does the agency report?** Every governmental entity sends documents somewhere, on a routine basis, detailing its everyday activities. These reports contain gems for reporters.

## 'Take over' agency territory

Now that you've gotten an idea of what an agency is all about based on its Web site, it's time to go native. Immerse yourself in the agency and learn how it operates by physically being there. Take a Friday morning and schedule a visit to meet each person in the office and learn what he or she does. Bring a box of donuts. Ask them what kinds of records they work with, and explain that you want to learn more about what they do and how they do it. Look at any forms they process. Find out what file cabinet or database the files are kept in, what information is in the documents and how far back they have been kept. Have them show you on the computer screen.

Pulitzer Prize–winning investigative reporter Eric Nalder begins a project by getting officials to work for him and "taking over" an agency. Nalder, senior investigative reporter for Hearst Newspapers, doesn't take charge, but rather becomes one with the employees. He requests a large number of records and then goes to the agency and sifts through the boxes, usually with someone present. Over time that person and other employees start to see the value of his work. He explains the public good of what he is working on. They join in. "They start telling me things they wouldn't normally tell me because they know me and understand the importance of the mission," he said.

## Pro tip | Look for longevity

Find the person who knows where all the records are hidden, including the archived records. A few years ago we represented a newspaper in the Midwest that was sued for libel. The plaintiff denied any and all prior criminal history. She came up clean at all of the local courthouses when our paralegal searched the municipalities in the area. When a veteran reporter at the newspaper heard of this, he asked us to let him take a shot. He went to the courthouse and talked to a different clerk who had been in her job forever. The clerk remembered some of the older court records were stored in antiquated microfiche format in dusty boxes in the courthouse basement. Less than an hour later, our reporter returned to the newsroom, caked in basement grime, with the court document that put the lie to the plaintiff's testimony. Within a week, we had a motion before the judge asking for the plaintiff to be sanctioned for hiding her criminal history. The judge issued a lengthy written opinion awarding legal fees to our client because of the plaintiff's evasive conduct. We later won the libel case.

—Charles Tobin, attorney, Holland and Knight, Washington, D.C.

Nalder's second technique is "reporting by hanging around." He hangs out at an agency for hours on end, observing, taking notes and learning. He used this technique in a 1997 investigation of the Seattle Police Department's office that handles arrest warrants. He went to the warrants office and sat in the lobby for a couple of hours and watched what people did. He came back another day and did the same thing. Staff members were curious, so they came up to him and started a conversation. Eventually his presence opened doors with workers who told him about systemic problems that allowed criminals to remain free. For example, once a person who was wanted for driving drunk staggered inebriated into the agency to ask about his warrant. The workers wanted to arrest him but could not because they were not given authority to do so. The drunk left the office, got in his car and drove away. By hanging around, Nalder could find out about these problems and the records that documented them.[1]

By going into an agency, you can find out how records are maintained so you know what you can request. For example, let's say your 8-year-old daughter or sister seems to be constantly talking about having a substitute teacher. You wonder what's going on at the school. How do you find out what records might exist?

Let's say you live in Utah, just to pick a state. Begin by going to the school district offices or calling the school principal, teachers or an administrator and asking what records are maintained, and in what form. Remember that the key is getting the proper name of the document, which in this case is "the substitute teacher master schedule."

A bit of research will reveal that as of 2009, the Salt Lake City School District used a database called "SubFinder®." Among other things, the program tracks how many substitutes each teacher has used and why that teacher was absent. Other Utah districts may use the same program or a similar one. If your district uses SubFinder®, the records custodian can query the records for your request. Consider asking that the records be exported into Microsoft Excel and given to you electronically. If the district does not use such a database program, ask what records are maintained and how.

If they are paper records—and in many states they will be—you will have a much more laborious task ahead. Having done it before, however, we can attest to the fact that once you're done you'll be able to tell your readers how many substitutes your district is using daily, weekly or monthly, and which classrooms most frequently have a substitute.

## Visit records' birth places

Seek the original forms and templates that give birth to the mountains of records. Government agencies typically create standardized forms for documents. Agency employees and citizens fill out the forms, which are then stored in file cabinets or entered into databases. Seek out a copy of the original blank form and you will have a pretty good idea of what the agency keeps and how the information might help you.

Find out if an agency has an office that is charged with developing, standardizing and photocopying forms. Many agency Web sites provide forms for the public. Simply type in the word "form" on the home page, and you'll find links to a variety of blank forms online.

For example, if you search for "form" on the Mississippi state government Web site, one of the first links is to a form for people trying to collect workers' compensation. People must fill in their occupation, average weekly wage, date and place of the injury, description of the accident and other bits of information. While the identity of the person is likely to be exempt from disclosure, the other information should be public. It could yield an interesting look at workplace accidents in Mississippi, perhaps even more telling than what's available in federal Occupational Safety and Health Administration accident data.

Another form on the Mississippi Web site instructs professional wrestlers to fill out personal information in order to be licensed to compete in public venues. Information includes age, weight, height, occupation, address, citizenship and whether the person is on parole or probation. Examining these forms could yield stories that deliver punch—along with a backhand chop and turnbuckle thrust!

### Scour document cemeteries

Just as records are born, so they die. Every record has a life span, and "retention schedules" lay out how long they'll get to live before being stuffed in the big file cabinet in the sky. In some cases, old records are required by state law to be maintained and archived for historical reasons. Many state archives departments establish the schedules for state and local agencies. Request retention schedules to find the existence of records.

Another benefit of retention schedules is that if an agency says it does not have a particular record because it was destroyed, you can request the retention schedule to see if it was destroyed on schedule.

It's easy to find retention schedules. For example, we went to the Iowa state government's Web site and in the search area typed "retention schedule." Up popped links to the State Records Commission, and on that home page is a link to "Current Records Retention Schedule." That link takes you to an 867-page list of thousands of public records in Iowa and how long they are to be maintained. For example, "executive correspondence" of agency heads is to be kept for two years by the agency, then archived permanently by state archives (see Box 4.1 for other examples). Archivists are wonderful people and can help you develop all sorts of records leads.

## BOX 4.1 **Sample records retention schedule**

Here is a summary of just some of the records listed in the Iowa Records Commission retention schedule (available at www.iowasrc.org). Many states have similar online retention schedules (look for a state archives or library office). Note the retention time of the first item (press releases), compared to the last item (criticisms of agencies).

| Documents | Retention orders for agency document |
|---|---|
| Press releases | 2 years, then destroyed |
| Governor's news conferences | 1 year, then archived permanently |
| Executive correspondence | 2 years, then archived permanently |
| Commission minutes | 5 years, then archived permanently |
| Department staff meetings | 2 years, then archived permanently |
| Organization chart | While current, then archived permanently |
| Surveys and studies | 2 years, then 8 years in archives, then destroyed |
| Requests to join associations | While current, then destroyed when no longer member |
| Emergency plans | While current, then destroyed |
| Awards to citizens for service | 2 years, then destroyed at agency's discretion |
| Criticisms of agencies | 6 months, then destroyed |

Similar to retention schedules, some states require that agencies maintain an index of their records to help keep track of the documents. In both cases, remember that these lists are often incomplete and sometimes government agencies don't follow them closely, keeping records longer than they should or destroying them before their time.

## Find records in records

After exploring the habitat and lifespan of documents, take a moment to consider how they reproduce. Documents beget documents. So when you're looking for records, a great place to look is . . . in other records.

Check the footnotes of government reports; they frequently refer to other similar documents. Check meeting minutes and agendas for mentions of reports and other documents that you can then request. If a city council member refers to a report during a meeting, request the document afterward. Some government reporters carry blank records request forms with them to meetings, so they can fill out a form and hand it to an official when the meeting ends.

### 'Interview' your documents

To look critically at documents and find more documents, try interviewing them. Sure, co-workers will wonder why you talk to paper and invite files to lunch, but if you interview records like humans, you will better understand their benefits and limitations. You might even make a friend.

Don Ray, a multimedia investigative journalist from Burbank, Calif., teaches journalists and law enforcement officers how to "interview" documents.

"When I encounter a document, it's in many ways no different than encountering another source, a human being," Ray said. "It's very easy to look past information in a document if you are not interested in it. So you need to get to know the document. Consider it a living thing, and it will give you more information."

When Ray was tipped off about alleged child molestation charges against Michael Jackson in 2003, he and other reporters got their hands on a document that included notes of an investigator's interview with a victim. Other journalists jumped straight to the last pages of the hand-written notes, where the graphic details were.

Ray, however, "interviewed" the whole document, including the first four pages, which seemed to contain nothing but boring typewritten bureaucratic jargon. "Who are you, document?" he asked. "What other information is out there that you know about?" As Ray questioned the record, he noticed a part buried in the jargon that everyone else had missed. It mentioned that another investigator was assigned to interview an additional suspected victim—child actor Macaulay Culkin. Because no other journalist noticed this piece of information, they missed additional records and a big story.

When I get a document the first thing I do is interview it. Ask your documents these 24 questions:

1. **Who's your daddy?** Find out who created the document and why.
2. **When were you born?** Find out the issue date and ask about updates.
3. **What language do you speak?** Make sure you understand the terminology.
4. **Where do you live?** You might need to make another visit to where it's stored.
5. **Who else is in your family?** Find out what other documents may be on file.
6. **Are you married?** Is there another document that is wed to this one?
7. **Why are you here?** Figure out the need for the document at the time of issuing.
8. **Just what is your job anyway?** Understand its purpose today.
9. **What information do you have?** Ask about every piece of information.
10. **Who told you this stuff?** It had to learn the information from someone.
11. **Who else are you allowed to talk with?** Find out if it's a public record.
12. **Did someone verify your information?** People can put what they want on a form.
13. **How do I know you're telling me the truth?** Yes, documents can also lie to you.
14. **What other secrets are you keeping?** Look for codes and other fine print.
15. **Who else have you been talking to?** Maybe there's a log of who's seen the file.
16. **If you don't know the answer, who might?** See if it leads you somewhere else.
17. **Are you legal?** Make sure you don't have a fake or altered document.
18. **How did you get here?** Find out the normal flow of the document.
19. **Are you retired?** Some documents have become obsolete.
20. **What's your life expectancy?** Check records retention policy.
21. **With whom have you been intimate?** Find out who has processed or handled it.
22. **Do you have any twin brothers or sisters?** There may be copies in other offices.
23. **Would you be willing to testify in court?** A certified copy will save court time.
24. **You're not planning on leaving town, are you?** Put your copies in a safe place.

—Don Ray, owner of Don Ray Media, information, news and investigations consulting, California (www.donray.com)

### Request the requests

When someone submits a public records request, that document becomes a public record. Even better, many agencies keep a log of public records requests to make sure they fulfill them and to track what has been settled and what is still outstanding. That log is public too, often as a computer spreadsheet.

Request the requests and you'll learn about hundreds or thousands of public records that other people found interesting and important enough to ask for. This was (and probably still is) a tactic some reporters use in large markets to see what the competition is working on.

Nalder had experienced this tactic firsthand when competing journalists requested agency FOI logs to see what he was working on. "I thought it was kind of a cheap thing to do," he said. Taken to its competitive extreme, Nalder could have requested to see the FOI log to see which competing reporters had requested the FOI log to see what records Nalder had requested. And they would see he requested the FOI log to see what they were requesting. Way too complicated. But over time Nalder realized, hey, these logs are actually useful for finding other stories. He saw in FOI logs lawyers requesting documents that might indicate lawsuit-worthy problems in an agency. Request logs are rich with documents and story ideas.

For example, looking at the U.S. Department of Homeland Security (DHS) FOIA logs for 2003–2005 (see Figure 4.1), we can see that a representative of presidential candidate John Kerry requested correspondence between the agency and four other presidential candidates, perhaps for political fodder in the campaign. We also see several journalists—from *U.S. News and World Report,* the (Manchester) *Union Leader* and News 4 of Colorado—requesting records regarding critical infrastructure, funding in New Hampshire and terrorism task force funding. It is also apparent that government watch groups were interested in decisions about detainees, and companies wanted information about baggage screening projects. All good potential stories—and all listed on just one page out of 70.

| Id | Date Received | Date Closed | Sender | Organization | Fee Category | Subject | Disposition (All internal disposition tracking notes have been redacted pursuant to (b)(2)) | Why (All internal processing/tracking notes have been redacted pursuant to (b)(2)) |
|---|---|---|---|---|---|---|---|---|
| 04-1 | 10/02/2003 | 10/30/2003 | Philip J. McGovern, Esq. | Mirick O'Connell | Commercial Use | Baggage Screening Explosive Device System Installation Project | | |
| 04-2 | 10/02/2003 | 10/02/2003 | Philip J. McGovern, Esq. | Mirick O'Connell | Commercial Use | Baggage Screening Explosive Device System Installation Project | | |
| 04-3 | 10/07/2003 | 10/07/2003 | Isabel Banner, Director | Oct. 97 Holdings Ltd | Commercial Use | when Eurocopter AS350BA cleared customs | | |
| 04-10 | 10/08/2003 | 10/08/2003 | David Maldonado | n/a | Other | vacancy announcement for Detention Enforcement Officer | | |
| 04-11 | 10/08/2003 | 11/03/2003 | Christopher H. Schmitt | U.S. News & World Report | Media Representative | critical infrastructure information | | |
| 04-12 | 10/08/2003 | 10/15/2005 | David Schnitzer | John Kerry for President | Commercial Use | correspondence with four Presidential candidates | | |
| 04-13 | 10/09/2003 | 10/30/2003 | Jordan Carleo-Evangelist | Manchester Union Leader | Media Representative | DHS funding in NH | | |
| 04-14 | 10/10/2003 | 10/17/2003 | Kim Neblett | INPUT | Commercial Use | FY2002 Domestic Preparedness Training & Technical Assistance Program | | |
| 04-16 | 10/10/2003 | 10/10/2003 | Natasha Geiser | n/a | Other | DHS information | | |
| 04-17 | 10/10/2003 | 10/27/2003 | Carisa Scott | News 4 of Colorado | Media Representative | Joint Terrorism Task Force conference locations and funding | | |
| 04-18 | 10/10/2003 | 11/20/2003 | Anna Feygina | INPUT | Commercial Use | RFP for Homeland Security Centers of Excellence | | |
| 04-20 | 10/10/2003 | 10/10/2003 | Dawn Parpart | Big Sky Computer Products | Commercial Use | IMPAC credit cardholders | | |
| 04-21 | 10/10/2003 | 10/10/2003 | Christopher Farrell | Judicial Watch | Other | decision to allow subjects of Saudi Arabia to leave U.S. after 9/11 | | |
| 04-22 | 10/07/2003 | 10/09/2003 | Gary Malyszek | n/a | Commercial Use | procurement | | |
| 04-24 | 10/07/2003 | 11/29/2005 | Edgar N. James | James & Hoffman | Commercial Use | documents responsive to OPM survey on employees with law enforcement duties | | |
| 04-25 | 10/14/2003 | 01/09/2004 | Maryiia Kelley | Tri-Valley CAREs | Other | MOUs with DOE | | |

This page is an excerpt from a 70-page case log spanning 2003 through 2005, obtained and posted online by the nonprofit government watchdog organization governmentattic.org (www.governmentattic.org). Note that DHS keeps the disposition (whether the records were provided or not) secret; most do not keep that secret.

*Source:* U.S. Department of Homeland Security, http://www.governmentattic.org/docs/FOIA_Logs_DeptHomelandSecurity_FY2004-05.pdf.

## Build on others' successes

Fortunately, a lot of great journalists, citizen activists and investigators have figured out where to find useful government documents. We can save ourselves a lot of time, and honor their achievements, by getting records ideas from those who came before us.

### Surf FOI-idea Web sites

Chances are other journalists have found great documents in their areas that you can find in your state, or localize to your community. Fortunately, many of these journalists have provided ideas online for others. Here are some useful examples:

- **Investigative Reporters and Editors (IRE).** This Web site highlights links to great investigative reporting, much of it document-driven. Become a member and get access to the IRE online morgue of more than 20,000 stories, searchable by keyword, along with online archives to *IRE Journal* and *Uplink* stories. The Web site also has more than 3,000 tip sheets from conferences that can be searched; the keyword "documents" yields more than 230 tip sheets (www .ire.org).
- **Data centers.** Look at the "data center" or "information center" parts of news organization Web sites to see what kinds of records and databases other journalists have gathered. See if the information is available in your state and get it. Gannett newspapers, in particular, have promoted their information centers aggressively. For example, at the *Cincinnati Enquirer's* data center you can find dozens of public records and databases on subjects including federal money earmarked for the area, property values, crime, smoking complaints, early prison releases and liquor licenses (http://dunes.cincinnati. com/data).
- **EveryBlock.com.** This innovative nonprofit project (now owned by the for-profit MSNBC) puts public data online so people can find out what's going on in their neighborhoods. As of 2010 this free service was provided in a dozen major metropolitan areas. For example, residents of Los Angeles can get information on restaurant

inspections, pool inspections, fire alerts, crime and liquor license revocations. The project was started by Adrian Holovaty, a journalist and Web developer formerly of washingtonpost.com, and purchased by Microsoft in 2009.

- **Free online records sites.** Companies gather public records and provide them online for a fee. Often they'll provide some information for free, or tell you the source of the information, which you can then go to yourself. Some of these great document-minded Web sites include BRBpub.com, Fedworld.gov, Newslib, Searchsystems.net and Zabasearch.com. Check out www.pipl.com and see the wealth of information about yourself or key sources. Think of where they got those records—then go get them yourself from the source.

- **IdigAnswers.** Joe Adams, a journalist in Florida and an FOI trainer for the Society of Professional Journalists, created a Web site dedicated to helping Floridians locate and use public records. Check out his "Joe's Hit Records" list of great documents for journalists (www.idiganswers.com).

- **Society of Professional Journalists FOI FYI blog.** This blog posts news about freedom of information and document ideas (http://blogs.spjnetwork.org/foi).

- **The Record Album.** We have provided hundreds of public records ideas on our blog for this book (www.theartofaccess.com). See the appendix for a sampling. In the list we provide examples of possible stories and where the documents usually reside.

### Follow record hunters

A variety of access advocates and nonprofits have gathered documents through FOIA requests and put them online for anyone to look at. These document vaults are rich with information and story ideas: wrongdoing by local companies, complaints against television shows and investigations into prominent newsmakers.

As journalists, we wouldn't actually use these records without requesting them ourselves and verifying the information, but they can provide great ideas:

- **The National Security Archive.** This independent, nongovernmental research institute, not to be confused with the federal government's National Archives, is based at George Washington University in Washington, D.C. The center collects and publishes declassified documents obtained through FOIA, usually shedding light on U.S. government policies. For example, you can find such records as "Rumsfeld's Roadmap to Propaganda," detailing psychological operations strategies and their possible spillover on American citizens, and "The Deep Throat File," an FBI memo detailing Mark Felt's involvement in the Watergate scandal (www.nsarchive.org).
- **The Government's Attic.** This Web site, launched in 2007, specializes in FOIA logs, so you can see what kinds of records have been requested from federal agencies, and by whom. Many names are redacted, but you'll find active requests by *The New York Times, Des Moines Register, The Seattle Times,* law firms and military newspapers. The other interesting postings include FCC complaints regarding television shows (for example, the file for "South Park" takes up considerable space) (www.governmentattic.org).
- **The Memory Hole.** This Web site has been around since 2002, dedicated to gathering important government documents and posting them for the public. In 2004 The Memory Hole obtained and posted 288 photos of war dead coming to Dover Air Force Base in flag-draped coffins, which caused a stir in military photo release policy. Recent postings include 500 photos and video showing cruelty at a horse-slaughter facility in Texas, gathered by a FOIA request to the U.S. Department of Agriculture by Animals' Angels. You might find similar documents posted about a company near you (www.thememoryhole.org).
- **Governmentdocs.org.** This site was launched in 2007 by Citizens for Responsibility and Ethics in Washington with a coalition of government watchdog groups. People who register can log in and review documents that these groups have requested and received. As of the end of 2009, the Web site was up to about 5,000 documents from 130 FOIA requests. This site is special because users can

comment on documents to provide insights and expertise for others (http://governmentdocs.org).

- **Local sites.** Look for local gadflies who gather public records from local or state agencies and post them online. If you can't find them, go ahead and start that service through your news organization. Maybe your company already does that—for example, archiving useful records online from City Hall. Many news organizations have started data centers, posting government data that are useful for citizens. Expand that service.
- **Google Advanced Search.** If you go into the Advanced Search of Google, you can search for specific types of files, such as .doc (Word), .xls (Excel) or .pdf (Adobe Acrobat). You can search for those specific types of files at government Web sites or domains, such as usa.gov, ny.gov or wsu.edu.

### Get help from librarians

Libraries are a good source of public documents and online resources to tap into public records. Many libraries, including university libraries, have access to LexisNexis, PACER and other powerful databases.

The federal depository library system designates more than 1,250 libraries nationwide to hold documents from all three branches of federal government. The volumes of documents and databases provided free include regulations, historical records, statistics, military records and presidential papers. These documents are used extensively by historians, academics, genealogists and all kinds of writers.

Ann Marie Sanders, depository librarian for the Library of Michigan in Lansing, said it's best to contact a federal depository coordinator to get a primer on the extensive resources. "Don't assume all the information is online, and if it is online it might not be easy to find," she says. There's a coordinator in almost all congressional districts and in every state. For more information, including finding a federal depository near you, go to http://catalog.gpo.gov/fdlpdir/FDLPdir.jsp.

Another great source of records is your state archives office. This agency stores all those public records that are often two years or older.

**Pro tip** | **Set up automatic FOI feeds**

To find new records and databases produced by an agency, subscribe to every communication it puts out, including e-mail alerts, department newsletters and RSS feeds. You have to consume a ton of stuff like that. For agency Web sites that don't have RSS feeds, use software, such as Update Scanner (a Firefox add-on) or Versionista, to automatically alert you when the site is updated with new information. Also, set up a Google News Alert to search for "database" or "records" and the agency name. It helps me find when they launch a new database, or a new technology project. You would be surprised what you get.

—Daniel X. O'Neil, "People Person" for Everyblock.com, in charge of gathering databases for the nationwide, neighborhood-level community information Web site

Even just checking your state archives Web site will yield ideas of interesting-sounding records. For example, the Oregon archives Web site (www.sos.state.or.us/archives) lists an index to the records it stores, has a section on genealogy records, describes its collection of governor records and provides details about records it maintains about adoptions, census, land, military and naturalization.

Also, at the federal level, check out the Government Printing Office's Federal Digital System (FDsys), which is available online for free (www.gpo.gov/fdsys).

### Mine the miners

Journalists are not the only document experts. Seek out all sorts of people in other careers who request records routinely, and take them out for coffee to share tips. Some potential allies include:

- **Genealogists.** Backgrounding relatives is document-intensive, so genealogists know their way around vital records. Just about every community has a society of genealogists with members skilled in the art of accessing government records, especially historical documents.

- **Historians.** Some of the most fervent supporters of public records are historians because they rely so heavily on written documentation for research. Contact your local and state historical societies and ask who are the records whizzes within the historian community. They can help you find out how to background the history of property and people through archival records and census/ immigration records, as well as identify the location of other documents you might not be aware of.
- **Librarians.** Librarians know how to find information, know their way around the Internet and are active in FOI issues. Meet librarians who work in the government document section of your local university library.
- **Private investigators.** These folks gather records for a living; they know the document terrain well. They also hear about a lot of interesting cases in town and might tip you off to a good story if it doesn't involve their clients. You can look up investigators in the phone book or, in some states, find detectives through government licensing data.
- **Realtors.** Looking for property records and documents helpful in backgrounding homes? Realtors know how to get through documents regarding property acquisition.

## Scan investigative stories

Learn about the best documents from the best journalists through document-driven story scanning. Here's how.

Browse lists of award-winning stories, such as Pulitzers (www.pulitzer .org), Society of Professional Journalists awards (www.spj.org/awards .asp) and Investigative Reporters and Editors awards (www.ire.org/ contest). Also, browse the "Extra! Extra!" postings of outstanding investigative reporting at the IRE Web site (www.ire.org/extraextra). To make it even easier, IRE has indexed all these great stories by beat and topic, such as "business," "broadcast" and "military." The Extra! Extra! story summaries also are keyword searchable. Each summary has a link to the story at the news organization's Web site.

**Pro tip** | **Submit standing requests**

Some agencies will allow you to submit standing requests, where you ask ahead of time for all future records produced regarding a certain topic. For example, in covering construction deaths on the Las Vegas Strip [Berzon's series[2] won a 2009 Pulitzer for the *Las Vegas Sun*], if a worker died I knew there would be a report out eventually, so I would submit my request ahead of time for the record as soon as it was available. That way I wouldn't forget later. I would always ask for things in advance. Get more rather than less.

—Alexandra Berzon, reporter, *The Wall Street Journal*

Based on the name of the author, news outlet, date and title of the piece, find the project on the media outlet's Web site. Often an organization will designate separate special report pages for award-winning projects, with sidebars explaining how the project was conducted and listing sources, including documents acquired.

Read the stories and look for attribution to records, the parts of sentences we usually ignore as readers. If you're short on time, do an electronic "Find" search for the words "document," "record" or "according to." When you find the references, think about where you might find similar records in your own community, and request them.

Take, for example, a 2006 project by Debbie Cenziper of *The Miami Herald,* exposing waste in the Miami-Dade Housing Agency. Online, the "House of Lies" project explains to readers how the reporters used a variety of documents, including housing project files, federal records, invoices, budgets, construction correspondence, canceled checks and audits. In a follow-up story posted online, a search for the word "records" zeroes in on references to audit reports and property records identifying the purchase price of a ranch. The newspaper even scanned in some of the documents for people to see for themselves.[3] The series won the Pulitzer Prize.

When Cenziper moved to *The Washington Post,* she produced another project in 2008 with database editor Sarah Cohen that exposed bad landlords, based on 1,000 court cases, 128,000 housing-code violation documents and hundreds of other government records. That seven-part series won the Goldsmith Prize for investigative reporting, which came with a $25,000 check.[4]

"I've mined thousands of government records for every investigative project I've published in recent years," Cenziper said. "I use budgets, invoices, contracts, grant agreements and audits to track government money. I use corporate, property and personal records to establish relationships between government officials and the people who have received money. It's like putting a puzzle together, and it's the best part of my job."

Cenziper is a pro at using records, and we can all learn from her and other great document-minded journalists. Once you know the law, figure out what records are out there and where they are, then go and ask for them.

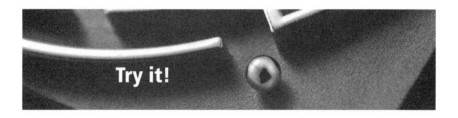

Try it!

**Exercises and ideas for journalists, newsrooms and classrooms to improve your skills and foster FOI in your community.**

### 1. Map an agency

Go online to the main Web page of a local government agency, such as the city, university or school district. Then start burrowing through the Web site, and on a piece of paper start mapping out the agency based on what you find. Answer the questions earlier in this chapter about what requirements the agency must meet and what documents it generates. Come up with at least two document-based story ideas.

### 2. Google Advanced Search document hunt

Identify a government agency you are interested in and find its online domain name (e.g., www.michigan.gov for the state of Michigan). Then, in Google, go to the Advanced Search function and search within that domain for different file types (.pdf, .doc, .xls., etc.). For example, a search of the michigan.gov domain yielded 1,630 Excel files, 8,150 Word files, and 111,000 pdf files. Browse them to see what records they have posted online. Find three records that could be the basis of stories.

### 3. FOI an FOI log

Pick a local government agency and request the requests for the past year or two. See if the log is kept in an electronic format, such as Excel, and try to get the disposition, including whether the records were provided, when they were provided and who asked for them. Then do a quick tally to see how many records were requested, what percent were provided, how long it took people to get the records and who tended to request the records (media, businesses, attorneys, etc.). Look for trends over time, or compare agencies to identify the most secretive and open local governments. Find three potential records that could lead to your own stories, and then request them.

### 4. Blank-form hunt

Search a local government Web site or your state's Web site, looking for all forms provided online; often state Web sites will have an actual link to forms from their home pages. You can also look for licensing renewal pages or search for the keyword "form." You will find hundreds of blank forms that people fill out. Print out two that interest you and use a highlighter to mark the parts that are most useful to your reporting. Then request to see the past year's filled-out forms at the agency.

### 5. Spin through The Record Album

Look through The Record Album at the back of the book and find three records you would like to request that could yield stories of interest to you. Request them. Also, check out the expanded listing on the authors' blog (www.theartofaccess.com) for more ideas.

### 6. Zaba and Pipl yourself

Pick a person: yourself, a professor or a key source. Then run that person through www.pipl.com, www.zabasearch.com and Google. Look at the vast amount of information available online that these Web sites gleaned, including date of birth, home address, home phone number, pictures and relatives. Notice how Google isn't really that helpful—that it's more important to know where records are kept. Try to figure out where the information came from, and then go get it yourself. Identify which information is inaccurate. Create a "profile" of the person based on what you found. Later, if a public official denies information to you, such as the date of birth of city employees or home addresses, then show that official his or her own "pipl" results displaying that information. The bottom line: If someone wants to find you, they will. As unpleasant as it is, keeping dates of birth and home addresses secret is futile—that horse is already out of the barn.

**Suggested links**

**Everyblock.com**   www.everyblock.com
Look through the wealth of data this outfit has collected from city governments and posted online. Request the same data in your town.

**Federal databases**   www.data.gov
The Obama administration began posting databases at this Web site in 2009. In December 2009 the president ordered all executive agencies to post "high-value" information, which could yield good stories.

**Federal records**   www.gpo.gov/fdsys
The Government Printing Office's Federal Digital System (FDsys) provides a wealth of documents online free for anyone to browse.

**The Government's Attic**   www.governmentattic.org
This Web site posts a variety of federal documents, including FOI logs from a number of agencies. Browsing the logs online will spur lots of records ideas.

**The National Security Archive**   www.nsarchive.org
This nonprofit group requests and posts online federal records.

**Online information collectors**   www.pipl.com
Check out pipl, zabasearch and other information collectors to get a sense of what kind of information is available.

**Uploaded documents**   http://governmentdocs.org
Citizens for Responsibility and Ethics in Washington provides this site for people to upload documents and review them.

# 5

# Strategies for effective requests

| ACCESS ACTION AGENDA |
| --- |
| ☑ Do your homework |
| ☑ Write effective letters |
| ☑ "Get to yes" through principled negotiation |
| ☑ Apply hard tactics if necessary |

You know what record you want, who has it and the law that says it's public. Now it's time to go get it.

You should be able to call or walk into an agency and just ask to see the documents, and often you can. Ask and you shall receive. But sometimes it isn't that easy. Sometimes *how* you request the information will determine whether you get it, or at least whether you get it in a timely fashion. It shouldn't be that way, but that is reality.

This chapter provides practical tips for effective public records requests, including preparatory steps, comparison of good and bad request letters and practical psychological strategies for dealing with your fellow humans.

## Do your homework

It pays to do a lot of work before asking for a document. It will save you—and the agency—time in the end. We suggest you walk through a series of steps in preparation of your request (see Figure 5.1).

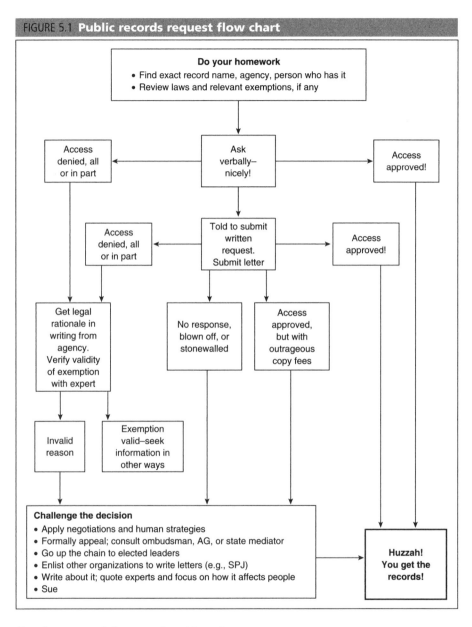

FIGURE 5.1  **Public records request flow chart**

**Do your homework**
- Find exact record name, agency, person who has it
- Review laws and relevant exemptions, if any

Access denied, all or in part

Ask verbally–nicely!

Access approved!

Access denied, all or in part

Told to submit written request. Submit letter

Access approved!

Get legal rationale in writing from agency. Verify validity of exemption with expert

No response, blown off, or stonewalled

Access approved, but with outrageous copy fees

Invalid reason

Exemption valid–seek information in other ways

**Challenge the decision**
- Apply negotiations and human strategies
- Formally appeal; consult ombudsman, AG, or state mediator
- Go up the chain to elected leaders
- Enlist other organizations to write letters (e.g., SPJ)
- Write about it; quote experts and focus on how it affects people
- Sue

**Huzzah! You get the records!**

## Get the name of the record and location

Your first task is to find out exactly what record you need, who has it and where the record is kept. A specific request is a good request. That requires reconnaissance.

Eric Nalder, senior enterprise reporter for Hearst Newspapers, tries to talk to government employees before requesting records so he knows exactly what to ask for, even on quick-hit stories. For example, in 1999 he got a tip that Washington state's ferries didn't have enough lifeboats to handle all their passengers. Only one in seven people could get in a lifeboat if a ferry sank—the rest likely would drown. An employee said the state keeps records showing lifeboat capacity.

"He said they're at headquarters," Nalder said. He continued:

> I asked where at headquarters, and he said in the general manager's office. I asked where in the office and he said in a gray file cabinet next to his desk. I asked which drawer—he said the top one. I asked where in the drawer and he said he thought it was toward the front. When I called the public information officer I asked for the records and she said she would check around and get back to me. I said, "Don't worry, the certificates of inspection are in a gray cabinet in the general manager's office in the top drawer near the front, and I'll come down and pick them up." I picked them up at 2 p.m. that day.

### Ask verbally first

Once you've identified what you want and know where to get it, simply ask for the records politely, preferably in person. Avoid e-mail or the phone unless you absolutely can't. It's much easier to deny someone via e-mail than in person. It's about people skills. "You can't just walk into a building and tout freedom of the press," said Marley Shebala, a longtime reporter for the *Navajo Times*. "It's just not going to work. You have to develop relationships."

Shebala has been a tribal journalist for more than two decades. As sovereign nations, tribal governments are not subject to state or federal public records laws.[1] She can't rely on the law, so she has to use people skills. For reporters covering nontribal governments, the same skills apply.

"If you know the clerk you can get records," she said. In the Navajo Nation, police records are mostly public—at least the ones the officers want to release. Budget information can take a couple of weeks to get. The "discretionary" slush fund for the Navajo Nation president and council remains secret. Getting records is a challenge.

That means talking to people and asking for records in person, not by letter. We should note here, by the way, that Shebala is no pushover. Early in her career with a tribal radio station she was given a choice of getting in line with tribal government or being fired. She took the firing. But she came back stronger to work for the *Times*. Her muckraking brought down two tribal presidents, sending one to prison in 1989.

The lessons she's learned can be applied on- or off-reservation, particularly in dealing with agencies in rural areas:

- Before asking for records, introduce yourself and share information about each other. The Navajo tradition is that when you first meet a person you explain your family origins, where you are from and what you are doing. That puts people at ease and gives them context and perspective.
- Show respect. "I was up at Mexican Hat, Utah, and I went way into this valley area with a medicine man and his wife," she said. "I talked with them for a while and I asked if I could take their picture. You just don't conduct yourself as if you have that right to freedom of information. There's a certain respect you show people."

When possible, developing relationships is a great way to smooth the way for records requests, in all cultures. With any luck, the custodian will hand you the records on the spot. If not, you might have to move to the next step—a written request.

## Write effective letters

Sometimes you'll ask for a public record verbally and you'll get the records immediately, but sometimes you'll be ignored or get the runaround, even when a verbal request legally constitutes a public records request in some states. If your verbal requests are ignored, or if the agency's policies require a written request, then it's time to submit a formal public records request.

A written request provides several benefits for you and the agency.

First, for most states and the federal government, a written request starts the clock ticking. Federal agencies are required to respond within 20 days of a written request. Some states require a response within three days; many states require a "prompt" request. By law, a written request is not supposed to be ignored. An agency must respond by providing the records, denying the request in whole or part by citing a legal exemption, or saying that more time is needed.

Second, a written request provides a paper trail and prevents miscommunication or bad memories in the future. If you send a certified letter you will have proof that an agency received it. A response to an e-mail request provides a trail.

Third, a written request forces you to put your thoughts down on paper, which can help you focus on what you want.

Also, a written request can be cc'd to others within an agency, such as elected officials or the state attorney general's office. That can send a message that others will also be aware of the request.

The agency might ask you to fill out its own records request form. That's OK—either way it initiates the same process, and it allows the agency clerk to show that he or she was required to give out the information because you submitted a formal request.

The form might ask you the purpose of the request—most state laws do not require the requester to identify how the records will be used with the exception of commercial use or mailing lists. Sometimes commercial users, such as marketers, pay higher fees. Lists are sometimes not allowed to be released for business uses, to prevent mass mailers from sending junk mail courtesy of government address lists. For federal requests, you can get a fee waiver if your purpose is for the public good, such as for journalism, so you would have to explain the purpose if you want a fee waiver.

### Find sample request letters

When you sit down to write a letter, consider borrowing templates available widely online for federal requests or state public records requests.

## Pro tip

### Beware of 'telegraphing'

In many cases, a specific FOIA request to a federal agency often speeds up the collection of information. However, be aware your FOIA might also tip an agency off to a story it doesn't want out. In a worst-case scenario, your FOIA may end up in the hands of an agency's public affairs office or a political appointee who may circle the wagons or launch a pre-emptive effort to undercut your reporting. A few days before *The Washington Post* published its high-profile exposé about the serious problems at Walter Reed Army Medical Center in 2007, they called the Department of Defense [DOD] and asked for statistics and interviews on the record. As soon as DOD found out about the soon-to-be published article, the agency called a pre-emptive press conference and invited everyone except *The Washington Post*, doing as much damage control as possible before the story came out. Some reporters sending FOIAs may not fully realize how sophisticated some agencies have evolved at managing their image, including through FOIA. Some federal agencies will refuse to release records, some may release only favorable records and some may undermine your story. One way to get around this obstacle is to regularly request several types of information so it is more difficult for an agency to determine your target. Another way is to work with a nonprofit organization that will submit a FOIA and follow it up, a cost-saving idea in these tough economic times when news rooms are short staffed.

—Paul Sullivan, executive director, Veterans for Common Sense

Two organizations, the Student Press Law Center and the Reporters Committee for Freedom of the Press, provide nifty letter generators online, tailored to your particular state (see Figures 5.3 and 5.4 on pages 95 and 96). Simply go online and enter basic information into the boxes, such as the agency address, what you want, how much you're willing to pay in copies, and your name and address. Choose your state and click a button. Up pops a formal letter ready for you to copy and paste into a Word file.

Also, other suggested templates for request letters are provided by a variety of organizations, including state press associations, coalitions for open government, state attorney general offices and Society of Professional Journalists chapters. Most of the letters share similar elements that should be a part of every letter:

- Address it to a specific person that you know will be handling the request. Don't address it broadly, like "Peoria Police Department" or "City of Peoria."
- Be as specific as you can regarding what you want, naming the records, how far back you want them to go and the format in which you would like them (paper, electronic, etc.). You might explain different options for providing the records (mail, e-mail, pick up, CD, etc.).
- Cite the relevant public records statute.
- Address whether you want to just see the records (usually free) or want copies. If you want copies, designate how much you are willing to pay; if the agency says it will cost more than that amount, ask it to contact you before making the copies.
- Note the statutory deadline for responding to the request, or politely give a deadline for when you would like the records.
- Ask for expedited review or copy fee waivers because you are working in the public interest. This is allowed under federal FOIA, and similar provisions are allowed in some state laws.
- Note that denial or redactions should be justified by a statutory exemption in writing.
- Provide contact information, such as an e-mail address or phone number, and offer to assist or answer questions.
- Some people add relevant case law, an attorney general opinion or other legal support for making the records public.
- Some people use the terms "any and all" or "included but not limited to" to make sure they get everything. They then can narrow the request from there. Avoid making it too vague, though, or it might be unwieldy and open itself up for denial.

### Choose your tone

You'll want to choose your tone for your letter, depending on the existing working relationship you have with the agency, what type of agency you're dealing with and how hostile the agency reacts to your initial verbal request.

We have seen three different tones of letters: friendly, threatening and neutral (see Figures 5.2, 5.3 and 5.4 on pages 94–96). When we ask

**Pro tip** | **Make it obvious**

Every written public records request should clearly state that it is an official legal public records law request, in the text and in a header ("RE: Public records request" or "Subject: Sunshine Law Request") so clerks do not dismiss it as an optional task or casual inquiry. In some states, such as Missouri, if a request does not state that it is a sunshine law request then the agency can legally ignore it.

—Jean Maneke, attorney for the Missouri Press Association

journalists and custodians which letter they think is most effective, usually most people say the friendly letter should be best. Makes sense; that's what we've always thought too. But we weren't sure, so we conducted two experiments.

In 2007 David Cuillier teamed with a college journalist who wanted to look at police use of force incidents in Arizona. Cuillier mailed out request letters to all 104 police agencies requesting the records. Half of the agencies, randomly selected, received the friendly letter (Figure 5.2) and half received the threatening letter (Figure 5.3).

Cuillier developed the friendly letter based on psychological principles of persuasion. It used subordinating language, such as "I know you are busy," or phrases to foster liking, such as "I want to thank you in advance," "I would very much appreciate a response by . . ." and "Thanks again for your help!"

The threatening letter, provided by the Student Press Law Center, began by quoting the FOI statute and ended with a reminder that non-compliance could result in litigation, fees, fines and paying attorney fees. The student journalist didn't know which agency got which version of the letter—he just collected the records and dealt with the agencies after the request letters went out.

Which letter worked best? The threatening one. Only half the police agencies even responded to the friendly letter, while two-thirds responded to the threatening version. Only 4 percent of the police agencies that got the friendly letter actually provided the records,

FIGURE 5.2 **Sample request letter: Friendly version**

*This letter is based on the principles of persuasion, intended to foster liking.*

Sept. 2, 2010

Cactus School District
450 West 6th St.
Prickly, AZ 85364

RE: Public records request

To whom it may concern,

I know you are busy, but I want to thank you in advance for helping me gather some public records regarding superintendents and high school coaching salaries. I am writing to request a copy of the contract for the district superintendent, including pay and any other compensation he or she might receive. Also, if your district has a paid high school head football coach, or several head coaches, I would like a copy of that person (or persons') contract, including pay and any other compensation they receive for their duties.

I would be happy to pay copying and postage fees and help in any way I can, but if the cost is more than $5, please contact me and let me know. If the files are available electronically and would be more convenient to copy and email, then that would be great too.

I would very much appreciate a response by the end of the month, and if there is information that I am not entitled to, please let me know. I understand that sometimes some information doesn't warrant disclosure for statutory reasons, and might need to be blotted out while releasing the public part.

If there is anything I can do to help with the request, please do not hesitate to let me know (email is the fastest way to reach me).

Thanks again for your help!

Sincerely,

John Jones
1212 Main St.
Needles, AZ 85745
520-555-1111
[e-mail address]

**FIGURE 5.3 Sample request letter: Legalistic, threatening version**

*This letter is based on the Student Press Law Center version, available at www.splc. org/foiletter.asp. You might remove the threatening paragraph toward the end.*

Sept. 2, 2010

Cactus School District
450 West 6th St.
Prickly, AZ 85364

RE: Public records request

To whom it may concern:

Pursuant to the state open records law, Ariz. Rev. Stat. Ann. Secs. 39-121 to 39-126, I write to request access to and a copy of the contract for the district superintendent, including pay and any other compensation he or she might receive. Also, if your district has a paid high school head football coach, or several head coaches, I would like a copy of that person (or persons') contract, including pay and any other compensation they receive for their duties.

If your agency does not maintain these public records, please let me know who does and include the proper custodian's name and address.

I agree to pay any reasonable copying and postage fees of not more than $5. If the cost would be greater than this amount, please notify me. Please provide a receipt indicating the charges for each document.

I would request your response within ten (10) business days.

If you choose to deny this request, please provide a written explanation for the denial including a reference to the specific statutory exemption(s) upon which you rely. Also, please provide all segregable portions of otherwise exempt material.

Please be advised that I am prepared to pursue whatever legal remedy necessary to obtain access to the requested records. I would note that willful violation of the open records law can result in the award of legal costs, including damages and reasonable attorney fees. See Ariz. Rev. Stat. Sec. 39-121.02.

Thank you for your assistance.

Sincerely,

John Jones
1212 Main St.
Needles, AZ 85745
520-555-1111
[e-mail address]

FIGURE 5.4 **Sample request letter: Neutral version**

*This letter is based on the Reporters Committee for Freedom of the Press online generator, available at www.rcfp.org/foialetter/index.php.*

Sept. 2, 2010

Cactus School District
450 West 6th St.
Prickly, AZ 85364

RE: Public records request

To whom it may concern:

Pursuant to the state open records act, I request access to and copies of the contract for the district superintendent, including pay and any other compensation he or she might receive. Also, if your district has a paid high school head football coach, or several head coaches, I would like a copy of that person (or persons') contract, including pay and any other compensation they receive for their duties.

I agree to pay reasonable duplication fees for the processing of this request.

If my request is denied in whole or part, I ask that you justify all deletions by reference to specific exemptions of the act.

Thank you for your assistance.

Sincerely,

John Jones
1212 Main St.
Needles, AZ 85745
520-555-1111
[e-mail address]

whereas 14 percent of those who got the threatening letter provided the records. The threatening letter also resulted in lower copy fees and faster response (nine days instead of 10).

A few months later Cuillier ran a similar experiment with school districts, asking for coaching and superintendent contracts of all 208 agencies in Arizona. He also added a third version in the mix—a neutral letter (the one put out by the Reporters Committee for Freedom of the Press, see Figure 5.4). Again, the threatening letter had the best response—74 percent instead of 50 percent for the friendly and neutral letters. The threatening letter also resulted in lower copy costs and faster turnaround. And agencies that got the threatening letter weren't rude or snippy about it.

So what's going on here? When looking closer at the data we noticed that a large chunk of the responses to the threatening letter came from attorneys and top officials. In other words, when clerks received the threatening letter they tended to automatically forward it to the powers that be. The attorneys would look at it and see that the information needed to be released, so it was released. Clerks who got the friendly letter tended not to take it seriously and were more likely to blow it off.

The lesson here is that it pays to highlight the law as a reminder that you are serious. You may or may not want to threaten litigation, but an authoritative letter certainly gets the job done in many cases.

Results may vary, and not every situation is the same. If you're coming in cold without a verbal request, a nonthreatening letter might be the way to go, and then work up from there. If you've had difficult times with the agency before and you know that only a club works, then bring out the club and remind the agency of penalties for noncompliance. Threaten to sue if you are prepared to do so and you think it is necessary. We find that smaller, more rural agencies tend to prefer a more friendly tone, although sometimes they are so busy and overworked they might ignore the letter anyway. Federal agencies are accustomed to the legalistic letters. The point is to give the letter a little thought and then send it out, following up to make sure the agency received it. Answer questions if they are unclear about what you are looking for. Now it's time to work with the agency, person to person.

## 'Get to yes' through principled negotiation

In our experiment, half the police departments and half the school districts didn't even acknowledge the written requests, violating state law. If our government officials, including the police, choose to break the law, what are we to do? Few people have the time or money to sue. And we'll talk more about how to handle denials in the next chapter. For now, it's worth looking at how we can use human tactics to achieve success with the initial request, and avoid denials and litigation later. Let's apply a little principled negotiation.

William Ury is an expert in principled negotiation, from family disputes to ethnic wars. He is a co-author of the bestseller "Getting to Yes,"[2] and co-founded Harvard's Program on Negotiation. Every requester should become fluent in the language of negotiation. These principles will help you build relationships with sources, which is important if you cover a beat, especially in a small town. We'll walk through some of Ury's key points, applying the principles of "Getting to Yes" to the art of accessing public records.

### Argue interests, not positions

Make sure the agency knows what your *interest* is, not your *position*. Here's the difference. A position would be "I want you to give me record

**Pro tip** | **Write your victory speech**

Do a thought experiment, imagining that the public official says "yes" to your request and then has to explain to their superior or peers or whomever they report to why they said "yes." Imagine what criticism or questions they might receive: "You gave them that? How could you?" Then imagine the best response they can make. If you can't imagine them giving a little "speech" that persuasively demonstrates why it was in the agency's interest, then you may need to do some work. If you want them to say "yes" to your proposal, it is your job to make it easier for them to make this "victory speech."

—William Ury, co-founder of Harvard's Program on Negotiation and author of such books as *Getting to Yes* and *Getting Past No: Negotiating with Difficult People*

XYZ by Tuesday." An agency might have its own position: "I'm too busy to get it by then," or "There is confidential information in those records I don't want out." When two sides take positions they often lock themselves in, and then it becomes a contest of wills: "I want that record." "No, I won't give it to you."

Another common example is when two sides argue over details in the public records law: "I think that exemption 3b says it's public," which is countered by, "I read exemption 3b to mean it's secret, based on court case *Jones v. City of Burkburg.*" Too often we argue over legal positions that go nowhere, or worse, lead to a lengthy and costly court battle.

Instead of taking a position, convey your *interest*. Your interest is that you want information that can help illuminate an issue important to the public. The clerks' interest is that they want to process paperwork efficiently without giving out information that will hurt someone. There are usually ways to provide that information while keeping private information secret (e.g., blotting out Social Security numbers with a pen). When you focus on your interests, then you can often work something out. Arguing over positions hurts ongoing relationships with sources, but negotiating interests builds relationships.

### Separate people from the request

It's important not to make the request personal, which is really tough for some people. Officials might take your request personally and see you as the enemy. You might see them as the enemy. That's unnecessary. Avoid this potential pitfall through a variety of techniques:

1. Act inconsistent with officials' perceptions of you. Be nice, empathetic and sincere. From their perspective, that might seem odd for a journalist!
2. Put yourself in their shoes. Always try to understand where they are coming from. That's why we have a whole chapter on that subject (Chapter 8).
3. Allow face saving. Don't box an official in a corner. Allow several outs for the records to be provided without losing face. "I know you want to be transparent and that you aren't hiding anything. Maybe the attorneys can look at the law and see if the information is disclosable."

4. Allow officials to vent, and don't react to outbursts.

5. Listen first, then repeat what you heard. That shows that you are listening and open to their concerns. Acknowledge their interests: "I understand you don't want to let personal information get out. I don't either. Let's figure out a way to redact that information so we don't let anything out that shouldn't be released."

6. Use "I" statements, not "You" statements. For example, say, "*I* think these records will be of interest to your constituents," rather than "*You* need to give these out because your constituents will appreciate it."

7. Try to talk with people informally side by side, rather than face to face. Avoid talking to a clerk on one side of the counter with you directly facing from the other side. The physical configuration sets up subconscious psychological opposition.

8. Ultimately, be hard on the problem but soft on the people. Don't blame. Listen with respect, express appreciation. Be firm but open.

### Use negotiation jujitsu

If officials play hardball and won't cooperate with your request, start a new game. If they attack, sidestep and deflect against the problem. Bend, like the flexible willow; don't break like the rigid oak. Here are some simple negotiating tips:

1. As you make your request, invite criticism and advice. Maybe a clerk will say the information won't be helpful to you. In that case, don't say, "I'll be the judge of that. Just hand it over, please." Instead, say, "I am interested in what you are saying. Why won't it be helpful? Are there other records that would be better to see?"

2. Use questions instead of statements. Statements of fact are threatening: "The law says you need to provide the information." Ask questions instead: "Can you show me where in the law it says that information is secret? I'm sorry, I must have missed it—which subsection would that be?"

3. Use silence after an unreasonable attack. Sheriff to you: "You ain't getting nuthin' because I'm the sheriff and I say so!" Let that statement sit there in silence. The official will often realize what was just

said, see that you aren't going to escalate the confrontation, and then cool down. It also gives you time to take a deep breath, compose yourself and not get angry.

4. Make yourself open to correction and persuasion: "Maybe I'm not understanding what is contained in the records—can you please explain to me what is in them, or better yet, show me an example of one so I can make sure I have this straight?"

5. Don't decide on the spot. If you request a record and the custodian says "no," don't argue, especially if you feel your hackles going up. Take notes on what the person says and respond: "I need to do some more homework to make sure I understand this. Let me get back to you."

6. End the conversation with a sincere compliment, no matter how it resolved: "I know you're busy and I thank you for your time. You folks don't get paid enough!"

7. If agencies use dirty tricks, call them on it. Raise the issue and question it, focusing on the action, not the person. Don't seek to teach a lesson.

8. Invent different options. Rarely is there just one record that you need. When you are requesting records, be open to the idea that there may be many different records that can satisfy your interest. Brainstorm solutions with colleagues and offer to brainstorm solutions with the agency over coffee. Make their decision easy by highlighting what they would get out of it.

## Apply hard tactics if necessary

Sometimes some people just don't want to work through principled negotiation. In that case, we turn to the "dark side." Robert B. Cialdini, a psychology researcher from Arizona State University, has identified what he calls "weapons of influence."[3] The psychological techniques are used by advertisers, marketers, public relations professionals and government strategists to influence the public—and journalists. Sometimes you have to fight back.

But before we get into these methods of persuasion, a word of warning is in order: Use these powers for good, not for evil. The intent here is not to "manipulate" people as if they are lab rats or consumers. Some of these principles are touted in books on "covert persuasion," the goal of tricking people without them knowing. Trickery is unethical in journalism.

The idea is to realize that the act of requesting records involves human interaction, where decisions are often arbitrary despite the law. Every day we act certain ways around others to get them to do stuff for us, even if it is just smiling and exchanging pleasantries. Is saying "Hi, how are you doing?" trickery? No. We say that because we want people to treat us well, not spit on us. That is the same idea here. We must understand the human elements of interaction between requester and custodian.

Below, we adapted Cialdini's weapons of influence and other principles of social psychology for getting public records. Always be honest, always be forthcoming and never lie. Wield these principles ethically for the public's good.

## Reactance

The idea behind reactance theory is people will resist being forced into a decision. Research shows that if you push people to act a certain way they will resist and act the opposite—that's where we get the concept of reverse psychology.

If you tell a custodian that he or she must do what you say and fulfill your request, then their natural reaction will be to resist. Avoid telling the person that he or she is wrong and boxing them into a have-to situation. Affirm the other person's view. First acknowledge the person's concern or position, then explain yours. This is consistent with principled negotiation jujitsu, but sometimes you have to be more overt and calculated about it.

## Reciprocation

When you give something to someone, that person feels obliged to reciprocate, often beyond the value of what you gave. That's why businesses offer free samples.

Now, we don't advocate that journalists buy off government officials, or even imply quid pro quo. We do, however, see how this psychological technique can be applied ethically.

For example, a reciprocation-based technique is the "rejection-then-retreat" tactic: Ask for a lot, and then cut it in half. "Can I see all documents you have regarding the budget for the past 20 years?" The clerk's jaw drops, thinking about the amount of time that is going to take. "OK," you say. "How about starting with just the expense reports for the past five years?" You are giving up something, so the clerk feels compelled to reciprocate by saying "yes."

In using this technique, we suggest you don't arbitrarily choose a huge amount of records just to be manipulative. As we've mentioned before, the best records requests are those that are specific and focused. If you ask for a large amount of information, perhaps to legitimately examine a broad issue, you should actually want to see all those budget records for the past 20 years. That can demonstrate trends. Also, it might be very easy for the agency to provide that material—stored electronically in Excel files that can be copied and pasted to an e-mail in an hour. It's just that you are prepared to accept less, and know that less will serve what you need if the agency is unable to provide you with your heart's desire. If you start big and give something up the gesture is appreciated and the person might be more likely to help you out.

Another application of the reciprocation principle is to offer to help the custodian as much as possible with the request. Volunteer to help make photocopies, or bring your own photocopy machine. While the custodian might not take you up on it, the good-faith gesture will be appreciated; he or she might even reciprocate by going beyond the minimum legal requirements to help you out.

### Commitment and consistency

Once people commit to something, they try to stick with it. Psychologists find that people have a difficult time acting inconsistently. This is the opposite of the "rejection-then-retreat" technique: Once someone has agreed to a small request, get a commitment for something bigger. Once they say "yes" it is more difficult for them to say "no."

Retail sales people use this technique all the time asking the simple question, "How are you today?" Most people automatically respond by acknowledging the question and affirming the person: "I'm great, thanks," even if they don't feel great. Once a person has gone along with one request it is more difficult to say "no" to the next question.

Here's how it might apply to records: "Could I see what a police report looks like? Great. Can I see what a case file looks like? Thanks! Ummmm, what does it look like in your computer system? Nifty. Any chance I could get an electronic copy of reports in Excel for the past year? Shoot, it appears you have all the data for the past 10 years. How about copying that too?"

Another use of the commitment principle is to discuss with the custodian the terms of the request and finish with, "Do we have an agreement?" or "Does this sound like something that will work for you?" Once agreed upon it is more difficult psychologically for a person to reverse a decision later.

Rob O'Dell, City Hall reporter for the *Arizona Daily Star,* uses this technique a lot on his beat. He routinely asks the city of Tucson for records, and officials get used to being asked. When he is working on deadline he gets what he needs quickly, without much hassle. For example, he requested e-mails among high-ranking officials and they printed out each one and gave it to him. "It's impossible to look through 1,200 sheets of paper to find what you are looking for," he said. So he wrangled with them and eventually got them to provide e-mails on a CD. "Then they told me that they don't have to do that every time, but I got them to do it the next five times." Then a controversy erupted where he knew he would need to see e-mails. "I told them that they should be able to provide them on a CD since they had done that previously. If I wouldn't have done that I wouldn't have gotten the e-mails in a timely manner."

Also, O'Dell said, if you routinely request records about less threatening information, the agency will get used to you and be less skittish when you put in a request for something controversial. "They'll be used to you and say, 'Oh, it's just another records request from this guy.'"

## Social proof

People are social animals who like to run with the pack. Peer pressure works. "Boy, all the other towns in the county provide this information. I wonder why it isn't open here?" Put together a list of agencies in your state or in the country that provide the information. What official wants to appear abnormal or deviant?

The principle of social proof is most effective when people are uncertain, so if they are not sure whether the information should be open they will often follow what other officials do.

Another example of social proof is playing up the patriotic duty of open government and the importance of the information to the community. Convey the idea that it's their duty as Americans to keep government open and free, and that their neighbors will appreciate their efforts.

Building on this thought, it is crucial during the request process for journalists to convey that the information is of interest to the whole community, not just the one reporter. It's easy for a custodian to say "no" to one annoying reporter; it's more difficult to say "no" to the 300,000 people living in the community. Talk about how city residents will appreciate seeing the information in the newspaper or online. Make it clear that if they say no you will put that in your story, and the agency will have to answer to its constituents, not one media organization.

### Liking

As much as we hate to admit it, people often make decisions based on how a requester looks. We see this time and time again in access audits, where records are denied to some requesters because they look "shady" or "disheveled." Appearing sneaky raises suspicions and increases denials.

Therefore, dress and act like your sources. Talk about similar interests. Research indicates that when people perceive similarities with others, such as the same birthday, they are more likely to approve of them.

Offer sincere compliments. Disassociate yourself from people perceived to use information irresponsibly (e.g., spammers, tabloids or identity thieves).

Some psychologists suggest that you go to lunch with someone and have a pleasant, nonthreatening conversation so that the person associates good things with you. They call this "classical conditioning" (remember Pavlov's experiments?). Pick a nice restaurant that the person likes, and pay separately to avoid a conflict of interest. Psychologically, the person will associate good things (e.g., cheeseburger) with you, rather than bad things (e.g., photocopying records).

**Pro tip** | **Deliver joy and goodwill**

To build relationships with sources, send holiday cards thanking them for their assistance. Also send thank-you letters, cc'ing to their bosses, about how helpful they were. I keep my naughty list and my nice list, and I mail them all cards. I think they appreciate it and it helps with future requests, even with the people who are difficult.

—Jaimi Dowdell, training director,
Investigative Reporters and Editors

Again, we don't want to perceive people as lab rats to be manipulated. It's just one of those functions of human interaction. Journalists, business associates and others do this routinely because they find it works—people will talk to them more. But we doubt they head out of the office saying they have to do some classical conditioning. We just don't usually consciously think of it in those terms. If you go to lunch often enough with custodians, then every time you approach the counter the clerks will start to salivate, as will you!

### Scarcity

Advertisers play on fear by saying their sales are available "for a limited time only." Likewise, make your request urgent and officials' response time limited: "I don't have time to wait until next week for you to check with the city attorney on this. My deadline is in six hours. I'm going to have to write a story for tomorrow morning's paper explaining that your agency is being secretive. And darn it, I would hate for you to look like you are hiding something when I know you aren't."

These techniques might not work every time, but like any reporting tool, they can improve your odds of getting the information you need, when you need it. Of course, use this only if you truly are on deadline and in a hurry. The custodians deserve to know that, as well as what might show up in the next day's paper.

## Authority

Authority can increase compliance. If you work for a small company, team with reporters from larger organizations. Cooperative requests increase pressure for release and serve everyone's interests. However, it might depend on the public official: Big-city media sometimes have it tougher in small burgs.

Titles convey authority. Have the request letter co-signed by the editor-in-chief or publisher. Government allies, such as the attorney general, can help.

Referring to the actual statute numbers of the public records law or FOIA conveys authority, increasing compliance with public records request letters. Writing "Public Records Request" on the top of your letter also amplifies the importance of the matter.

Also, research has found that authority symbols, such as clothing, height, maleness and nice cars, increase persuasiveness. Unfortunately, that is something out of most journalists' control, unless the publisher is open to buying a company Porsche in the name of FOI.

## Choosing soft vs. hard

Now, let's say you were pleasant and reasonable with an agency and have a legal right to the information (and triple-checked with legal experts), and the agency still balks. When do you use soft tactics and when hard tactics? That's something you'll have to figure out through practice, and it depends on the circumstances. But here are a few thoughts.

We believe it's important to first apply the "Getting to Yes" ideals of principled negotiation and avoid needless confrontation. That doesn't mean coddling or backing down, but rather finding solutions that meet everyone's needs.

"The good thing is for them to see you as principled and fair," said Michael Jonathan Grinfeld, an associate professor at the University of Missouri School of Journalism and co-director of the Center for the Study of Conflict Law and the Media. "You want them to see you as a smart and good person who wants to make things better for the community."

## Pro tip — Mark your calendar

When you send a records request, mark on your calendar or use Google Calendar or another electronic system to check back in a week so you don't forget. I called back 10 days after I requested water line inspection records and the official said, "I thought you didn't need the information anymore." Officials will try to take advantage of when we forget about requests.

—Yang Wang, reporter for KHOU-TV
Channel 11, Houston, Texas

Grinfeld suggests people avoid the hard tactics if they can because they will lead to mistrust. But if principled negotiation doesn't work, then journalists have an obligation to acquire the information for the public. "I'm not against hard tactics, but it's a last-ditch effort," he says. "If they use hard tactics on you then you use them. You don't have to get mad. Just move step by step. The natural thing is to flip someone off, but you have to work at it. Manage your emotions, and move forward with greater resolve."

Psychological research indicates that authority wins over liking, so if the liking doesn't work it might be time to break out the big stick. If you can't afford to sue, then you might have to apply more heavy-handed tactics to convince custodians it's in their best interest to follow the law.

Mike McGraw, special projects reporter at *The Kansas City Star,* says that sometimes a journalist must pummel an agency into submission. Harsh? Maybe. Will custodians cringe at the suggestion? Sure. But sometimes, with those few officials who knowingly violate the spirit and letter of the law, it's the only option.

For example, McGraw had asked a public university—one that was across the country—for a document that outlined how much funding was provided to women's and men's sports, showing favoritism toward men's sports. The university could have mailed it, and McGraw was willing to pay for expenses. But the university didn't like his request because it might have made the university look bad, so officials told him he would have to fly across the country to get the records. Instead, McGraw called the university's campus newspaper, told reporters about the document and story idea and asked them to mail a copy of the report once they finished their story. After the campus newspaper and *The Kansas City Star* both published their stories, McGraw called the university public information officer back and said, "Now you have two negative stories about you. So there."

We hope the tips provided in this chapter will prevent you from having to punish an agency, or flip someone off. But the reality is some agencies, like McGraw's university, will give you a tough time and deny a valid public records request. For that, in the next chapter we will talk about how to deal with denials.

Try it!

**Exercises and ideas for journalists, newsrooms and classrooms to improve your skills and foster FOI in your community.**

## 1. Create letter templates

Go to the Reporters Committee for Freedom of the Press (RCFP) online letter generator (www.rcfp.org/foialetter/index.php) and the Student Press Law Center letter generator (www.splc.org/foiletter.asp), and create different versions of public records request letters. At the RCFP Web site create a federal FOIA letter and a separate state public records request letter. Copy and paste the letters into Word files and keep them handy for when you might need them, along with your own tailor-made letters based on the letters discussed in this chapter. Figure out what tone you like best and then set aside two separate letters—one for federal FOIA requests and one for state/local requests. Photocopy the forms and carry them with you to fill out on assignment at meetings or at agency offices. Make them available to your classmates or co-workers.

## 2. Build a request kit

When you are on the beat covering agencies and you are in a document state of mind, you will begin to request records on the fly—when a source at City Hall mentions a report, or a school board member refers to an audit during a board meeting. In those cases you need to be ready to submit a public records request immediately. Prepare a packet to have with you at all times, or at least while you're at government agencies and meetings. Put the following items in a folder to bring with you:

- ☑ **Blank public records request forms.** If an agency you cover has its own forms it prefers people to fill out, bring copies of those forms.
- ☑ **Thumb drive or flash drive, and a blank CD.** So a clerk can transfer electronic files for you.
- ☑ **Camera or portable handheld scanner.** To capture images of documents at the agency rather than paying for copies.
- ☑ **Copy of your state public records law.** Go to www.rcfp.org/ogg and click on your state. On the left is a link to your state statute. Copy it to a Word file and reduce the font, then print it out.
- ☑ **Summary of supportive case law.** In that RCFP guide at www.rcfp. org/ogg you'll find explanations by an attorney about each element of the law and case law supporting openness. Create a one-page sheet of paper that lists key elements and the cases that support openness. For example, maybe a court case in your state ruled that electronic records are subject to the public records law. Be able to cite the case.

## 3. Learn how to understand others

Hone your people skills by checking out books that will improve your ability to work out disputes with others. These skills can help you in your working and personal relationships as well. Take notes as you read them and boil down the tips for your co-workers or fellow students. Here are some good books to read:

- ☑ Babcock, Linda, and Sara Laschever. *Women Don't Ask: The High Cost of Avoiding Negotiation—and Positive Strategies for Change.* New York: Bantam, 2007.
- ☑ Cialdini, Robert B. *Influence: Science and Practice.* Needham Heights, Mass.: Allyn and Bacon, 2001.

☑ Fisher, Roger, William Ury and Bruce Patton. *Getting to Yes: Negotiating Agreement Without Giving In.* New York: Penguin Books, 1991.

☑ Mnookin, Robert H., Scott R. Peppet and Andrew S. Tulumello. *Beyond Winning: Negotiating to Create Value in Deals and Disputes.* Cambridge, Mass.: Belknap Press, 2000.

☑ Stone, Douglas, Bruce Patton, Sheila Heen and Roger Fisher. *Difficult Conversations: How to Discuss What Matters Most.* New York: Penguin Books, 2000.

## 4. Record yourself

We rarely know how we interact with others because we can see only from our own vantage point. So record yourself asking for records. If a clerk is willing to be recorded while you ask for records, great, but it's probably likely that they won't want to be recorded or would act unnaturally. So practice with a colleague or student. Simulate a records request, using an audio recorder or video recorder to capture the exchange. Examine how you act. Note whether you use "I" statements or "You" statements. Go down the list of negotiation principles presented in this chapter and see if you are following them. Note how you can improve, write it on a piece of paper and keep it with you to practice when you are interacting with sources and requesting records. This is also a good technique for improving your interviewing techniques.

## 5. Host a soda session

Some of the best resources for FOI strategies and records ideas are in the neighboring cubicles. Get your co-workers or classmates together for cookies and soda, and share public records ideas and request strategies. It's amazing what we can learn about our communities simply from our colleagues. Come up with two document-based story ideas and one new strategy for each person.

## 6. Practice psychology for real

It's one thing to read about psychology and persuasion, and it's another to try it out and see it work in practice. Test out some of these simple persuasion principles and see if they work:

- ☑ **Authority.** All week go to class or work wearing nice clothes—more formal than the situation calls for. Note how people treat you. The next week wear grubby clothes—less formal than the situation calls for. Note how people treat you then.
- ☑ **Reactance.** One day tell your friend what to do: "You need to drive me to the mini-mart for a soda." A week later, try the same task, but phrased differently: "I guess I don't have a way to get to the mini-mart for a soda today . . . hmmm. I wonder how I can get there?" See how your friend responds. Discuss it with your friend.
- ☑ **Liking.** For one week make an effort to smile and give people sincere compliments. Note how they respond and treat you. Then in another week make an effort not to smile and not give compliments. Any difference in how you are treated?

Think of other ways to test these psychological principles. Take good notes, and then tell the other person what you did so you can both learn. If anything, this will arm you with the knowledge to defend yourself from marketers, advertisers and manipulative acquaintances who may try to use these tactics on you. These aren't guaranteed to work every time—humans are not machines. But see if they tend to work most of the time. Above all, don't seek to manipulate. Seek to be a good person. People like that.

**Suggested links**

**Federal FOIA letter generator**    www.rcfp.org/foialetter/index.php
   Use this site by the Reporters Committee for Freedom of the Press
   to create a simple federal FOIA request letter online. It's simple and
   quick.

**State public records request letter**    www.splc.org/foiletter.asp
For a state public records request letter, tailored to your state, use
this online letter by the Student Press Law Center.

**Strategies from everyone**    http://wikifoia.pbworks.com/How-To-Guide
WikiFOIA provides a spot for anyone to provide their suggestions
for requesting records.

**Tips for effective letters**    www.rcfp.org/fogg/index.php?i=pt1#b
The Reporters Committee for Freedom of the Press provides tips for
effective letters.

# How to overcome denials

### ACCESS ACTION AGENDA

- ☑ Understand the nature of "no"
- ☑ Respond to common denials
- ☑ Play hardball

With the power of state and federal public records laws, access should be simple: Just go and ask for the public records you need. We wish it were that easy.

To use FOI laws is to deal with denials, often offered up seemingly without reason and designed to buy time while you stew. Sometimes denial—repeated, mindless denial—can dampen the enthusiasm of even the hardiest records requesters.

While overcoming denials every time might not be easy, it is achievable. Just ask Scott Reeder, a managing editor for the Franklin Center for Government and Public Integrity, a nonprofit news organization that covers state governments. When Reeder was the statehouse bureau chief in Illinois for The Small Newspaper Group, he requested documents from all of the state's 876 school districts regarding teachers who had been disciplined. How many districts provided the records?

All 876. He did it through persistence and applying some of the techniques you'll read about in this chapter.

First, Reeder mailed out request letters, which got about half the districts to respond. Then he faxed a second letter to get 25 percent more to provide the information. Then he hit the telephone, hounding superintendents until they complied with the law.

"One district I had sent more than 20 faxes and letters and they ignored me," Reeder said. "So I got the cell phone number of the FOI officer and just kept calling. When he was at volleyball practice. At home for dinner. Finally he got exasperated and just handed over the data."

After shaming some districts into complying ("Hmmm, about 860 districts provided the information, why won't you?"), Reeder was down to a few holdouts, including Chicago officials who cited privacy as an exemption. So Reeder walked over to the office of the state Senate majority leader and asked if he could talk to the mayor's office. "Within minutes the phone was ringing," Reeder said. "It was the school district saying, 'Mr. Reeder, we'll have the information for you this Monday.'"

You, too, can get 876 school districts to comply with the law, or even that one recalcitrant sheriff's office on your beat. This chapter explains how to respond when public officials illegally deny valid public records requests. It then describes common denial excuses and how to respond, including a list of strategies for turning "no" into "yes." At the heart of the strategy is turning access requests into a bit of a game—rather then wallow in misery in the aftermath of a denial, FOI stalwarts told us again and again that they see denials as the beginning of the chase.

## Understand the nature of 'no'

Some government officials turn your "right to know" into their "right to no."

As in "no way are you getting that document."

That's why it's so important to understand the prevalence of denials, *why* some agencies deny valid records requests and what to do about it.

### Denials gone wild

First, let's start with the fringe denials, the loony ones that leave journalists fuming, gasping and occasionally laughing. Wacky denials illustrate how far some public officials will go to assert total control over their domains and say anything to thwart transparency.

**Sticking their necks out.** In 2002 Ryma the giraffe, a beloved public favorite at the Smithsonian Institution's National Zoo, died at age 16, long before the giraffe's life expectancy of 25 years. *The Washington Post* requested the medical and pathology records. While the zoo gave a general description of the death (Ryma apparently died of a digestive illness caused by eating bamboo), officials refused to hand over the specific records, saying that disclosure would violate the giraffe's privacy, as well as animal-zookeeper confidentiality. The Smithsonian was able to get away with the denial because a court ruled that the nonprofit organization is not subject to FOIA. In a similar case, the *San Jose Mercury News* lost a lawsuit in the 1990s after suing over pet licenses. The court agreed with Santa Clara County's argument that releasing pet license data would invade dogs' privacy.

**Protecting porn profits.** A public school teacher from Wisconsin was fired for viewing pornographic images on his classroom computer. When the *Milwaukee Journal-Sentinel* asked to see the computer files, the teacher went to court to stop the disclosure of the images, arguing the school couldn't release copies of the commercial porn images because it would infringe on the copyright held by the porn producers. In May 2007 the state Supreme Court ruled in the newspaper's favor, saying compliance with the public records law is fair use and therefore release of the pictures wouldn't violate copyright law and wouldn't financially hurt pornographers.

**Adopt-a-highway.** You know when you drive down a highway and you see those "adopt-a-highway" signs that state that the local Kiwanis club or the Jones family has adopted that section of the road to clean up? Ever wonder whether they actually do the cleaning for that prime free advertising? Jennifer LaFleur did when she worked for the *San Jose Mercury News,* so she requested the database of all the adopt-a-highway volunteers to find out how the program worked and who was involved. The state refused to make the list public, saying it would invade the volunteers' privacy for the public to know they had adopted a section of state highway—even though their names are posted on highway signs for everyone to see.

**Secret Santa.** We trust our government to protect us from terrorists and other bad people, so when they say information has to be kept secret because of national security we assume that is true. Or is it? In 2003 the National Security Archive combed through declassified federal documents to find a December 1974 CIA "Weekly Situation Report on International Terrorism" that had been blotted out to protect national security. Yet when the declassified version was made public it revealed an internal office joke about a potential terrorism attack on the North Pole by the "Group of the Martyr of Ebenezer Scrooge" (see Figure 6.1). National security? Bah, humbug. More like an office holiday joke.

If public officials like these are so brazen at trying to keep public records secret with outrageous excuses, imagine how often they deny valid requests through seemingly benign reasons, through dubious reliance on exemptions and sometimes through good, old-fashioned stonewalling.

### Prevalence of denials

OK, so we pointed out a few extreme examples of silly secrecy. Is secrecy really that much of a problem? You bet. Despite state and federal laws requiring government officials to honor public records requests, the reality is that many don't.

Secrecy has been on the rise for decades. About 200,000 documents are classified annually at the federal level, and tens of thousands of FOIA requests wait in backlogs, some pending since 1992.[1]

Helen Thomas, a political columnist for Hearst Newspapers and a journalist since 1943, said that in her nearly 70 years in the field she has seen the government gradually get more and more secretive.

"We had a lot of access in the Johnson era and the Kennedy era. We used to walk down the street with Carter," Thomas said. "But more and more it's become difficult. There's too much secrecy in government, and I think the news organizations have gone along with it. I don't play ball like that. . . . People have a right to know."

Secrecy has become ingrained in our government, from the top down.

An examination of 32 state public records audits conducted from 1997 through 2004 showed widespread noncompliance with public records laws.[2] Citizens and journalists visited police stations, school districts and city halls and asked for different kinds of records. In many cases the responses were hostile and illegal. Among the 32 audits, agencies complied

**Classified version**

SECRET
No Foreign Dissem/No Dissem Abroad/Controlled Dissem

VI.  Terrorist Threats and Plans:  Worldwide

---

**Declassified version**

VI.  Terrorist Threats and Plans:  Worldwide

Target:  GONP Courier
         Flight

Place    Unspecified

Date:    24-25 December
         1974

** A new organization of uncertain makeup, using the name
"Group of the Martyr Ebenezer
Scrooge," plans to sabotage
the annual courier flight of
the Government of the North
Pole.  Prime Minister and
Chief Courier S. Claus has
been notified and security
precautions are being coordinated worldwide by the CCCT
Working Group.  (CONFIDENTIAL)

*Source:* The National Security Archive, www.nsarchive.org.

with the law only 59 percent of the time. That means four out of 10 times public officials illegally denied valid public records requests.

Cities were fine at handing out city council minutes—93 percent of the time. But good luck trying to get copies of crime logs—police agencies complied with the law only 29 percent of the time (see Table 6.1). If police don't follow the law, who will?

And if it isn't bad enough to simply say "no," some officials get downright rude. In a 1999 Illinois audit, after requesting a public record an auditor was pulled over by a sheriff's deputy and told, "You can't come to a small community like this and act like that." In another state, a sheriff crumpled up a request letter, tossed it in the garbage and told the citizen auditor, "I don't have to give you nuthin'." In some cases, people requesting public records have been detained by police and even cited for disorderly conduct.

Why in the world would our public officials act like that to citizens, their bosses, who have a right to ask for *their own* public records?

**TABLE 6.1  Compliance varies by record type**

| Record type | Average compliance rate |
|---|---|
| City council minutes | 93% |
| Restaurant inspections | 86 |
| Expense reports | 74 |
| Travel vouchers | 74 |
| Coach salaries | 68 |
| Superintendent contract | 66 |
| City employee overtime pay | 60 |
| Jail log | 58 |
| Crime incident report | 55 |
| Crime log | 29 |

*Source:* David Cuillier.

*Note:* This analysis of 32 state public records audits, completed between 1997 and 2004, showed that average compliance rates varied depending on the type of record and agency.

Unfortunately, there are lots of reasons, including lack of staffing, orders from the top, entrenched secrecy and plain old arrogance.

According to research by Wendell Cochran of American University, about two-thirds of the time federal agencies deny FOIA requests citing privacy exemptions. About 15 percent are denied to protect ongoing law enforcement investigations, and 23 percent for other reasons. Only 1 percent of denials are attributed to national security.[3]

But those are just the *apparent* reasons. When a denial appears to be arbitrary, there are usually more subtle reasons at play. In Chapter 8 we'll go through in much more detail some of the reasons why officials hide records, but for now, regardless of the reason, you need to figure out what to do. It's time to respond and get those records.

## Respond to common denials

So we know there's a good chance a public official will deny a valid public records request. So what do you do? Don't give up. The worst thing you can do is walk away because the agency will use the same excuse on the next person, including *you* the next time you request a public record. Instead, look at the initial denial as the beginning of your response rather than as the final answer.

### Don't get mad, get busy

It can be difficult to stay calm when you're denied public records. Investigative reporting guru Don Ray tells journalists "don't embrace obstacles." Maybe the information is available elsewhere. Don't fume and focus on the denial. Focus on getting the information.

Sometimes journalists are quick to pounce on reluctant officials by threatening a lawsuit or writing nasty stories about denials. This may be necessary, but at the very beginning it might box the agency into a corner, forcing it into a win-lose scenario: roll over or fight. Most cornered animals fight. One way to prevent the agency from digging in its heels early on and battling all the way to court is to provide an easy escape hatch. Enable the agency to save face and it might drop the files in your hands and scuttle off unscathed.

An example of face-saving is acting like "Columbo," a humble and seemingly harmless character from a 1970s television detective show. Ray said that when a low-level clerk denies copies of a record, there's a good chance that the clerk doesn't know whether it's public or not, but chooses to play it safe by denying access:

> When they do that, I say, "No problem. I don't really need it that bad. Besides, I can leave earlier than I expected and get home sooner." I start to walk away and then put my hand to my forehead and do a "Columbo" move. I return and say, "I just realized that my boss is going to want to know why I came back empty handed. If you could be so kind, would you please tell me the law or regulation or court case that says the record isn't public?" They'll usually say, "I don't know." Then, I say, "Oh, well then maybe you'd let me talk to someone who knows. Could I ask your supervisor?" I'm never threatening— always nice and friendly. Usually, the supervisor comes and also doesn't know. Then I ask nicely for the supervisor's supervisor. By the time the chief clerk or the office manager comes to the desk the original clerk is intrigued. What often happens is that the head honcho person looks at the request and says, "It's public record. Make the copy for him."

As we discussed in Chapter 5, focus on the "interests" of what you want, and the interests of the clerk. Investigative reporter and editor Scott North of *The* (Everett, Wash.) *Herald* suggests journalists quickly identify the sticking point. "Identify the problem they had with the request, why they are reluctant to give it up," North said. "If it's not a problem for you, give it up and open the logjam. Sometimes instead of going at it at ramming speed, look at it as a maze."

Here are a dozen ways of working yourself through that labyrinth, of responding to those common denials.

### If the agency says . . .

#### 'Nah, it's our policy not to give that out.'

That's nice, but what does the *law* say? Have the agency provide its denial in writing, citing the relevant state or federal statutes that allow for the secrecy. In many states this written legal citation is required by law.

When an agency is forced to cite the exact law it often realizes that there is no such law. Once it provides the written denial, check the law yourself to make sure it's a valid exemption. Sometimes officials cite a law that does not apply. Or court rulings might interpret the exemptions narrowly, as they should, which might contradict the agency's application of the exemption. Still unsure? Run the denial by your state FOI coalition, a media attorney or a fellow FOI junkie.

### 'Chirrrp, chirrrrp.' (Crickets chirping from the silence of the agency's nonresponse.)

You submit your request but don't get any response. Nobody calls you, e-mails you or sends you a letter. In many states the public records law requires a response within a certain time limit, usually from three to 10 business days. If the agency fails to respond it is breaking the law. Call to find out what happened. If you get the runaround, send another letter, this time to the head agency official and elected officials. Mention you have gotten no response from a previous letter, in violation of state law. Maybe even send it on your organization's letterhead, or better, from your organization's lawyer. If you have sources within the institution, enlist their help. Be firm and consistent, not militant. Ask them if they need a little more time rather than going straight for the jugular.

### 'The description of what you requested is overly broad or inadequate.'

Narrow your request so it is clear what they need to provide you. In some states officials can deny records requests that are overly broad. It helps to meet with staffers to find out exactly what records they have, down to the form number, so you can be specific in your request. Discuss in detail the ways that you could limit the scope of the request, and be willing to take suggestions from staffers in government, who can really be a great help in the process.

### 'The record doesn't exist.'

If you are sure the record does exist and your letter was clear, then give the agency more guidelines and clues for where it might find it. Try to be patient because some agencies are short staffed or disorganized, and the person you talked to might not even realize the agency has such records.

Find the right person who knows where the record is. Get past the clerk by asking who would have generated the document. Ask around: Don't take the word of a single employee at City Hall.

### 'We'll get back to you' (20 years from now).

Access delayed is access denied. If the records aren't available by deadline then that hurts the story, and a lot of public officials know that. Studies show that federal agencies in particular will delay FOIA requests for months or even years, with some of the longest requests pending more than 20 years.[4] Help the agency speed its response by being specific in exactly what documents you need, and which ones you need first. If an agency is dragging its feet for no apparent reason, consider the request denied and ratchet up the heat.

### 'Some of the materials are legally exempt from disclosure, so we can't give you the record.'

The agency can black out, or redact, the exempt material but still let you see the other parts of the record that are public. In databases, this entails simply deleting exempt columns, such as Social Security numbers. Check the fields that are being redacted and make sure you really need them before you insist on getting them. Sometimes you can offer up a field you don't need to ease the negotiations and speed things along.

---

## Pro tip | Play the patriotism card

When officials balk at giving out information, remind them of the heritage of openness in our past. This is true for tribes too. For a long time back our people knew everything that was going on in their community. That's our history. When we have a ceremony you tell the truth about your sickness so everyone will know exactly how to pray. Everyone knew who did something really good and who did something really, really bad, even if it was deviant. Then we can deal with it in the proper way—everybody can be brought back into harmony. Those are the Navajo teachings.

—Marley Shebala, reporter, *Navajo Times*

**'Here you go, with a few redactions' (all blacked out).**

Sometimes government agencies go overboard on redactions, blotting out everything whether it is exempt by law or not. If you feel they redacted more than they should have, but you don't know because you can't see the blacked-out material, first ask the nature of what they blacked out and what statute allows them to keep it secret. If you get vague excuses, ask for the justifications in writing with specific laws cited for blotting out the information. Some state public records ombudsmen can review the unredacted documents *in camera* (in private) to determine whether the agency followed the law. A judge could do the same if you sue. Another possibility is to request the same record from different agencies. Sometimes they redact different parts, enabling you to piece together the public material.

**'Our hands are tied. An exemption in the law forces us to keep it secret.'**

First, check with an expert to make sure the exemption is being applied correctly. If so, still see if you can work something out. Exemptions are usually discretionary, not mandatory. Agencies are not required by law to withhold the information, except in some circumstances. For example, some privacy laws require government to keep certain records secret, such as grades or medical records. But in most cases, officials can choose to waive the exemptions and release the material if they wish. In some cases the public interest overrides privacy or other competing interests.

**'We don't have time to get that for you.'**

While many public agencies are strapped for resources, this is not a valid or legal excuse for denying a public records request. Have them point out the "no time" exemption in the law. When they can't find it, offer to help them make photocopies and prioritize the records so they can provide them on a schedule. We've even offered to come sift through records—and been welcomed to do so.

**'Where does it say in the law that I have to give you that record?'**

Nowhere. But that's not how public records law works. Remember that the presumption is that government records are public unless there are laws saying they are secret. So show the official the statute and ask where in the law it says the agency can keep the record secret. If you forward the request to the agency's attorney, that can clear things up fast.

**'You can have the records if you sign this contract.'**

Be very wary of contracts or agreements with agencies. Avoid signing them because they often allow the agency to withhold the information if it deems the use as "inappropriate." Some agreements even allow the government to come into a newsroom and look at the computer and records to make sure the information is being used appropriately. Either the records are public or they aren't. The law is the law. Don't let the government con you into data agreements that allow for intrusion and censorship.

**'We don't know how you'll use it. You might not use it in a way we like.'**

Tough noogies. In most states, records requests can not be denied based on who the requester is or how the information will be used. The exception is in the case of commercial mailing lists or business use, but news gathering is exempt from the commercial restrictions and higher copying costs. Access audits have demonstrated that officials get suspicious when requesters won't say who they are or why they want the record, so if it doesn't matter, feel free to tell them if you want and it might speed things along. However, if you don't want them to know, and they really have no business asking, then just respond, "I wouldn't want to determine the story before I have all my facts. I'm just doing my job at gathering information." If you request records routinely from the agency then it will be no big deal and the agency will be less likely to question you. Get in the habit.

**'We think that legally we can keep it secret because of [privacy, national security, personnel, internal memos, under investigation, etc.]. So we'll agree to disagree and not give it out.'**

Check with an expert. If the agency is right, get the information other ways. If it is wrong, it's time to turn up the heat.

BOX 6.1 **Ten ways to reduce or eliminate outrageous copy fees**

Sometimes an agency will provide records but charge thousands or millions of dollars to get copies. Most state public records laws require agencies to charge "reasonable" copy costs, often just for the paper, toner and machine use, not staff time. We guarantee you can work around unreasonable fees and get what you need on the cheap or even for free. Here are 10 ways:

1. Ask for a waiver because of the public good (federal FOIA law allows such a waiver of fees for the news media).

2. Instead of getting copies, bring a notepad and look at them for free.

3. Narrow your request by selecting only the documents that you really need.

4. Ask for the records in a digital format. Transfer the files onto a flash drive or CD-ROM, or have the files e-mailed.

5. Photograph the documents with a digital camera, or use a portable scanner. Bring your own photocopier.

6. Make the agency justify the actual costs of copying through a line-item list. Request the contract with its copy services company to see how much it pays per copy. If commercial copy businesses charge 10 cents a page, and make a profit, then a reasonable cost for a nonprofit government agency should be that or less.

7. If the agency won't provide justification, help it out with your own list:

   - Paper: Box of 10 reams (500 sheets each ream), at $35.99 = 0.7 cents per page.

   - Machine: Xerox WorkCentre 5225 costs $4,299 and produces 75,000 copies a month. Assuming two-year life, that's 0.2 cents per page.

   - Toner: $172.00 for 30,000 pages, or 0.6 cents per page.

   - Electricity: Negligible.

   Total cost per copy: 1.5 cents. Now, that's reasonable!

8. Survey all the local agencies in your area and do a story about the inconsistency in fees and ways officials rip off the public. Interview average folks who pay the fees and ask elected leaders why they think it's necessary to overcharge citizens to access records they've already paid for through their taxes.

9. Contact your state public records ombudsman or attorney general's office to talk some sense into the agency.

10. Sue or lobby for legislation specifying lower, reasonable fees.

## Play hardball

So you've haggled with officials and they still don't want to provide information you believe you are legally entitled to. It's time to ratchet up the pressure.

### Go up the ladder

If a manager or clerk is denying the records request, go to the person's supervisor or the elected governing body of the agency. Sometimes line workers are reluctant to give something out because they fear getting in trouble from superiors. Those in charge have more authority. Also, those in charge have more to lose from the appearance of secrecy or a public records lawsuit. Ask each of the city council members or school board members what they think about the agency keeping the records secret from the public. Gain advocates for your position further up the institutional food chain, then call in the firepower.

### Rally allies

Work with other journalists or other interested parties, such as genealogists, librarians, building contractors, private investigators or neighborhood gadflies. A unified front from diverse groups can be persuasive. Legislators also are good allies, as Scott Reeder found out in Illinois for his school district records project. Unions and nongovernment public interest groups can also make good allies on public records requests.

Find an attorney in your state attorney general's office or auditor's office who knows the open records law. Have that person talk to the agency. Also, find guides to public records produced by the state attorney general or the cities association in your state. Often those guides will explain how the record is public. E-mail the agency a page from the guide, or send it the whole document. Then the agency doesn't have to take your word for it; the agency is hearing it from authoritative government employees.

### Shame the agency

Find out whether other agencies provide the records in question, and then shame the deviant agency into making it public. Maybe every school district in the county or state provides teacher disciplinary reports but one. Peer pressure can be effective. Also, sometimes it helps to remind the agency about the purpose of the public records law, open government and transparency in a democracy. Wear a flag pin on your lapel and talk about freedom. This is America, after all, not Nazi Germany or Stalinist Russia.

A lot of officials don't realize that breaking the public records law puts an agency at risk. Point out other jurisdictions that denied public records, were sued and had to pay hundreds of thousands of dollars in penalties or attorney fees. In other words, secrecy creates a potential liability for the agency, not only in bad publicity but also in tax dollars. When you see in the news an agency lose a public records lawsuit, note the details in a running file and have that list on hand to provide to reluctant officials. Point out that you (and taxpayers) would hate the agency to become the state's next poster child of secrecy.

## Pro tip | Find old documents to leverage new information

I was involved in a massive project on the Louisiana environment some years back that showed safety problems with oil and natural gas pipelines. The thing that popped out of the records was that inspections were not as frequent as they ought to be and that the risk factor in failure in some of these pipelines was a lot higher than we thought. There have been several pipeline explosions over the years that could have been prevented. Since then, reporters I've worked with have tried to get plans for water system security, which you can't get anymore—officials cite the new critical infrastructure exemption. A lot of times I think it's just overreaction to a perceived threat, or basically they don't want to release information that will embarrass them. But I've found that sometimes you can get around that by finding older documents that may not be as up to date, but you can use them as a foundation for asking for more specific or penetrating questions. Sometimes small libraries that serve as repositories will have those documents still. You'll find that they've forgotten to remove those documents from the shelves. Or interview former agency officials— sometimes they'll still have a lot of documents with them and will let you see them. Just be as resourceful as possible. Don't limit yourself to the official agency that is responsible for that document. Documents get sent out all over the place. Sometimes you have to be imaginative.

—Sonny Albarado, projects editor, *Arkansas Democrat-Gazette*

### File more requests

Some journalists assume that if an agency routinely denies a valid public records request then the officials must have something to hide. And if they are hiding this document, what else are they trying to keep hidden? That's why Eric Longabardi, an investigative television reporter, digs even deeper if he gets a denial.

"If they delay and are deliberately making things difficult, send 400 requests via e-mail in 10 minutes," Longabardi told a crowd at the 2007 Investigative Reporters and Editors national conference in Phoenix. "They'll want to get you off their back and they'll get you what you asked for."

Also, you might try lobbing some "FOI clusterbombs." Request the same documents from other agencies that might have them. Or think of other documents that would have the information you are looking for, maybe even from the same agency.

Mike McGraw of *The Kansas City Star* used this technique when he was trying to get records regarding food poisoning caused by tainted beef. The Centers for Disease Control (CDC) refused to provide records that included the names of food poisoning victims. So instead McGraw requested all correspondence between the CDC and attorneys regarding food poisoning. He then contacted the attorneys who represented the victims, and they were more than happy to get the reporter in touch with their clients.

Lawyers can be great sources of documents that might have been gathered during the discovery portion of a lawsuit, in preparation of making their cases. Find out if an agency or group has been sued, and then call the plaintiff's attorney to find out what records were gathered during discovery.

Another tip is to request e-mails and memos regarding your request to see if officials talked about why it was denied and mentioned other records they did not give you. The correspondence will give you a good sense of whether the agency actually denied the records for a legitimate reason or is trying to hide something. You may learn information that allows you to submit a new request that is more focused.

### Write about it

One of the most effective ways of overcoming a public records denial is to tell people about it.

It's too bad more journalists don't follow through. Some hesitate to write stories when government hides information from the public, saying it's "inside baseball" or a conflict of interest to write about disputes between journalists and government.

We disagree. The government isn't saying "no" to the journalist. It's saying "no" to the thousands or millions of people in the community. As proxies for citizens, journalists are entrusted to tell the public when government keeps information secret. They have a duty to tell the public. Even a little story is better than nothing, and then the editorial writers can take it from there and slam the secrecy.

Other journalists say the public doesn't care.

We disagree again.

Survey research shows that people care about open government, especially when the documents concern tax dollars or public safety.[5] Journalists must demonstrate, again and again, the value of public records in everyday life, and highlight attempts at unwarranted secrecy, every single time.

In Chapter 9 we explain in more detail how to write about FOI issues in ways that make sense and are not inside baseball. If you don't tell people about the secrecy, who will?

## Appeal

Federal FOIA and a lot of state public records laws provide the ability to appeal a denial officially. In some cases it's not that helpful because you end up appealing to the head of the agency who might have been the same person who denied you the record. But in other cases the appeal is heard by the state attorney general or an outside commission.

Regardless, if that is an option in your state, take it. Always. It's free, it's easy and it can work.

American University professor Wendell Cochran looked at FOIA requests in 2006 among 15 federal agencies and found that among the 240,000 denials only 6,600 people appealed. Of those who appealed, a third got more information.[6] It pays to appeal.

## Pursue mediation

One way to work through disputes without caving in or going to court is through mediation. About half the states have some type of formal or informal mediation process, such as a public records ombudsman or person within the attorney general's office, with varying degrees of success.[7] Few have strong powers to compel the agency to provide the records, but often they can convince the officials to do the right thing and follow the law. Some state ombudsmen also have the power to review the documents in private to see if the agency's denial or redactions are justified.

For a great overview of the different states' ombudsman positions, see a report by Harry Hammitt for the National Freedom of Information Coalition at www.nfoic.org/white_papers.

In general, the idea is that if a requester and an agency disagree over a records request they can invite an independent third party to negotiate a solution. The difficulty of this process is that both sides have to agree to mediation, but the decision is not binding—whoever ends up losing doesn't have to concede.

Daxton "Chip" Stewart, a journalism professor at Texas Christian University, studies the use of mediation in resolving FOI disputes. With a law degree and a background in newspapers, Stewart sees the usefulness of journalists avoiding court if they can. Also, mediation can be used to build long-term working relationships between news organizations and agencies, without giving up the watchdog roles that journalists must play. That's why Stewart doesn't focus on formal mediation. Instead, he suggests journalists apply the general principles that make mediation work in an informal way.

A key element for working out disputes is trust. "That's hard for journalists," Stewart said. "It's not in their DNA to trust government officials, and maybe they shouldn't." Likewise, government officials often don't trust journalists, either. No wonder records requests so often end up in angst. The key, Stewart said, is to develop a trusting relationship with clerks to the point where "they call you and give you records you didn't know about." Or they might lower or waive fees.

### Sue

The last resort for a denial is litigation, mainly because it takes so long and is expensive, ranging from $250 to file a complaint in federal court to $50,000 or more, depending on how high it climbs up the courts. Yet it's one of the most important and effective responses to a blatantly illegal

**Pro tip** | **Threaten litigation if you can back it up**

It's often difficult to obtain information about issues relating to national security without litigation. But litigation, and sometimes even just the threat of litigation, can persuade a reluctant agency to process a request that it would otherwise ignore, or to release records that it would otherwise withhold. Many of the records that the ACLU obtained relating to surveillance and torture were obtained only after we brought suit.[8] You shouldn't threaten litigation unless you can make good on the threat, but if litigation is an option, sometimes just letting the agency know that you're considering it is enough to make the agency a little more cooperative.

—Jameel Jaffer, director of the American Civil Liberties Union National Security Project

denial, and it is crucial that news organizations routinely incorporate the costs of litigation into their budgets. Sometimes the records themselves are not as useful by the time a case is litigated or settled, but simply filing the suit sends a strong message. Officials might think twice before denying you records in the future.

News organizations choose their cases carefully because they don't want to establish bad case law if they lose. So when considering litigation, make sure it's a slam-dunk win. In some states, the government may have to pay attorney fees, penalties or both if you win in court. If your news organization doesn't want to sue, look around for an attorney who might handle the case for free. The Student Press Law Center (www.splc.org) provides free legal advice to student journalists. Or team up with other organizations that might want to sue for the information.

Filing a lawsuit in federal court over federal FOIA is actually pretty easy and affordable. You don't need an attorney or that much money. The Reporters Committee for Freedom of the Press outlines the steps and even includes the forms to fill out (www.rcfp.org/fogg/index.php). The mere act of filing a lawsuit in federal court will often pry the records loose.

Michele Earl-Hubbard, an attorney in Washington state who litigates public records disputes, said the chances of winning increase if journalists keep a detailed paper trail of their quest for documents. "The most important thing is good record keeping," she said. "Keep your requests and don't alter them. Make your requests in writing. Keep track of everything. If you talk to them, create a written record of what was said."

Earl-Hubbard also suggests journalists act politely and reasonably with agencies as they deal with denials. If it does go to court, a judge will notice if a reporter is being a jerk or has an ax to grind.

### Make it easier for agencies to comply

Ultimately, the key to overcoming illegal denials is to be persistent and not back down, using a combination of some or all of the techniques provided in this chapter.

Rob O'Dell, City Hall reporter from the *Arizona Daily Star,* said tenacity is the key to getting what you need: "My philosophy is that you have to show them that it's going to be more work to deny the records then to comply with the request."

For example, sometimes an agency will say it can't get a record because it would take too long for a staff member to look through all the documents to find what you need. And the agency will say it will photocopy everything for you but at a high fee. So just look at the documents yourself. In response, O'Dell said, an agency might insist that it has a staff member on hand to make sure you don't damage or take documents. "I'll say, 'OK, I'll be there every day starting at 9 a.m.,'" he said. "On the first day's it's fine. The second day it's fine. The third day it's fine. But by the fourth day they'll come up to me and say, 'Is there another way we can do this?' They realize that maybe it's easier to just comply and give me what I asked for rather than have someone sit there with me all day."

O'Dell said that if you develop a reputation as someone who does not simply go away when denied, then you will be denied less. "You have to show that you are going to get the records, that you are consistent and that you aren't going to go away. If they know that you will keep coming and won't give up, then they will figure out a way to give you what you need."

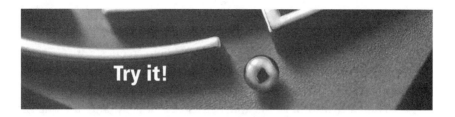

**Exercises and ideas for journalists, newsrooms and classrooms to improve your skills and foster FOI in your community.**

## 1. Conduct an FOI audit

Show citizens the prevalence of illegal public records denials by conducting an FOI audit in your community, college campus or state. Audits show the extent of agencies not following the law and often lead to new legislation and openness. Gather other journalists and citizens together and develop a protocol for what records you will request and how you will do it. Choose records that yield good stories. Then publicize the audit results and make sure legislators get copies in case your state laws need strengthening. To get a sense of what other audits have accomplished, check out a list of some at the Freedom of Information Center (www.nfoic.org/audits-and-open-records-surveys). To get detailed tips and instructions for conducting your own audit, check out the FOI Toolkit produced by Charles Davis for the Society of Professional Journalists (http://spj.org/foitoolkit.asp).

## 2. Quantify the price of secrecy

Demonstrate the price of secrecy by developing two lists to share in your newsroom or as a class project, or even as a news story:

- ☑ Important public-interest stories that couldn't have been done without public records, or stories that won't be able to be done because of secrecy.
- ☑ Big payouts by the government in penalties and attorney fees after losing public records lawsuits.

These lists can be used when convincing an agency to provide records, writing about denials, pushing for better laws or arguing cases in court.

Provide a summary paragraph for each instance with the basic details and links to any stories or supporting materials. Compile the anecdotes for a story that can be published during national Sunshine Week, held every mid-March. For an example of stories that couldn't have been done without public records, see Jennifer LaFleur's 2003 report on "The Lost Stories" for the Reporters Committee for Freedom of the Press (www .rcfp.org/loststories).

## 3. Do a double take

For your next document-driven story, identify a document that is held by two different agencies, such as a boating accident report (e.g., your state boating safety commission and the U.S. Coast Guard), and request the same document from both agencies. Note how the different agencies handle the requests and compare what information each agency redacts and makes public. This will enable you to piece together a more accurate picture for your story and better understand the inconsistencies of how different agencies, and perhaps different people within agencies, provide records.

## 4. Dig those declassifications

Dig through declassified documents to get a sense for what is kept secret. Did it really need to be kept secret, or was it as benign as the Secret Santa memo? A great Web site that posts declassified documents is The National Security Archive, based out of The George Washington University (www .nsarchive.org).

## 5. Analyze the FOI logs

Request the FOI logs from an agency you cover or local jurisdictions that interest you, such as your city, university or school district. Request to see the logs for the past three years. Make sure the logs include dates and disposition—when the person requested a record from the agency, when the agency responded and ultimately whether the person got the records or not. Also try to get the reason for denial if the request was denied. Create a spreadsheet (if the log isn't already in one), and tabulate the average length of time it took the agency to respond, the percentage of requests where the agency didn't respond within the time required by law, the percentage of requests that were denied and the most common reason for denial. See if the denial percentage is increasing or decreasing (trends), and compare to other similar agencies to find the most secretive one in your area. Write a story showing the state of access in your community, interviewing people who requested records.

**Suggested links**

**Federal appeal/lawsuit forms**    www.rcfp.org/fogg/index.php
The Reporters Committee for Freedom of the Press has provided forms online to appeal a FOIA denial, as well as a form you can fill out to actually file suit yourself in federal court.

**Federal FOIA ombudsman**    www.archives.gov/ogis
If you are stonewalled or denied by an agency, get help from the federal FOIA ombudsman, officially the director of the Office of Government Information Services. In addition to the Web site, you can e-mail at ogis@nara.gov or call 301-837-1996.

**Learn about mediation**    www.nfoic.org/white_papers
Look at the report "Mediation without Litigation" by Harry Hammitt to find out if your state has a mediation system.

**Students can get free legal help**    www.splc.org
The Student Press Law Center will provide free legal assistance to student journalists who have problems getting public records.

## Going digital
### Strategies for getting data

**ACCESS ACTION AGENDA**
- ☑ Become familiar with data
- ☑ Get the database
- ☑ Counter cyber-denials
- ☑ Teach yourself database journalism

When is the last time you saw a typewriter? Maybe in a museum or your grandparents' garage?

The days of ink are gone. It's all about zeros and ones now.

Chances are, nearly everything your local government officials record is in a computer. So you need to know how to get at those electronic records, transfer them and use them. That includes e-mails, Excel spreadsheets, pdf documents, Outlook calendars and just about any other computerized file in a government PC or mainframe.

In this chapter we will focus on the art of accessing electronic data, specifically databases that journalists can analyze to identify trends and community challenges. We call it different things—computer-assisted reporting, database journalism, power reporting—but it's all the same thing: showing people what is happening through quantifiable evidence rather than relying on anecdote or he-said, she-said quotes.

The stories are harder hitting, the topics more serious and important. This is reporting at its best, and something every journalist can do.

If we can do it, we know anyone can. The benefits are just too good to pass up.

- **Find bad people in good places.** Get a copy of every criminal conviction in your county or state for the past five to 10 years, or longer. Match the data to other databases to find hardened criminals in positions of trust where they don't belong. Classic matches include school bus drivers, daycare workers, high school coaches and people allowed to carry concealed weapons. For example, in 2007 *The Columbus* (Ohio) *Dispatch* matched criminal records to a database of school bus drivers to find 167 drivers who had records of drunken driving or drug abuse.[1]
- **Identify trouble spots.** Government tracks everything that goes wrong in society, so there are a lot of accident data available for analysis: train wrecks, car wrecks, plane crashes and more. Government also inspects everything, so you can download and analyze inspection data for bridges, nursing homes, gas pumps, restaurants and other areas of public interest. Government tracks crime, so you can identify trends and problems in your community. For example, the *Tulsa World* examined police data to find that calls to schools increased 44 percent from 2005 to 2009, including fights, drug use and weapons incidents.[2]
- **Monitor government performance.** Databases allow you to assess how well government is operating. Request budgets, audit numbers and citizen complaints. Look at performance data to find out if an agency is doing what it says it's doing. Andy Hall, executive director of the Wisconsin Center for Investigative Reporting, once found through state gaming records that a pet adoption agency was selling retired racing greyhounds for cardiac research experiments rather than adopting them out to families.[3] "Always assume there is a record or data to help you look into an issue," Hall said.

Anyone can acquire government data with a little initiative and tenacity. Requesting government databases poses special challenges you don't find with paper documents,[4] so in this chapter we will cover basic elements of data, how to find data, how to write request letters specific to databases, how to counter denials and outrageous programming costs, how to transfer data and how to teach yourself the art of electronic access.

## Become familiar with data

While database journalism has been around since as early as the 1950s, it is far from being a common tool for examining government information.[5] By 1994, about two-thirds of journalists were using computers to find information on the Internet. That grew to 90 percent by 1998.[6] That's great, but only 10 percent of journalists analyzed government data in spreadsheets and only 4 percent acquired and analyzed databases.[7]

Today, more journalists are examining government information using basic spreadsheet software, such as Microsoft Excel, said Brant Houston, former longtime director of Investigative Reporters and Editors and the National Institute of Computer-Assisted Reporting. But still, relatively few journalists are going after databases.

"We've made a huge amount of progress with the Internet and spreadsheets," said Houston, who now teaches investigative reporting at the University of Illinois at Urbana-Champaign. "The focus now continues to be in training people to use database managers."

Anyone can do it, but before you request specific government data, it's good to have a basic understanding of the format and terminology of what you are likely to get.

### Examine the pieces

First, almost all databases are set up in a grid pattern, just like you've probably seen in Microsoft Excel or another spreadsheet program. The "fields" are the columns of information going up and down, labeled with a "header" at the top saying what it is.

So let's say you have a database of city pet licenses. Headers for the columns might include "Identification number," "Dog name," "Breed" and "License expiration." When you request data you want to know every field contained in the database—the whole list—so you know what you can do with it.

The information running horizontally in our grid, from left to right, is called a row, and each row represents a different record. In the case of our basic example, each row represents a different licensed dog.

| FIGURE 7.1 | **Spreadsheet sample: Pima County, Arizona, dog license data** | | | | | | |
|---|---|---|---|---|---|---|---|
| **Name** | **Breed** | **Expiration** | **Age** | **Gender** | **Address** | **Zip** |
| Snuggles | Schnauzer | 2006 | 9 | F | 5567 W Dove Loft Dr. | 85653 |
| Zappa | Airedale | 2007 | 5 | M | 4786 W Saguaro Cliffs Dr. | 85745 |
| Thor | Beagle mix | 2004 | 2 | M | 2748 N Pacific Dr. | 85705 |
| Freedom | Rottweiler mix | 2007 | 1 | F | 1022 N Palo Verde Rd. | 85716 |
| Princess | Rottweiler mix | 2005 | 1 | F | 4500 N Paseo DeLos St. | 85745 |
| Hans Solo | Beagle mix | 2006 | 5 | M | 1440 Irvington Rd. | 85746 |
| Boo Bear | Heeler | 2004 | 13 | F | 10040 E Mary Dr. | 85730 |
| *Source:* Pima County Animal Control, Tucson, Ariz. | | | | | | | |

In our example of dog licenses, we've provided a sample of public data acquired from Pima County Animal Control in Arizona (see Figure 7.1), comprising actual records from the agency database, including Snuggles the schnauzer and Hans Solo the beagle mix. There are relatively few fields in this database, including name, breed, age, gender and address, but the number of individual records, or rows, number 65,536. We provided just seven of the records, but you can get a sense of what a database "looks" like.

### Learn the lingo

To communicate within this world of electronic geegaws, it doesn't hurt to speak the language. You don't have to be fluent, but you should at least know what to write down so you can ask a techie later.

- **Data:** Any information kept in a computer, although we think of it as organized information kept in a database in rows and columns. The word "data" is plural, as in "Government data are awesome." Sounds funny in some contexts, but you can write around it by using the word "database."
- **Database:** An organized collection of information in rows and columns. You might also hear it referred to as a "table." The database

looks like something you would see in Excel, with information organized in a grid format that can be sorted.

- **Field:** The column in a database (going up and down) that represents a piece of information that each individual record has, such as identification number, date or other variables. In our dog database, "Name" is a field, as is "Breed."

- **Record:** The row in a database (going across), representing an individual record, such as a dog in a pet license database, or a single nursing home's inspection report. In our dog database, "Thor" the beagle mix constitutes a single record.

- **Record layout:** This describes the fields contained in the data, including each field name, the field's width and the field's type—such as date, numeric (numbers that you can add and subtract) or text (numbers and letters that you don't add or subtract, like telephone numbers and names).

- **Code sheet:** Also called a data dictionary, this document provides explanations for any codes in the data. For example, perhaps in the "Gender" field 1 represents Female, 2 represents Male and 99 represents Unknown. You need the code sheet to be able to understand coded data.

- **Tab-delimited text file:** This is the most easily transferable format of data because it can be imported into just about any spreadsheet or database manager software. Each field is separated ("delimited") by a tab symbol, allowing Excel, Access or other programs to easily flow the data into its grids. The data are in plain text characters that any program can read. Sometimes data are provided in *comma*-delimited text files, where each field is separated by a comma instead of a tab symbol.

- **Fixed-format data:** Some databases, particularly older, main frame–oriented databases, are in fixed format. This means that each field is allowed a certain number of digits, and when you import the data you will need to tell the program how many digits each field has been allocated. Make sure to get the record layout that would list those numbers. You don't see this format so much anymore—a tab-delimited text file is easier to import into Excel and Access.

## Get the database

When Steve Doig teaches computer-assisted reporting classes at Arizona State University, his students often have an idea of what they would like to look into, and they'll ask, "Is there data out there to look at, and where do I get it?"

"I'll say, 'I don't know. You have to go find out,'" said Doig, who helped *The Miami Herald* win a Pulitzer Prize through his data work. He tells his students to do their reporting and go find what data exist. "They need to think of what agency might have it, and what they might keep."

Ultimately, the computer is not the important part of computer-assisted reporting—it's just a tool. The key is to figure out what questions need answering, and then list the pieces of information that would be needed in a database to answer those questions. If you want to identify trends you'll need a date field to look at change over time. If you want to see if there is racial profiling in traffic stops you'll need a field identifying race and ethnicity.

In Chapter 4 we focused on how to find documents, and the same strategies apply to data—looking at forms online, scanning journalism tip Web sites, mapping the government, talking with sources, etc. However, when trying to identify electronic records, take a few extra steps that go beyond just asking for paper documents.

### Get to the wonk

Every government clerk knows how to run a photocopy machine to provide you copies, but few know how to export data onto a CD-ROM, or program in Structured Query Language. That's why it's crucial to find the techies at an agency who actually work with the data.

This can be a challenge because some public information officers (PIOs) and agency officials will want to be the go-between. So you end up asking for a certain database in a certain way and the PIO relays the information to the technician—sometimes the wrong information, so the technician says that doesn't make sense, relaying it back to you. Then you have to clarify. Back and forth it goes, frustrating everyone.

Eventually the PIO might finally let you talk directly to the computer programmer, sometimes all together in a room. That's fine. Even better, if you're unfamiliar with programming, bring your news organization's techie or someone else who can help you work through the issues.

Most computer programmers at government agencies are helpful. They often don't get a chance to work with journalists, so it lends importance to their job. Bring them donuts. Visit them and learn what they do and what kinds of information they work with. Ask them the exact name of the database and understand what's in it. Take a real interest in their job—people love to explain their work to others. That will help you provide a specific request that will be processed quickly.

### Get the record layout

Most agencies keep a "record layout" of each database, basically a roadmap or table of contents for the data to help keep track of the different pieces of information the agency collects. Always try to get this record, preferably before you request the database, because it will help you see what is in the data and make sure the agency isn't leaving out key fields and not telling you.

Some layouts are simple, listing the name of each field, the type of field (date, numeric or text/character) and the width of the field. Some layouts provide a brief description of each field, along with any codes and how to interpret the codes. The U.S. Department of Health and Human Services, for example, provides nursing home inspection data online for anyone to download (www.medicare.gov/Download/DownloadDB.asp).

In addition to downloading the data, you can snag the record layout, which describes the different tables, including a simple table that lists when each nursing home was last inspected (see Box 7.1). Notice in the figure that the layout includes the field name, its type and its width (how many digits are allowed for that particular piece of information). This layout also provides a short description, which is helpful.

Increasingly, some agencies are trying to keep record layouts secret and are arguing that they are not public records. We're not sure why this is, except that they may want to make sure you don't know what information they keep, so they can selectively pick the fields of data they want you to have and leave out the information they would rather keep secret. Don't let agencies get away with this. Always try to get the record layout,

**Sample record layout: Nursing home inspection data**

Table "dbo_vwNHC_SVRY_DT" contains eight (8) fields. This table lists the three most recent survey dates for each nursing home. Here is exactly how the record layout describes the fields in the database:

1. **ProvNum:** varchar (10).
   Lists the nursing homes by their provider identification number.

2. **SurveyDate:** char (8)
   Lists the date the survey was performed.

3. **NursingHomeName:** varchar (50)
   Lists the name of the nursing home that corresponds to the provider identification number.

4. **Street:** varchar (50)
   Lists the street address in which the nursing home is located.

5. **City:** varchar (28)
   Lists the city in which the nursing home is located.

6. **State:** varchar (2)
   Lists the two-letter code representing that state in which the nursing home is located.

7. **ZipCode:** char (5)
   Lists the five-digit numeric zip code that corresponds to the nursing home.

8. **PhoneNumber:** char (10)
   Lists the 10-digit numeric telephone number, including area code, that corresponds to the nursing home.

*Source:* U.S. Department of Health and Human Services.

especially for large, complicated databases, even if you have to file a for-mal FOI request to get it.

### Get a printed sample

Ask for a printed-out sample of the first dozen records or so, just to get a sense of what you'll be getting. Make sure it's what you want before you go through all the trouble of having it exported and delivered.

Find out exactly what the records cover, how far back they go, how many records there are and how big the files are in megabytes. Also make sure to ask if there are any limitations to the data, such as certain fields where clerks enter the information in different ways or accuracy problems known by the agency. Data are only as good as the people who enter it.

### Write data-specific letters

After doing your homework and talking with the agency's data wonks, you should know exactly what information you want and how they will be able to give it to you. They might be able to simply provide it to you without a formal written records request, but sometimes you'll need to write a letter.

Or maybe the agency is not helpful in explaining its data and how it stores them. Remember, there is no law requiring anyone to explain what information they have—only that they provide copies of records. So if you don't know what data the agency has, and the agency isn't telling you, then you will have to send a letter requesting the data.

Request letters for electronic records tend to be longer and more detailed than letters for print documents. Sarah Cohen, former database editor for *The Washington Post* and now a journalism professor at Duke University, said she makes her request letters as detailed as possible, identifying the exact names of the database or records and specifying the different formats that it could be provided on. When she asked the Washington, D.C., mayor's office for a database containing nuisance complaints from citizens, she was clear to point out that she wanted database "727-1000" (see Figure 7.2 for her letter and how she put it together). The database shed light on trouble-spots in the city, enabling the paper, for example, to produce an online "rat map" that highlighted areas of heavy rodent infestation.

### Transfer the data

When Brant Houston started working with computer data in 1985, he transferred files on 5 ¼ floppy disks, if he was lucky. They could hold about a megabyte of data, equivalent to a 40-page Word document today. Good luck getting a court database of criminal convictions for the state!

If the database was larger than the little floppies could handle, he used his company's mainframe, or a $5,000 9-track reader, loading large, movie-like magnetic reels and watching them spin for hours downloading a 500 megabyte database, something that fits on a cheap flash drive today and is transferred in seconds.

FIGURE 7.2 **Sample records request for government data**

Peggy Armstrong
Director, Office of Communications
Executive Office of the Mayor
One Judiciary Square, Suite 1100S
Washington, D.C. 20001

**Address to specific person**

Dear Ms. Armstrong,

**Cite the law**

Pursuant to the D.C. Freedom of Information Act, D.C. Code 1-521 et seq., I hereby request an electronic copy of the service request database maintained as part of the customer call center informally known as 727-1000.

**Name the specific database**

In particular, I am requesting all records and all fields from the database from its inception to the present, including but not limited to:

**Keep it open-ended**

The location of the problem (including quadrant, street number and street name), the proximity or description of the location, the service requested, any additional description of the problem, the tracking number, the date of the request and all data elements associated with tracking, correcting or otherwise acting on the request.

**List specific fields, in this case identified by looking at the blank form on the Web**

**Always ask for code sheets**

I am also requesting any lookup tables, code sheets and other documents needed to interpret the data.

If you regard any of the requested records as subject to exemption from required disclosure under the Act, I ask that you exercise your discretion and disclose them nonetheless. If you find that any exemptions do apply, please be aware of the specific requirement under D.C. Code 1-1524(b) that you provide any reasonably segregable portion of any record after deletion of the portions claimed to be exempt.

**Remind them to cite the law for keeping anything secret**

I am requesting that this data be supplied in any common electronic form on any common medium, such as an ASCII text file on CD-ROM, tape, Jazz or Zip drive. I am happy to supply you with any materials you need to comply with the request. As an alternative, we have an FTP site for just these requests.

**Make it easy to transfer the data. Substitute Jazz or Zip drives (dated) with an external hard drive**

**Give them a sense of what it's about, to build trust and justify a fee waiver**

I am making this request on behalf of The Washington Post, a newspaper of general circulation in the Washington, D.C. metropolitan area and throughout the United States. The records disclosed pursuant to this request will be used in the preparation of news articles for dissemination to the public.

Accordingly, I request that, pursuant to D.C. Code 1-1522(b), you waive all fees in the public interest because the furnishing of the information sought by this request will primarily benefit the public and is likely to contribute significantly to public understanding of the generations or activities of the government. If, however, you decline to waive all fees, I am prepared to pay your normal fees to newspaper requestors, but request that you notify me if you expect these fees to exceed $100.

**Make fees clear to avoid surprises later**

**Offer to help and make it as easy as possible for the agency**

I understand that this system is based on a common relational database format that should not take significant work to copy. I am happy to work with your office to make this request as simple as possible and to eliminate any unnecessary work. Please call me before you undertake any programming or other difficult work—we can probably find an efficient solution while minimizing your effort.

If you have any questions about this request, please do not hesitate to contact me at the above telephone number. I look forward to your response within the ten (10) day statutory time period.

**Remind them of the statutory response deadline**

Sincerely,

**Be polite and provide contact information**

Sarah Cohen
Database editor
(202) XXX-XXXX

Life is much better today. Transferring data has become a lot easier because of the Internet's larger storage capacity, CD-ROMs and flash drives.

"The biggest change was the Web and the ability to get data out there for everyone," Houston said. "Sometimes the agency management didn't even know it was up there. That was a great leap forward."

The most common method of transferring electronic records is via CD. Also you can transfer files on flash drives, download data from the agency Web site or have a file sent to you via e-mail. Carry around a portable hard drive for huge files.

If the file is large, say a gigabyte or more, and you can't make it to the agency's office, the agency might be able to post it on its Web site for you to download. Some agencies might still use "ftp" Web sites, which stands for File Transfer Protocol—a way of allowing someone to download data via the Internet.

Avoid accepting electronic records in pdf format because it can be tricky to pull into Excel or Access. A number of programs can do it, such as PDF to Text and Able 2 Extract, but if you can get it as a tab-delimited text file you'll save yourself time and hassles.

When you finally do get the data, and you've imported them into Excel or Access, make sure to check to see if you got everything you were supposed to get, and spot check them against paper files to make sure they're accurate.

## Counter cyber-denials

Electronic records can be trickier to acquire than paper documents because of technical hurdles that may block your access. Here are some of the common denials specific to requests for data and ways of dealing with them.

### 'We can't technically do that'

Often when you request data from a government agency you might be the first person to have asked for it. That will throw some agencies for a loop.

The first response might be "we don't have data." The clerk might not have ever worked with a database, only what comes across the desk or what is showing on the computer screen. Instead, the clerk, accustomed to dealing with the day-to-day reports, will instead offer to provide you all the records in paper, totaling 2,435 pages (at 25 cents a page). The clerk then prints you out a report summary, pulls it from the printer and hands it to you as an example. "That's nice," you reply politely. And then, putting on your best Columbo impersonation, scrunch your face a little and say, "Shoot, I might not be following everything here, but where did that printout come from?"

After the clerk realizes it's silly to say there are no computer data, after having just printed out information from the computer, the next line is usually, "That would be a ton of information. There's no way we could ever provide that to anyone." The clerk is envisioning a warehouse of records. But in reality, the data can fit on a flash drive the size of your pinkie.

"Well," the clerk says, "we just don't have any way of making a copy of what you are asking for in the format you're talking about. We have our reports, and that's it."

That's when you have to start getting to the techies—the people who understand the structure of the data that the printouts are based on. There's *always* a way to get a copy of the data.

Steve Doig said the next excuse is sometimes "It's not our policy to give out this information." "That's incredibly bogus," Doig said. "That's like saying 'it's not our policy to follow state law.'" Refer to Chapter 6 on denials when the rejection is based on policy issues rather than technical obstacles.

### Proprietary software

Some agencies will say their software is proprietary and does not allow them to make copies or export data. Usually this is the case of a PIO who doesn't understand the software, or a computer technician who doesn't want to take the time to export the data. It's usually a bogus claim—most software today can export data in some form. Assuming most agencies like to have backups of their data, ask for an extra copy.

Or you might have to work with the private vendor to get the data if the agency isn't used to copying or exporting its own data. Jaimi Dowdell, a database trainer for IRE, said she is usually able to get around the "proprietary software can't export" excuse by contacting the private vendor who made the software. "I ask for the name of the software and I look up the company online and call them up. I say, 'I was just on the phone with one of your clients and they say your software doesn't export into anything.' They usually say, 'Oh my gosh, our software can do back flips.' They offer to train the agency and make sure it can be done. Then I call the agency back and tell them the company is open to helping them do it."

## Personal information

Often government databases include fields that are legitimately secret, such as Social Security numbers and bank account numbers. If an agency says it won't give you a database because it has personal information in it, simply ask the agency to redact, or delete, the private information and release the public information. Just like a paper document.

Sometimes PIOs don't realize that redaction of fields is pretty easy. In Microsoft Excel or Access, simply click on the field and then click on "Delete." A lot easier than using a black pen!

It becomes more difficult, however, when there is a field that includes narrative—explanations and descriptions—that have a mix of public and private information. When you're looking at databases that can include millions of records, it's a lot to ask of an agency to read through each record and delete the private materials. It all depends on how important it is and how much you are willing to pay for redaction time if your state allows that to be charged to requesters.

Sometimes you want a unique identifier for each person in a database, to tell the John Smiths apart from one another. This is common when comparing criminal data to other databases, such as school bus drivers. You generally can't get Social Security numbers anymore because of fear of identity theft. But you might ask for the last four digits of Social Security numbers, or that the agency substitutes each Social Security number with a randomly generated unique number. The key is to stress that you want to make sure you get it right, and those key identifiers prevent you from mixing up people who have the same name. It's diffi-cult for an agency to argue against accuracy.

### Creation of a 'new record'

Sometimes an agency will deny a request for data because it claims that copying certain fields of information from its computers is creation of a new record, and state laws generally don't require agencies to create new records for a person.

Remind the agency that all you're asking for is a copy of its existing data. Writing a computer program to copy data to a CD is the process of copying data, just like walking to a photocopy machine, opening the lid and pressing the green button is the process for copying a print document. It's not creating new data—the information is there in the computer. You're just getting a copy of it, as allowed by law.

Where this becomes tricky is when you want to substitute a unique identifying code for names in a database. For example, to see if schools are advancing students who fail their classes, you might want to look at raw grade information of students and whether they were passed along to the next grade. Identifiable grade information is secret under the Family Educational Rights and Privacy Act (FERPA), but if you take the names out you can have the information. Some agencies will argue that substituting a random number for a student name is creating a new record, and they don't have to do that. Most agencies will carry out the substitution. It doesn't take much work, and it protects the privacy of the people in the data.

### High programming costs

It would seem that costs for transferring data should be lower, given the move away from mainframes and the ease of copying and pasting an Excel file and shooting it off in an e-mail. Yet many agencies will find ways of charging for "programming time" to copy data.

Or worse, an agency might charge a fee by the record as it would for photocopies, or a per-record fee, such as police reports. Steve Doig remembers when he worked at *The Miami Herald* and wanted driver's license information (when it was still public). The state would charge $2 if someone wanted to see one record, so the agency charged him $2 for each record in the database—all 13 million records—for a copy fee of $26 million. "They said statute required them to charge $2 per record so their hands were tied. We didn't buy it," said Doig. He found out the state routinely sold the database to companies so the newspaper bought one of those copies for cheap. Funny that an agency can readily make a copy of data for companies that will then use it for marketing purposes, but give citizens and journalists a tough time for wanting to analyze it for the public good.

When Jason Grotto, a projects reporter for the *Chicago Tribune*, worked for *The Miami Herald*, the local school district wanted to charge an outrageous price—in the thousands of dollars—for a copy of data. First, Grotto tried to narrow the request by looking at the record layout to see if there would be fewer fields that he needed. As they continued to negotiate he found out that the school district provided a routine audit report for internal uses, which happened to have the same basic information he needed for his analysis. He simply asked for a copy of the audit report data, which cost far less than a special request.

## Teach yourself database journalism

Brant Houston has done more for helping journalists learn database journalism than any other person on this planet. We wouldn't exaggerate. He's taught thousands of reporters how to crunch spreadsheets, query data and create geocoded maps.

As former director of the National Institute for Computer-Assisted Reporting (NICAR), Houston hosted weeklong boot camps at the University of Missouri–Columbia School of Journalism and traveled the country conducting workshops for newsrooms. He says all journalists can learn database journalism, starting on their own and working up. In this section we'll suggest ways to get started in computer-assisted reporting. Anyone can do it!

### Learn Excel

First, you can teach yourself a lot of the basic skills of database journalism through Microsoft Excel. Get familiar with the concept of columns (fields) and rows (records)—like the dog license database earlier in the chapter.

Anyone can learn Excel, then download government data and do simple sorts and calculations. Excel also allows you to do basic statistics,

## Pro tip | Scrape the Web for data

If an agency won't provide data in a spreadsheet, database or text file, but the information is displayed online, then try Web scraping. You can get software that will automatically capture information from a Web site and put it in a spreadsheet or other format that you can analyze. You can download Web scraping extensions for the Firefox Web browser, such as OutWit Hub, or dedicated software like Web Scraper Plus+ and Kapow. You can master a scripting language—for instance PHP, Perl, Python, C#, Ruby or Visual Basic. In Denmark we use Web scraping software from Kapow Technologies. It may be the best way to go if you can't write code or if you don't want to or don't have the required time to learn it. Today Kapow also exists in a free version, OpenKapow, which is used by journalists in at least the U.S., Denmark and Norway. Before scraping, contact the site owners and tell them that you plan to scrape the site and ask which time would be preferred so you don't bog down their site. Try to scrape in the evening or in the middle of the night or weekend, when few users are using the site. Remember to check your data in every possible way. It's easy to create errors. And when you find strange occurrences in your scraped dataset, double check against the original data. Ask the data owner for an explanation. Very often journalists can tell data owners about errors in data they didn't know about. Learn more about scraping through the National Institute for Computer-Assisted Reporting at Investigative Reporters and Editors (www.ire. org), including online tip sheets with more details about how to scrape data.

—Nils Mulvad, editor, Kaas and Mulvad (media consultants in computer-assisted reporting in Denmark), and associate professor at the Danish School of Media and Journalism

pivot tables and other functions that start moving into more advanced data analysis. A lot of journalists do great work with data simply using Excel, particularly when analyzing government budgets or spending. It's an outstanding program for working with numbers and calculations. We aren't saying that because of any deal with Bill Gates. That's just what most database journalists use. It works and is a common program.

One of the best ways to teach yourself Excel is to get the book "Computer-Assisted Reporting: A Practical Guide," by Houston and available through IRE (www.ire.org). We use this book in our courses, and it works, thanks to the relevant examples and sample data provided online for practice.

Eventually you are going to acquire large databases that Excel can't handle, or you'll want to do more advanced analysis. Then you'll need to learn a database manager.

## Learn Access

Once you have Excel down, Houston says a NICAR boot camp or other intensive immersion training is a good way to learn how to use database managers, such as Microsoft Access. The program doesn't matter that much—in the 1990s most database journalists used FoxPro and then migrated to Access. A new program could evolve in the future replacing Access. Don't get fixated on the program, but rather the functions that you need for analyzing data.

The advantage of a database manager is that it can handle larger databases than Excel and is able to quickly group information together. You can also learn Structured Query Language to create your own programmed queries for analyzing data.

Learning how to apply that kind of software to data analysis can take longer to learn on your own, although a lot of journalists have trained themselves, using self-help books and discipline. Taking a class or going to a NICAR boot camp might get you started off right.

A few hardcore data heads will delve into the world of statistical software, such as SPSS or SAS; mapping software, such as ArcGIS; social-network analysis software and other high-powered analytical tools. This is more difficult to learn on your own, but many journalists have done it, and again, IRE can help. By the time you get to this level you will need to know where to find resources for teaching yourself these skills.

## Tap into the computer-assisted reporting network

Computer-assisted reporting journalists are great about helping each other, so feel free to learn from the best. Your first stop is the National Institute for Computer-Assisted Reporting (NICAR) (http://data.nicar .org).

The NICAR listserv allows you to post questions when you run into problems. First, like many listservs, check the listserv archive to see if the question has already been asked (and answered). The archives are available to IRE members, so make sure you join. Chances are the topic already has been covered and there's no need to waste space in a lot of people's e-mail inboxes. One of the best parts about subscribing to the listserv is reading about great database story tips and debates over the proper use of data and data practices.

The NICAR Web site also provides tools for working with data, tip sheets and databases that you can buy for cheap. It's a great deal because they've already done the acquisition and cleaning. All you have to do is pay a reasonable fee—as cheap as $15, depending on the size of your organization—and you get the data ready to crunch for your community.

Attend a computer-assisted reporting conference put on by NICAR. You'll also learn about the latest application of software and data analysis in journalism.

Be on the lookout for a Better Watchdog workshop put on in your area by IRE.

| Pro tip | Join computer groups |
| --- | --- |

When you're learning software join computer users groups. You'll get a lot of tips, pick up the lingo and the agency techs will realize you are capable of doing it. It's kind of like nerd bonding.

—Jennifer LaFleur, director of computer-assisted reporting, ProPublica

### Find a stats guru

Grotto, while still at *The Miami Herald,* analyzed 10 years of data regarding each time a person accepted a plea agreement or deferred prosecution. He found through logistic regression and other sophisticated statistical analysis that whites were likely to get more lenient sentences than blacks and Latinos with the same criminal background. He had two university professors help him with the number crunching. "Anytime you do analysis of that level you need to have a guru check it," Grotto said. He even gave all of his analysis to the Department of Corrections so it could double-check it, and it found he had done a solid job in his analysis.

Over time, as you acquire databases and overcome the hurdles in doing so, you will develop a strong electronic document state of mind. Now that you know how to find records (both paper and electronic), request them and overcome denials, it doesn't hurt to figure out the perceptions of those on the other side of the counter. We will cover this in the next chapter. Understanding public officials will make you better in the art of access.

**Exercises and ideas for journalists, newsrooms and classrooms to improve your skills and foster FOI in your community.**

### 1. Join the NICAR listserv

Join the National Institute for Computer-Assisted Reporting listserv (www.ire.org/membership/subscribe/nicar-l.html), and get a membership to Investigative Reporters and Editors (www.ire.org) so you have access to listserv archives. Search the archives for five tips about acquiring government databases (you'll find a lot!).

### 2. Browse the data library

Check out the NICAR database library (http://data.nicar.org/node/61) to get a sense of what kinds of government databases are out there—dozens are listed on the Web site. You can download a 100-record sample of each database to get a sense of what's in it. Look at the fields and brainstorm potential story ideas. You know you have a good shot at acquiring these datasets because NICAR already did it. Go ahead and request a database, or buy one from NICAR.

### 3. Get extra database ideas

Go to Investigative Reporters and Editors' Web site and click on the Extra! Extra! portion of the site (www.ire.org/extraextra). Look for the subject archives on the right part of the Web page and click on "CAR" (computer-assisted reporting). Browse through the nearly 1,000 CAR story summaries, each containing a link to the actual story at the news organization's Web site. Find five database stories that you would like to do and go request the data.

### 4. Learn Excel through your home budget

A great way to teach yourself Excel is to create a home budget for yourself, tracking where you spend your money each month. Create a worksheet, and across the top label each column (field) for a month. Then, across the rows provide the main categories of expenses in your life (e.g., rent, food, entertainment, utilities, car insurance). Create a TOTAL column and have Excel keep a running total as you add in figures for each month in each expense category. Also have Excel calculate the total of all your expenses for each month. Include a row for income and see if you end up in the red or black each month. If you're running in the red, you can easily see why by examining your expense categories. No more mochas!

### 5. Census primer through 'Elima-Data'

One of the best ways of learning how to download and analyze government data through Excel is through the census. This exercise enables you to find which city in your state has the highest percentage of men and which city has the highest percentage of women—a good way to find out which city would give you the greatest odds of finding a significant other. Here's how:

1. Go to the census site (www.census.gov).
2. Go to "American FactFinder," then "Data Sets," then "Decennial Census." Select the Census 2000 Summary File (SF-3)—Sample Data, and click on "Detailed Tabs."
3. Create a table by Place (cities) for your state. Choose the P8 file (Sex by Age), then "Download."

4. Unzip the file and pull into Excel.

5. Calculate the percent of residents for each town that are women. Do a sort to find the towns with the greatest percentage of women and the towns with the greatest percentage of men. Notice anything about those towns that might stand out—good or bad?

6. If you want, calculate the percent of men or women in a certain age range, depending on your dating interests!

**Suggested links**

**Access by state**    www.rcfp.org/ecourt/index.html
Reporters Committee for Freedom of the Press summary of access to electronic records by state.

**Beat Page**    www.ire.org/resourcecenter/initial-search-beat.html
Shawn McIntosh's now-famous page listing links by beat. Try this one for a broad overview (hosted by IRE's Reporter.org). You will find links to records and resources by beat.

**Database journalism help**    http://data.nicar.org
The National Institute for Computer-Assisted Reporting, housed within Investigative Reporters and Editors, can provide you help in getting data, cleaning it and analyzing it. Online you can also find tip sheets on doing CAR. You must be a member to purchase data from IRE and download tip sheets.

**Drew Sullivan's databases**    www.drewsullivan.com/database.html
Drew Sullivan has compiled a list of interesting, free, downloadable and searchable databases on the Internet. Good for finding raw data.

**Power reporting**    www.powerreporting.com
Bill Dedman provides links to helpful information for journalists and the use of data.

<section>Chapter

# 8

# Understand how public officials think

<section>┌─────────────────────────────────────────┐
**ACCESS ACTION AGENDA**

☑ Comprehend bureaucratic culture
☑ Identify agency constraints
☑ Help them help you
└─────────────────────────────────────────┘

Government officials aren't that bad, really. Sure, we've talked a lot about how to get around stubborn clerks and overly secretive elected officials, but they are not the enemy.

They are like us. In some cases they *are* us. As university professors, we are government employees. We have relatives who are government employees. We even socialize with some government employees.

Crucial to requesting records is understanding the folks we are dealing with: their attitudes, day-to-day problems and perceptions of requesters. Once we know where they are coming from, we can better communicate and make the process work more effectively for everyone involved.

In this chapter we will explain a little about government culture, common reasons for why officials feel like they should deny records requests and suggestions from officials for making the process go a lot more smoothly. There will always be a natural tension that comes between government and the watchdogs. But we *can* get along.

## Comprehend bureaucratic culture

Government agencies, like any collective group of humans, have their own culture—a mysterious set of assumptions, norms and unwritten rules only understood by those within. Fortunately, you don't have to go into the cubicle jungles and live among these cloistered tribes because others have already done so.

Michael G. Powell, who got his doctorate in anthropology from Rice University in 2006, wanted to understand the culture of government records clerks and information flow.[1] He studied the records request process in Poland and the United States and found that bureaucracy generates paranoia—those outside the agency are paranoid that the agency is up to no good and those within the agency are paranoid that others (e.g., journalists) are out to get them.

"I wanted to investigate how the FOIA process may obscure more than it clarifies," Powell said. "FOIA may produce paranoia." He found the interplay between requester and FOIA officer creates suspicion on both ends, and he found the barrier to be enormous in Poland, where "there is a pervasive belief that all government is corrupt."

Powell said FOI is a great idea, but the bureaucratic process gets in the way of transparency. Forms, laws, regulations, procedures: All create barriers that enable secrecy. "As a brand, freedom of information is really a sexy thing," Powell said. "We're going to open up the archives and get at the truth. But the reality is the bureaucratic culture makes it difficult." Powell said he didn't find any proof that FOI reduces corruption—it might just make corrupt officials better at hiding information because most citizens don't have the skills to ferret it out.

What we learn from Powell's work is that the system inherently has some conflict and tension built into it, no matter what you do, whether you live in Poland or Poughkeepsie. It's just the dynamic between people and their government. Understanding that helps journalists remember that the individual humans they deal with are a part of this systemic tension, not a cause. Just like requesters, records custodians don't come to work with horns and cloven hooves.

### The power of process

Bureaucracies by their nature inherently hamper the flow of information. Information is power, and why would anyone want to give up power? The act of shuffling paperwork efficiently for the agency's sake, not necessarily the will to help society or further the marketplace of ideas, often drives decisions to keep records secret.

That's what Michele Bush Kimball found when she studied the FOI behaviors of law enforcement clerks in Florida. Kimball, who teaches media law at the University of South Alabama, sat in police lobbies and watched the processing of hundreds of public records requests. Then she interviewed the clerks to understand their motivations and to learn why they handed out some records and kept others hidden.

She found that most of the clerks were motivated by making sure they processed information quickly and accurately to help their co-workers.[2] Processing requests is perceived by many as processing widgets for the good of the bureaucracy, not democracy. Whatever helps that process is good; things that get in the way of that, such as vague, large requests or difficult people, are bad. If clerks expressed a higher calling, it was in maintaining confidentiality to protect individuals, not to get information out.

Less-experienced clerks tended to be more cautious about what they released. Some of the custodians said that when in doubt they kept records secret, because they would be less likely to be faulted for keeping something secret than for giving something out.

While all the clerks said they follow the law when deciding what to make public, the reality was that many of their decisions were arbitrary and based on how they felt about the requester or people named in the documents, usually crime victims. If the custodians felt sympathy for the requester, they would grant preferential treatment. All clerks said they give free copies to crime victims, and if the victims had children they got even better treatment. One clerk said she denied a request if she didn't think the requester needed to know the information.

So it's important to understand that from a clerk's perspective, he or she is thinking about the request as an office process—how am I going to get this done quickly so I can get all my other work done too? Also, the clerk is going to be thinking about the ramifications of giving out the information—is this going to hurt someone or get me in trouble? The more you can do to allay those concerns the better.

### Full-time vs. part-time

It's important to understand that there is often a difference between full-time FOIA officers and agency workers who handle records requests part-time in addition to other duties.

Suzanne J. Piotrowski, an associate professor of public administration at Rutgers University in New Jersey, surveyed nearly 200 federal FOIA officers in 2003 and found that these full-time access professionals truly supported open government.[3]

"Taken as a whole, I think these people are earnest," she said. "They want to release the information. You don't become an FOIA officer if you believe in secrecy—otherwise you go work as a classification officer." Still, Piotrowski said she found that full-time access officers tend to be caught between requesters who want the information and higher-up officials who don't want to give it out. "In many cases, they want to release the information. They just need a reason to do it."

In contrast, some government employees who are tasked with handling requests part-time, often at smaller agencies, might see a public

**Pro tip** | **Empathize with FOIA officers**

One problem in a lot of agencies is that the FOIA office is not the most powerful office in the agency. A lot of people in government are so busy doing their jobs that they aren't thinking about disclosure of the very records they are creating. The FOIA officer is starting his or her job with an obstacle: asking people to interrupt their work to do something else, to hand over the records. If requesters understand that the people they are dealing with in the FOIA office are also in effect making a request, that might make them feel a little more empathetic. A little bit of understanding on both sides can help the process.

—Miriam Nisbet, director, Office of Government Information Services, U.S. National Archives and Records Administration (the federal FOIA ombudsman)

records request as less important and something extra, a hassle and burden on their day—because, from their point of view, it is.

### Tone from the top

Leadership can affect the openness of an agency. Just ask Anne Weismann, who litigated freedom of information lawsuits for the U.S. Department of Justice under three presidents, Democrat and Republican, starting in 1981. A requester would sue for records and she would defend the government's right to keep them secret. As a lawyer, she did her best to follow the law, and higher-ups rarely said to do otherwise. That is, until 2000. When George W. Bush was elected, everything changed.

"Secrecy became pervasive and reflexive," said Weismann. "We were told to stake out a position of secrecy." Weismann said that when the American Civil Liberties Union and others wanted the names of detainees held in secret there was a great deal of "high-level involvement" in the cases.

In 2001, fed up with the political interference, Weismann left her job as a government attorney. She is now the chief attorney for a nonprofit watchdog group, Citizens for Responsibility and Ethics in Washington. Now she faces her former co-workers in court as she sues to open records. She and other FOI insiders say that the tone appears to have changed with President Barack Obama's administration, but culture takes years to adjust and change, so she'll wait to see if federal agencies begin opening up.

If an agency wants to take a position of secrecy, then it can easily work its way around the laws, Piotrowski said. One trick is just not to make records. People within an agency will tell each other, "Hey, that information is FOIA-able, so don't write it down so we don't have to release it."

Tone and directions from the leaders of an agency can seep into all recesses of an organization. You can see it in the most innocuous places. For example, in spring 2009 the Department of Homeland Security posted a job announcement for a public information officer on the American Society of Access Professionals Web site (www.accesspro.org), which serves freedom of information officers. The posting said the agency was looking for someone who could "promote a culture of privacy awareness."

Tone starts at the top, for good or worse.

## Identify agency constraints

Just as bureaucratic systems and culture affect how an agency responds to records requests, so too can other barriers to access, many of them outside the control of the clerk handling your query. Have you ever worked a job where you had too much to do with not enough time or resources? Most jobs are like that these days, including in journalism, right? So we can empathize.

Longtime freedom of information attorney Thomas Susman has found that delays in FOIA requests are usually caused by a number of factors, including inadequate resources and training for processing requests, pressure to mask information that might embarrass the agency, complexity of some requests, the need to consult with other agencies, little incentive to release documents and punishment for releasing too much information, bureaucratic largesse and a tendency to discourage requesters—particularly journalists—from requesting records in the future.[4]

Let's talk about some of those barriers.

### Lack of resources and training

Most government agencies aren't rolling in dough. They have enough to do without digging through a bunch of files and making photocopies. Lack of resources is one of the biggest problems in handling records requests, according to government freedom of information officers.[5]

Also, a lot of public employees, including municipal attorneys, don't know much about their state public records law. They don't teach it in law school, few states require public employees to have training in open records laws and it's not the kind of thing that comes up every day for most public employees.

### Fear of embarrassment

Nobody wants to be embarrassed or lose their jobs. So is it any wonder public officials might be wary when a journalist comes a-calling?

Studies indicate that journalists are more likely to have longer delays and more trouble requesting records than other types of requesters, at least when potentially controversial information is involved. Alasdair Roberts,

## Pro tip  |  Help train government employees

As president of the Idaho Press Club and founder of Idahoans for Openness in Government, I have worked with the attorney general, cities and counties to get our open meeting law fixed and to educate public employees on open records and meeting laws. The training in conjunction with the AG has worked extremely well, including seminars and online videos and DVDs. We've had hundreds and hundreds of local officials come from around the state and have their eyes opened. It's presented in a fun and interesting manner so it's not threatening. We don't have a hammer coming down saying, "You're wrong." All these people in government, whether it's the clerks or the attorney general, are just human beings. We can relate with them, we can connect on a human level and we can talk and come to an understanding. I think most public officials realize the reason they are there is to serve the public. Really, what we in the press want and what they want as elected officials is all the same. We want good government that functions, that people can participate and have knowledge. There are always going to be a few who don't get it, but I think most do. The whole point is to bring people together, to work on something we have in common.

—Betsy Z. Russell, Boise bureau chief, *The Spokesman-Review,* and president of Idahoans for Openness in Government (www.openidaho.org)

a professor at Suffolk University Law School in Boston, examined thousands of public records requests in Canada to find that journalists had more difficulty getting records and receiving them in a timely manner because agencies delayed release so they could have time to rebut critical stories.[6] Roberts found that agencies face two competing pressures: the legal requirement to disclose information vs. the pressure to control information to manage public perceptions and save face. He calls this "message discipline."

"In a perfect world the request system would be user-blind," Roberts said. But that's not the case. If a request for information comes from a journalist or a political entity, then that request is likely to undergo more scrutiny and delay because the agency will want to make sure the information doesn't lead to negative perceptions.

Piotrowski agrees, based on her conversations with records custodians. "Most officers are always suspicious if a journalist asks for something," she said. "If you have a journalist asking for something they will think, 'Hmm, maybe there's something controversial here. '"

## Parental controls

Some public officials believe it is their responsibility to look out for the people mentioned in their records, like a father or mother over their children. They see the records as their own documents, and they feel responsible for how they are maintained and used. They don't want anyone included in their records hurt—for example, through identity theft or stalkers—on their watch.

In the Florida clerk study, all of the clerks told Michele Bush Kimball that they based all their decisions on the law, yet she noticed arbitrary discretion in approving or denying requests. She saw clerks withhold records to protect crime victims whose names were included in the documents. She saw them provide files for some people, particularly people they already knew, but deny others the same information if they felt they would not use the information properly. One clerk said she asked requesters why they wanted the information, and then, "If I don't feel that they have a real need to know, then I just tell them, 'I'm sorry, but we don't release that information.'"[7]

## Punishment for disclosure

We know of no records custodian who got a promotion for releasing too much information. The punishment for releasing a document that shouldn't be released is usually greater than the penalty for not releasing a document. Government employees have little legal incentive to follow the law. A 2007 study of the penalties and response requirements of state public records laws showed that 38 of the 50 states had meager and inadequate repercussions for illegally withholding records.[8]

Time and time again, citizens and journalists complain that when they are denied records they have little recourse because they can't afford to sue. Anthony Fargo, a journalism professor at Indiana University, led a study that interviewed 218 people who had problems getting records and tried to get help from the state public records ombudsman. Fargo found that 91 percent said the No. 1 problem was lack of teeth in the law.[9]

Worse, the penalties are often more severe for *providing* information than for keeping it secret. For example, violating the public records law in Arizona is a Class 2 misdemeanor, which is equivalent to not having your driver's license handy when pulled over by police. Yet a government employee who accidentally releases a public record that contains the home telephone number of a police officer or judge faces a Class 6 felony charge—equivalent to aggravated assault or abusing a child, with punishment of up to a year in prison. With laws like that, what clerk wouldn't favor secrecy over disclosure?

### Walls of denial

Finally, the reality is that some public officials are just like some journalists—arrogant and resistant to questioning, probably because of having to interact with so many angry people all day.

Alexis Lambert, deputy general counsel for sunshine and public records in the Office of the Attorney General of Florida, gets about 1,500 inquiries a year regarding disputes between requesters and agencies. Often the heart of the dispute is a personality conflict. "Usually the spicy disputes are in small towns," Lambert said. "I mediated this ongoing spat between a requester and a city over a huge volume of documents. Most of the back and forth was, 'You know, her sister spread rumors about me,' and 'You know, she was rude to me.'"

In most cities a few active citizens with a grudge against officials can make clerks wary of other requesters. Every city has at least one persistent gadfly. That still doesn't excuse an illegal denial. It just helps you understand one possible reason for the secrecy, and possible avenues for getting the records you need.

### Help them help you

Aside from systemic bureaucratic tendencies that might get in the way of access, sometimes officials perceive the problem to be with requesters. And sometimes they're right! A few rotten apples can sour clerks on anyone asking for records. Don't be a rotten apple. Learn their peeves and avoid doing them if possible.

Colleen Murphy, executive director of the Connecticut Freedom of Information Commission, recalls an individual whose repeated requests to a police department for a broad swath of records reached the point of harassment. "He would ask for every incident report for the past 20 years on a certain date, such as March 15, of every year, from the

## Pro tip | An insider's guide to FOIA

As director of the U.S. Department of Justice's office that guided all federal agencies for more than 25 years on how to implement the FOIA, I've seen a lot that requesters can do to improve their odds of getting what they want. Here's my "top 10" list:

1. Remember that the FOIA is administered on a decentralized basis, meaning that each agency, or major component of a large agency, processes requests for its records according to its own practices and procedures, which lawfully can vary significantly from one place to the next. Don't assume that what works at one agency will work at another.

2. There is no substitute for doing some careful research before writing your FOIA request. No longer does a requester need to comb through agency regulations in order to find out exactly where to mail a FOIA request. This can be done through FOIA Reference Manuals that all agencies are required to maintain, and keep up to date, online.

3. Under recent FOIA amendments, getting your request to the exact correct office within an agency (which sometimes is not so intuitively obvious) has great significance for both time deadlines and potential penalties on the agency for noncompliance, so it pays to focus on it.

4. Don't just send your request through the U.S. mail. These days, even more than eight years after the anthrax terrorism of 2001, much mail to federal addresses is subjected to electronic screening, usually at a site far removed from the agency's location, which can greatly delay your request's receipt. It is the receipt and "logging in" of your request that matters under the law, not the date that you place on the letter or the date of the envelope's postmark. Try wherever possible to send your request letter by fax.

5. Research the possibility that one or more other federal agencies could have copies of the records you are looking for, and know the exact terms used by the agency for dealing with the subject matter of your request, so as to minimize the chance of denial on mere semantic or rigid computer-search grounds.

period of 12 p.m. to 2 p.m., and the clerks thought he was doing it to harass them," Murphy said. It didn't help that he also wrote expletives in his request letters, such as "thank you, a-hole," and that he wrote his request letters on toilet paper.

6. Be aware that each agency, or individual agency component, is required to maintain a distinct Web site devoted to its administration of the FOIA. Browsing those sites often helps.

7. Pay careful attention to the exact wording of your FOIA request, because you can be fairly certain that the agency will. In doing so, realize the significance of words and phrases such as "any" and "related to." Use them to make your request all encompassing where you mean to do so (and to limit an agency's ability to interpret your request unduly narrowly), but be alert that with such expansiveness can come larger volumes of truly unwanted document pages, higher fees and greater delays. In other words, be careful what you wish for—but at the same time be careful not to allow your request to be read more narrowly than you actually intend.

8. When it comes to not just the wording but also the very structure of your request, don't be shy about breaking it down into subparts. This not only helps make clear exactly what you're seeking, it also allows the agency to give you partial responses in stages instead of holding off until everything is ready for the entirety of the request.

9. Remember also that in some cases your FOIA request is just your "opening bid"—an effort to "place things on the hook" at an early stage, subject to negotiation. Agency FOIA officers like nothing more than to get requesters to narrow their requests (it creates a feeling of true accomplishment, and it is strongly encouraged by certain provisions of the 1986 FOIA amendments).

10. Lastly, never forget that there can be an enormous difference in what you receive, and how quickly you receive it, according to how cooperative you are perceived to be by agency FOIA personnel. Be friendly, as if you're all in this together. And by all means, use the telephone to have "human dialogue" with them (which does *not* include voice mail) every time you possibly can. All agencies now have "FOIA requester liaisons" as a carryover from the lip service to openness that was paid by the Bush administration. Try to use them to the max: to learn, to clarify, to cajole and only when push comes to shove, to start shoving.

—Daniel J. Metcalfe, founder of the U.S. Department of Justice's Office of Information and Privacy in 1981, and now executive director of the Collaboration on Government Secrecy, the anti-secrecy center at American University Washington College of Law

While the swearing toilet-paper man might be unusual, other factors that turn clerks against requesters are pretty common, Murphy said. The FOI Commission handles about 800 complaints a year over public records and meeting disputes, and mediates disagreements, seeing a variety of misfires on both sides of the counter. Sometimes a clerk is not going to be happy no matter what a requester does, but some angst is avoidable with a little effort on the requester's part.

In previous chapters we've discussed the importance of human interaction and playing nice. Here are some suggestions for speeding requests along, based on what clerks say they would like to see from requesters.

## Be polite and respectful

It's funny that we even need to mention this in the book, but it's something we hear over and over from requesters and custodians alike: "You can catch more flies with honey than vinegar." If we hear that American proverb again we'll beat ourselves senseless with a paper shredder. At the same time, we think it makes sense.

If an agency has a full-time public records officer, get to know that person well. Go chat over coffee and be nice to him or her. If you do it's likely the person will be on your side, responding faster and offering suggestions for other documents you could request. If you're rude the officer will have no need to be on your side and could drag out the request, or follow it to the letter, like a genie following the instructions of a wish literally: "Ohhhhh, you wanted the incident reports from our police department in Springfield, *Illinois*. Your letter didn't specify the state, so that's why I got you the reports from Springfield, *Oregon*. Sorry about that, and good luck with that story of yours."

Catherine Starghill, executive director of the New Jersey Government Records Council, said that in her state it's particularly helpful to be nice because state law requires requesters to ask for a specific record by name. If a person doesn't know what a document is called the agency has no obligation to respond. That means it's important to get a custodian to explain what records are available. "The spirit of the law, in my opinion, requires them to help the requester," Starghill said. But that's just the spirit, not the letter—and some clerks will follow the letter of the law if they can get away with it.

"While I totally believe that requesters shouldn't have to bend over backward—it should be the custodians who bend over backward—it's really difficult for a lot of custodians to embrace open records," Starghill said.

Regardless, being pleasant almost always is to a requester's advantage, Murphy of the Connecticut Freedom of Information Commission said. "You can't really deal with what the other person can do, but you can do a lot to make the situation more positive, which usually yields better results," she said. "Help make it less onerous."

That doesn't mean you have to be a pushover. Just be polite, persistent and knowledgeable. Remember how we learned in Chapter 5 that an authoritative request letter is more effective than a friendly letter? You want to quote the law to show you are serious and know what you are doing. But at the same time, you can be polite about it.

"You don't want to be confrontational in tone, but make it clear you know the law," Piotrowski said. That combination is the key. You can be firm, but polite.

### Consider explaining the purpose

Most public records laws do not require the requester to reveal the purpose of the request, but sometimes requests seem so random and oddball that without some explanation the whole task appears to be harassment. When a clerk understands that all the work he or she is about to do has an actual purpose then he or she is more likely to do a better job. Explaining the purpose of the records usually speeds things along. It's quite likely the

**Pro tip** | **Actually pick up the records**

Clerks will take a lot of time, sometimes months, to track down records, photocopy them and prepare them for the requester, then the person never comes back to get them. Sometimes they call a journalist to pick up the records and the reporter says the story is long over so no need to bother. The clerk is thinking, "Why do I even bother to do this if the person doesn't even come get it?" If you request records, always, always, pick them up, even if the purpose has long lapsed. It's possible the documents might yield other stories, and it increases the odds that the agency will comply with future requests.

—Colleen Murphy, executive director, Connecticut Freedom of Information Commission custodian will refer you to other records that you didn't know about that would be more helpful.

While you don't have to prove the records are public, it can help if you cite relevant case law that clearly makes the documents open. That makes it easy for the FOIA officer to have a clear legal justification for convincing the higher-ups who might be reluctant to disclose. If the records have been disclosed in the past, provide examples. If other states release the records, bring stories that illustrate that as well.

At the very least, include a phone number and e-mail address so they can reach you if they have questions or need clarification. We always attach a business card to any request.

### Be specific

Broad requests slow things down. Maria Everett, executive director of the Virginia Freedom of Information Advisory Council, remembers one person who requested all e-mails sent to and from all the town council members over a five-year period. The cost of working through all those e-mails was $10,000 in staff time. Everett found out that the requester was just interested in a particular e-mail between one council member and the town manager, so the citizen narrowed the request, speeding the process and making it far less expensive.

Piotrowski agrees, saying that specific requests are more likely to get processed faster. "I think a lot of requesters are unreasonable," she said. "They ask for everything regarding the Iraq War over a broad time period, or every memo regarding torture."

### Avoid arbitrary requests

Some people ask for a lot of records, a lot of the time, and it tends to bother some clerks. Records custodians call these requesters "frequent fliers." It might be a neighborhood activist, someone mad at police or a disgruntled former employee. Maybe it's an antigovernment group acting out its frustrations, or a prison inmate seeking documents to help get an early release or simply to harass.

In 2008 and 2009, citizens critical of the mayor in Akron, Ohio, filed more than 100 public records requests for e-mails, expense reports and other information in preparation for a recall, costing the city an estimated

$200,000 in staff time. City council members and supporters of the mayor criticized what they painted as a waste of tax dollars. On the other side, critics of the mayor said the records were necessary to bring truth to light.[10] More recently, in her resignation speech in July 2009, Gov. Sarah Palin of Alaska lamented the heavy costs incurred by her state for records requests seeking to examine the details of her tenure.

Many frequent fliers do good for their communities. But from the other side of the counter a flood of FOI requests can be perceived as a drain on taxpayers' dollars and clerks' time, and that argument is convincing to a lot of people, including legislators. That's why many states have considered adopting laws to discourage frequent requests and "abusive" requesters.

### Communicate often

Call the FOIA officer after you submit your request and make sure it is clear. Keep the informal communication flowing.

"When we get cases to mediate, by and large the greatest reason for problems is that people stop talking to each other," Murphy said. "They put in a request and don't hear a response as quickly as they like, so they file a complaint. Then the agency feels like it's in litigation mode and stops talking."

Try it!

**Exercises and ideas for journalists, newsrooms and classrooms to improve your skills and foster FOI in your community.**

**1. Check out ASAP**

Go online and look at the American Society of Access Professionals (ASAP) Web site (www.accesspro.org). Read the introduction "About

ASAP" page, then browse the job announcements to get a sense of what agencies look for in access/privacy officers. Read the newsletter to get a sense of what issues access professionals discuss and find important. If you're serious about being an FOI pro, join ASAP.

## 2. Find a former custodian

Talk to FOI officers at local agencies and ask who they replaced, and where their predecessor landed. Track down the person and ask the person to coffee for an honest conversation about how access worked in the agency when he or she was employed there. You'll find that the former custodian is usually more open than the current one about how things actually work behind the scenes. The former custodian also might provide ideas for records that would help the public and lead to great stories. Leave with three document-based story ideas. Also, talk to current FOI officers and ask them for their suggestions. You'll be amazed how grateful most of them will be just for being asked.

## 3. Attend access training for officials

Find out when access training is scheduled for local or state officials in your community and see if you can attend. Some state ombudsman offices provide training for clerks. At the federal level, ASAP offers training (www.accesspro.org/index.html#programs). Attending these sessions will provide new insights into the law and allow you to see how government officials view access issues.

## 4. Foster FOI in government

Initiate a dialogue with government leaders (attorney general, secretary of state, mayor, legislators, city council members, university administrators, etc.) to discuss an issue that you have in common—good government. Work toward several goals, which could be announced with fanfare during national Sunshine Week in mid-March:

☑ Ask legislators, city councils or executive leaders to reaffirm their commitment to open government through proclamations, resolutions and opinion pieces. Get them on the record for how they stand on freedom of information in the abstract, as well as specific provisions in the law that might need changing.

☑ Help create or enhance training sessions for public employees on open records laws. Co-sponsor training with government groups. Also do training sessions and public forums for citizens.

☑ Work together toward developing improvements to your state's open records and meeting laws.

☑ Translate FOI guides and other materials into different languages, such as Spanish, to help underserved populations in your community understand their rights to information.

### 5. Get involved with your state FOI coalition

Nearly every state and the District of Columbia has an open government coalition, and some have multiple groups. Find your state's group and get involved. You can find a list of them at the National Freedom of Information Coalition Web site (www.nfoic.org/nfoicmembers). Most of the coalitions are composed of people from a variety of backgrounds, including government, and most have boards that meet regularly. Attend a coalition board meeting and get involved.

**Suggested links**

**Access group**   www.accesspro.org
Scan the Web site for the American Society of Access Professionals.

**Collaboration on Government Secrecy**   www.wcl.american.edu/lawand gov/cgs/
Find resources about access in past and current presidential administrations.

**Federal FOIA ombudsman**    www.archives.gov/ogis
    If you are stonewalled or denied by an agency, get help from the
    federal FOIA ombudsman, officially the director of the Office of
    Government Information Services. In addition to the Web site, you
    can e-mail at ogis@nara.gov or call (301) 837-1996.

**FOI coalitions**    www.nfoic.org/nfoicmembers
    The National Freedom of Information Coalition lists its members
    by state so you can find government officials in your state who
    support access.

# Putting it together
## Writing the FOI story and FOI ethics

### ACCESS ACTION AGENDA
- ☑ Create great record-based stories
- ☑ Do the right thing: FOI ethics
- ☑ Anticipate public reaction
- ☑ Write about FOI
- ☑ Become an FOI warrior

Whew! You have gotten far in the art of access. You've learned how to get in a document state of mind, find out where records are located, figure out the law, request documents, overcome denials and handle data. You have a bunch of documents sitting in a box or in a computer file folder. Now what?

It's time to put it all together. In this chapter we will explain some techniques for writing effective stories that are relevant to citizens, handling ethical dilemmas that arise with records and anticipating public reaction to the publication of documents and data, particularly online.

Once you get the records, the work isn't over. It just begins. And it gets more fun!

In this chapter we won't go through all the ways of producing compelling stories in a sound ethical framework—multitudes of great books already cover writing and ethics well. Instead, we will cover issues and news-you-can-use tips specific to incorporating government documents in storytelling, ethics and news judgment.

## Create great record-based stories

While good writing is good writing, regardless of its source, stories based heavily on public records could end up dry if you're not careful. Don't let it happen! Remember why you've put so much work into researching, requesting and negotiating for records? Because they contain information that's important to people's lives. Now's your chance to devise a fascinating presentation of that information that will grab people and compel them to read or watch.

The beauty about document-based stories is that if they're done right they can resonate with readers. Research shows that stories with authoritative sourcing are better liked and perceived to be of higher quality than stories merely based on anecdotes. Readers are skeptical of stories based on questionable information, such as hidden cameras, anonymous sources and paid informants.[1]

For example, in a study published in 2000, a third of the participants read a story that attributed information to authoritative expert sources; a third read the same story, except the information was attributed to anecdotal evidence; and a third read the same story, with the information attributed to an analysis of data by the reporter. Study participants found the story that was based on the reporter's data analysis was less readable and less likable than the stories based on anecdotes and authoritative sources.[2] Sometimes we can get too bogged down in statistics and reports, so make sure to also provide authoritative expert sources and make it more readable with human-interest anecdotes. Take advantage of the sourcing, but don't let the government jargon wash away the life from your words.

Let's walk through some steps in putting together your story.

### Organize the piles

They're in the garage. Stacked around tables. Perhaps there are 30 boxes in a newsroom storage area. Eric Nalder has a tendency to accumulate documents. "It's terrible how many trees I've destroyed," said Nalder, senior investigative reporter for Hearst Newspapers, who's gathered records for more than three decades. "One of my wife's biggest nightmares is the number of papers I bring home. I keep them for as long as my wife and newspaper tolerate it."

## Pro tip | **Spot time holes with Excel 'date' field**

With a large number of records, sort through them and enter important developments and events in Excel in a "date" field. Then you can easily sort by date to see the holes and where the agency might not have provided you all the records. I also create a field by topic area, so when I write the project I can easily identify the records for different story angles. For example, for our investigation of the Maricopa County Sheriff's Office (which won a 2009 Pulitzer for local reporting[3]), I labeled some records as "cash" because I knew they would help in a story about the money. It's a matter of managing all those records.

—Ryan Gabrielson, former reporter for the *East Valley Tribune*, Mesa, Ariz., and investigative reporting fellow at the University of California, Berkeley

Gathering that many documents can be daunting for writing a story. How do you sort through all that material and make sense of it?

First, Nalder suggests trying to collect as much information as possible electronically so you don't have to sift through so much paper. He keeps the information on two computers and backs it up on an external hard drive.

The next step is organizing the key bits of information in a computer spreadsheet, such as Microsoft Excel. Some journalists make separate files including the most crucial information they plan to use in their stories. If you're working on a large project with multiple reporters, create an online shared editing system, such as through Google Docs, that allows different reporters to add and edit material. Make sure to note important information from documents as you go along, or it will be a nightmare when you sit down to write.

### Focus on your main point

Have a clear focus on the most salient point that you want people to get, which can be difficult if you are dealing with a massive amount of records. Find that focus through two steps:

1. Dig into the data and records and absorb it all. Immerse yourself in your records. Interview the records.
2. Back off. Let your project sit for a day or two if you can. Think of the one main point that jumps out, the one thing you would tell your roommate or mother. Try to describe your project to a friend. The first few sentences are likely to be your main point. Start drafting without looking at your notes. Don't get caught up in the details.

### Avoid documentese

As you start writing the story, approach it as you would any other story—not a document-based story.

We asked Roy Peter Clark, senior scholar at The Poynter Institute and industry writing guru, how he would make an interesting story that was heavily based on government documents. That might sound like trying to make broccoli taste good. But it can be done by taking extra steps to simplify and humanize the information (see Box 9.1).

---

**BOX 9.1  Roy Peter Clark's 12 tips for writing document-based stories[4]**

1. Take responsibility for what readers or viewers know and understand.
2. Imagine an audience of civilians and not specialists.
3. Slow down the pace of information.
4. Use only essential numbers.
5. Translate jargon.
6. Unclutter leads.
7. Have a conversation with the reader.
8. Focus on the impact.
9. Keep the boring parts short.
10. Find the microcosm, a particular example that expresses a larger reality.
11. When possible, tell a story.
12. Use graphics to unload the heavy cargo from the text.

He suggests writers keep jargon and numbers to a minimum, slow down the pace of the story and imagine they're writing for their neighbor (not the city budget manager who provided the records). Writers should use graphics liberally and humanize the story with a real person's story. They should let the story hang on the authority of the documents, but they should not make the story about the documents.

## Humanize

The key to any good story is, well, a good story. That includes real people and action, the "plot" that will move your story and your readers along. So humanize your work. Find a gripping, emotional example that will capture your readers. Human beings aren't "decoration" you're adding to your story for exploitative purposes; the impact of this information on real people is the essence of why your story matters and is worth public attention. So show it. Readers can easily see through flimsy evidence, and stories that are purely emotional don't resonate with them. The best stories are compelling *and* provide solid analytical facts, such as those found in public documents.[5]

You don't want anyone to click on your story and say, "Wow, look at all these documents." You want them to turn to a friend and say, "Listen to this story!" Great narrative stories can be written based heavily on documents. Here's an example from Tony Kennedy and Paul McEnroe of the *Minneapolis Star Tribune,* who in April 2009 wrote a four-part narrative series about Minneapolis police corruption:

### *The Informant*

Word on the street was that some Minneapolis cops were dirty, tipping off drug dealers. Investigators knew one man who could help them figure out if that was true: gang leader Taylor Trump.

His presence filled a city block.

It wasn't that Taylor Trump was physically huge—he was 5 feet, 10 inches and 260 pounds. It wasn't even the range of his avocations, the way he could savor discussing Buddhist and

Hindu philosophers one day and swing a crack deal the next.

It was that Trump was comfortable in his own skin, even when he had absolutely no right to be. Even on a hot summer night when trouble lay straight ahead.

As he walked down N. 4th Street in downtown Minneapolis, FBI agents focused cameras on him from afar. His underclothing was laced with their surveillance wire. A lot was riding on what he was about to do.

With national standing in the Gangster Disciples gang, Trump was used to maneuvering through dicey situations.

But now he was trapped. It was August 2007, and federal prosecutors knew they had enough pinned on him to send Trump away for more than 20 years. They had forced his cooperation in a complex federal corruption case with serious implications if even half of what Trump and another informant claimed turned out to be true: Minneapolis cops allegedly taking bribes to provide inside police information to gang members, who paid them off with cash and prostitutes.

The *Star Tribune,* through confidential police and court documents, has retraced the inner workings of that public corruption probe from its origins on the streets of Minneapolis in late 2006. Dozens of interviews were conducted with police officials and sources close to the investigation. . . . [6]

In addition to interviewing dozens of people, the series was based on transcripts from internal affairs interviews with police officers, an FBI report, a deposition in a civil lawsuit, memos, letters between police and attorneys, a federal indictment of a police officer, overtime records and court files.

Great job putting a face—in this case, Taylor Trump—on an important story.

### Attribute clearly

While the goal is to make a document-based story *not* read like a document, you want to make sure readers know the source of all relevant information. Some writers streamline too much by just writing "according to records. . . ." Readers don't know what to make of that—they have to trust you. That's like writing "according to people. . . ."

Just as we are specific about identifying people sources, you should be specific about identifying document sources without bogging the story down in long titles. For example, instead of writing "according to county records," be specific by writing "according to a property tax record obtained through a public records request from the Clark County Assessor's Office."

That tells the reader exactly where the information came from, so he or she can obtain the information as well. It lends authority to your reporting. It also shows readers that public records are important. If someone proposes making property tax records secret, maybe people will think, "Hey, I see the news mentioning those records—that might be a problem if those are no longer available."

One way to attribute information to documents without bogging down a gripping, emotional narrative is to write something we call a "doc box." This is a side breakout box that runs with the main story. It states where the story documents came from and how readers can access them, including address and office hours of the agency. It's authoritative, and news you can use for readers!

### Provide the records online

Take advantage of the Web by including the original documents for readers as pdf files or searchable data. It's simple to scan files, or create pdf files using Adobe Acrobat or other software. Let people see the actual records on which you are basing your story. Turn data into clickable maps or searchable online databases.

Some reporters carry portable scanners with them so they can scan documents for later perusal, avoiding copy fees and providing the records for the public. It's a great idea, and some portable, handheld, pen-like fold out scanners cost less than $100.

*The Idaho Statesman* used public records well in its coverage of the Larry Craig scandal in 2007. Craig was a Republican U.S. senator from Idaho when he was detained at a Minneapolis airport for allegedly propositioning an undercover police officer for sex in a bathroom. Craig denied the allegations, saying it was a misunderstanding. The police officer said otherwise. A he-said, he-said story.

So the newspaper let the readers make up their own minds by posting public records online, including the audio-recorded police interview with Craig at the airport. Readers could hear the flimsy reasoning in Craig's voice. They could read the actual arrest report. Craig resigned, and the *Statesman* was a Pulitzer finalist for its coverage.[7]

## Do the right thing: FOI ethics

We don't mean to get preachy, but it's important to think about what is right and what is wrong. It's what we call FOI ethics. You can't expect people to believe and trust your stories unless you've been trustworthy in reporting and writing them. Ethics is permanently tied to excellence in all types of journalism, of course—but when you have documents that expose the unethical behavior of others, it's even more important that your own behavior be beyond reproach.

Gathering and disseminating government documents can lead to ethical dilemmas that are important to think through carefully. Every situation is different, but most of us can agree on some basic moral principles and ethical guidelines that make for better decisions that we can explain with confidence to angry citizens, sources and Mom.

### Exercise your right to know

"Seek truth and report it" is the first edict in the Society of Professional Journalists (SPJ) Code of Ethics.[8] That means it is incumbent upon journalists—and citizens—to aggressively seek out information.

We believe it is unethical to walk away from a records request denial if the information is important to the public.

We also believe it is ethically responsible for journalism organizations to actively and aggressively pursue government records through litigation if necessary, to lobby for better laws and to write about secrecy.

"Promoting freedom of information is an ethical imperative for journalists," said Jane Kirtley, the Silha Professor of Media Ethics and Law at the University of Minnesota and former executive director of the Reporters Committee for Freedom of the Press. "There are so many ethical implications to *not* getting information."

For example, Kirtley said that closed records mean journalists rely more on leaked documents and unnamed sources, which can lead to unreliable information. She added that for some reason journalists consider it OK to sue for records, which often creates case law for FOI, but are reluctant to lobby or testify for changes to public records laws. Why treat the legislatures differently from the courts? If the public has an interest in having public records, then journalists should fight for them at all levels. At the very least, publishers and editorial writers can fight for open records.

News organizations can even cover access to information as a beat or part of a beat. When Andy Alexander, ombudsman for *The Washington Post*, was Washington bureau chief for Cox Newspapers, he assigned a reporter to cover government transparency full time. "This is an issue that will win you readers," Alexander said. "Managers need to reassert the importance of FOI. It's a citizenship issue. It's a democracy issue."

We urge news organizations to band together to fight for access to public records that help society. We urge collaborations with other like-minded organizations as well, such as government-watchdog and civic groups. It's a journalist's duty.

### Exercise your 'right to no'

Just because a record is public doesn't necessarily mean you need to make it public. Though it can be hard to remember when you've fought weeks or months to obtain documents, the "right to know" is not a mandate to publish everything you have, just because you have it. We can say "no" to publishing documents that could hurt people without providing public benefit, or pieces of documents that might not be crucial for the public to know.

This is particularly true of information that includes personal information about individuals, sometimes accidentally left in by custodians. We need to balance the public interest and benefits of disseminating the records against the harm it could do to individuals.

Sometimes we can apply Aristotle's Golden Mean and find ways of telling the truth without harming individuals, such as redacting bank account numbers, Social Security numbers, dates of birth, home phone numbers and other information that might have slipped into the records.

We can also balance public good against harm. Following the terrorist attacks of September 11, 2001, newsmakers had to make tough decisions on what records to publish. For example, in 2002 *The Los Angeles Times* received leaked documents detailing the U.S. government's nuclear strategies against China, Russia, Iraq, North Korea, Iran, Libya and Syria. The records also included the inventories of the U.S. nuclear arsenal, with specific numbers and types of warheads.[9]

Editors postponed the story for 10 days as they verified the information, looked for newsworthy information, consulted experts and thought about the ramifications of publication. Ultimately, the *Times* decided the information was important for people to know, so it published stories explaining countries viewed as threats but included no details of the U.S. arsenal.

### Get it right

A lot of information in public documents and data—particularly crime data—contains errors. In the computer-assisted reporting world they call it "dirty" data.

Yet we're amazed at journalists and other requesters who gather data and documents and then slap it on their Web sites without any vetting, cleaning, verification or context. We understand the pressures of daily (and hourly) deadline journalism, but that is simply unconscionable. You wouldn't publish a spoken defamatory accusation against someone without checking its accuracy, so apply the same skepticism to documents, even legally privileged documents such as police reports and court records.

The very first bullet item in the SPJ Code of Ethics (out of 37 bullet points!) states: "Test the accuracy of information from all sources and exercise care to avoid inadvertent error. . . ." We must verify information. That's what separates reporters from repeaters.

## Pro tip

**Compare data to paper**

No database is perfect, and some can give the totally wrong impression. We got one database that was so inaccurate and so incomplete that it was misinformation. It was almost libelous, so we didn't put it on the Web. You can't expect data to be perfect, but you have to make sure it doesn't give the wrong impression. Make sure to compare your data to the paper files—and sometimes you'll find that the electronic records are more accurate than the paper files. Compare your data to the record layout and agency's description to make sure everything matches. Pull some records and verify them through other reporting methods. Find some people to talk to who intimately know the data—the landlords and tenants who were involved in a building code dispute, or the victim of a crime that is represented in the data. Nothing replaces human reporting to find holes in data. You don't need many of these interviews to pinpoint a lot of problems. Run your analysis and findings past the agency to make sure you got it right—they might find errors that would completely negate your story. Better you find out before you publish it rather than later.

—Sarah Cohen, Knight Professor of the Practice of Journalism and Public Policy, Duke University, and former database editor of *The Washington Post*

Yes, if you acquire a public record or data and there are errors (we guarantee there will be), and those errors are defamatory, you are generally protected from libel suits because the information is already public and contained in official government documents.

But ethically, you have no choice but to make sure you verify and check the veracity of all information. At the very least, spot-check the records and make it clear to readers that the information might be incorrect. It's the right thing to do.

## Anticipate public reaction

You've figured out that we really, really believe in the public's "right to know." Did we give it away somehow? But we also have seen where blind adherence to that phrase not only can hurt people but lead to *less* openness.

You see, not everyone agrees with us. In fact, many citizens (including some of our own friends and family) would say we're nutters. We understand their concerns. Through surveys and other research we have asked thousands of people what they think about public access to a variety of government records. Our conclusion? People like the idea of openness, but when you start getting specific their attitudes get complicated. Documents displayed publicly without context can lead to severe citizen backlash—leading to legislatures closing records.

Take, for example, concealed weapons permits. Since the 1990s media organizations have acquired gun permit databases and analyzed them to find trends and instances where felons are given permits to carry guns that they aren't supposed to own. In our country, it's still a privilege to be able to secretly carry a gun—we trust the government to make sure crazy killers aren't legally allowed to walk around with revolvers in their jackets (at least, that's the goal).

Some of these media organizations have posted this data on their Web sites. Sounds useful enough. Anyone can see if their co-workers, coaches, babysitters, customers, students or ex-lovers are carrying guns around. And if it's a public record, why not?

That's what *The Roanoke Times* thought when it posted concealed weapons data on its Web site in March 2007 to commemorate national Sunshine Week, to herald the beauty of public records. But citizens were outraged, saying it was an invasion of privacy.

As a result, the legislatures in Virginia and South Carolina closed those records. The same thing happened in Florida in 2005, when a television station posted similar data on its Web site, and again in Tennessee in 2009 and Arkansas that same year. And on and on and on.

If the public benefits don't outweigh the perceived privacy invasion, then people will call for closure of public documents.

That's why it's important to understand how citizens think about these issues, at least to ensure that the public-interest purpose of the information is clear and outweighs perceived harm to privacy or public safety. Based on our public opinion research, here is what we've been able to figure out.

### People support access in the abstract

Every public opinion survey about FOI usually asks about people's general feelings about secrecy and openness, and every time citizens say they strongly believe in openness. In a 2009 Sunshine Week survey by Ohio

University, 79 percent of nearly 1,000 Americans surveyed said they agree with President Barack Obama's call for more transparent government, and 77 percent said they think FOIA is a good law.[10] Other studies show even larger majorities of open-government support. A 2002 survey of Washington state residents found that 98 percent said they agree that government meetings and records should be open.[11] It's a no-brainer. Who *wouldn't* support openness?

According to the Sunshine Week survey, only 6 percent of Americans have actually ever requested information under FOIA. So despite having little firsthand experience with accessing public records, the public strongly supports the overall concept of open government. That's great!

### People dig safety and accountability

People *love* public records that warn them of public safety hazards. They want to be safe, and they appreciate it when government, the media or watchdog groups post records and data that help them assess the safety of their neighborhoods. In survey after survey, citizens strongly support public access to neighborhood crime reports, dam inspection data and registered sex-offender data (see Table 9.1).

Citizens also demand that their governments spend their money wisely and do it in the open. Surveys show that support for openness is high for records pertaining to officials' expense accounts, public employee salaries and even government officials' work e-mail.

### People don't like privacy invasion

Any government records that contain information perceived to be personal should be kept secret, most Americans believe. And the definition of "privacy" keeps shifting toward the less personal. Home addresses, home phone numbers, dates of birth and other basic information are now considered off limits by a lot of people.

Some of the fear has to do with identity theft and criminal stalkers. Ironically, some of it has been spread by the media in sweeps-week consumer pieces warning citizens of all the information available about them in public records.

Fear leads to darkness. One study showed that the more fearful a person is about privacy invasion the less supportive he or she is toward

| TABLE 9.1 **Public support for records** | |
|---|---|
| **Record** | **Mean** |
| Crimes in your neighborhood | 9.23 |
| Registered sex offenders | 8.59 |
| Officials' expense accounts | 8.44 |
| Location of hazardous chemicals | 7.93 |
| Public employees' salaries | 7.52 |
| Vulnerabilities of dams | 6.90 |
| People's water use | 6.32 |
| Officials' work e-mail | 6.10 |
| Property tax records | 5.73 |
| Driver's license records | 3.38 |
| Divorce court files | 3.34 |

*Source:* David Cuillier.

*Note:* Results are from a 2006 phone survey[12] of 403 U.S. adults, on a 0–10 scale, with a higher number indicating greatest support for public access (5 is the neutral midpoint).

the press's right to access government records.[13] People consistently oppose the disclosure of records such as divorce court files, driver's licenses and files that contain the identity of victims, particularly victims of sexual crimes.

The lesson here is that if you seek records that include any hint of personal privacy invasion, then you'll have to make a strong case for why the public interest outweighs the personal.

### People vary

While we find general trends for public support by type of record, we also find that people's support varies depending on values and demographics.

Research indicates that the people who tend to be most supportive of FOI tend to be skeptical and cynical, active in their communities, frequent users of information online and educated.[14] Also, older people tend to be more supportive of access to government finance records than younger people, and women tend to be more supportive of safety-oriented records than men.

Some research indicates that political liberals are more supportive of FOI, but the findings are inconsistent. After all, many conservative individuals and groups champion the cause of FOI as a check on big government. So don't assume liberal lawmakers will support your access and conservatives won't. Most likely, libertarians are supportive of FOI, whether they are liberal or conservative.

Support can vary under different conditions as well. One experiment showed that the thought of death amplified people's attitudes toward FOI, so those who tend to value secrecy become even more supportive of secrecy and those who value openness tend to be more supportive of FOI.[15] So perhaps under times of mortal strife, such as war or terrorist attacks, the public might become more polarized over access to government records.

The key is to remember that people view FOI differently, and under different conditions, and we cannot assume everyone believes that government records should be freely disseminated.

Before making a public stink about a records denial, or before proudly splashing records or data on your Web site for all to access, think about how the public might react. It might not be on your side. But if you explain the practical need for the records to be out in the open—for public safety—then you might just win the public over.

## Write about FOI

We want to end this book with one last thought, and probably its most important point: Fight for everyone's right to access their government.

When an agency says "no" to you it is saying "no" to your whole community. Fight for your community by aggressively pursuing records, writing about denials and suing if you have to. Empower the public—your family, co-workers, neighbors, fellow citizens.

Too often we see journalists give up when denied records, or say they can't write about denials because it's simply a press issue. Phooey.

If you are denied public records, tell your community and let it decide what should be done. Chances are if the matter involves public safety then citizens will demand transparency. If the records involve personal privacy of citizens they might side with the agency. But regardless, tell them what is at stake.

You can write about FOI and not be biased. Here are tips for writing legitimate stories that need to be told.

### Find the news peg

A lot of journalists struggle with writing a story about a public records denial because the news peg is not apparent—it feels weird to write a story that involves you. In general, journalists try to stay independent from the story. You need a peg other than the fact that an agency wouldn't give you documents. We're not talking about making up news—instead, look for the possibilities and don't immediately discount a story because it happens to involve *your* public records request. Here are several legitimate news pegs:

- **Law breakers.** It's newsworthy and ironic when government knowingly breaks the law. Don't we report when the mayor embezzles tax funds? Don't we report when politicians skirt campaign finance laws? Why is it different when a public official breaks the public records law? Verify, using experts, that the agency is breaking the law; get the agency's response and focus on why it matters to the public.
- **Rogue agency.** Find out how other agencies in the county or state handle the dissemination of the same records. You might find that everyone else provides it. It's newsworthy when an agency is deviant.
- **Under investigation.** Contact your state's attorney general, auditor, governor or other official whose job is to oversee compliance with public records laws. Ask if they are looking into the matter. If so, you have a news peg: "Attorney general investigates mayor's refusal to provide text messages."
- **Board questions staff.** Ask each member of the elected governing body what he or she thinks about the staff keeping the information secret. If a city council member says the information should be public and raises the issue at a public meeting or by memo, write about it.

- **The anecdote.** Find a real person affected by the denial and write a news feature story focusing on that anecdote. Stories about human angst and injustice are newsworthy. For example, if police won't release a report about a violent crime or a serial rapist in a neighborhood, interview neighbors to see what they think about the lack of information.
- **Mass noncompliance.** Conduct a public records audit in your county or state and find how all agencies respond to requests. Methodical research is newsworthy. See the SPJ FOI Toolkit for tips on doing an audit (www.spj.org/foitoolkit.asp).
- **Party to a lawsuit.** Sue the agency. That's news.

### Hang it on experts

Once you have a solid news peg, bolster your story with authoritative sources who can speak to the legality of the denial. You can't say the school superintendent has rocks for brains, but an expert can. Here are some good sources for, well, good sources:

- **Legal minds.** Talk to the top media law attorneys in your state. Lawyers can't provide legal advice unless you are a client, but they may be willing to give you their opinion for a story. Also, get to

## Pro tip | **Provide appropriate weight**

Sometimes journalists frame access/secrecy issues as if there are two equal sides when the sides aren't always equal, misleading readers. Often a records denial is just plain wrong—being used to hide embarrassing facts. It can be misleading to frame it equally, as if the agency has a legitimate right to keep the information secret. If you do a story about a public records denial, and you read the law and have experts saying the agency is breaking the law, then tell readers that. Too often journalists try to make the story appear "balanced," but it gives the readers the impression that the records actually should be secret, when that's not the case.

—Patrice McDermott, director, OpenTheGovernment.org

know an FOI-friendly attorney at your state attorney general's office who can provide context and quotes.

- **National FOI organizations.** Charles N. Davis, executive director of the National Freedom of Information Coalition (www.nfoic.org) and co-author of this book, provides fiery quotes that will singe the hair off secretive public officials (daviscn@missouri.edu). Also, contact the Reporters Committee for Freedom of the Press (www.rcfp.org, legal defense hotline: 1-800-336-4243). If dealing with education records, contact the Student Press Law Center (www.splc.org).

- **Prod a prof.** Find a journalism professor at a nearby university, perhaps one who teaches media law, computer-assisted reporting or public affairs reporting. Go online to the university's journalism department or communication college Web site and search through the faculty list. Check all the major universities and colleges in your state. Professors are usually willing to speak out on issues, especially tenured professors.

- **SPJ Sunshine Network.** SPJ FOI Committee members (including both of this book's authors) will give great quotes. Find their contact information online at www.spj.org/foi.asp. Also, find your state SPJ sunshine chair at www.spj.org/sunshine-chairs.asp.

- **State open government groups.** Find your state's coalition for open government at www.nfoic.org/nfoicmembers.

- **State press associations.** For a press association in your state, check out a list online by SHG Resources at www.shgresources.com/resources/newspapers/associations.

### Make it relevant

The most important thing to remember when writing about denials is to focus on how the issue affects everyone, not just you.

Why should people care? What public good is served by the records being open that overrides privacy or national security issues? Find an average person who is affected by the secrecy and focus on him or her.

So the next time a public official denies you access to public records that you and the rest of the public are entitled to, don't slink away quietly.

Find the news peg, call the authoritative sources, focus on how it affects the public and let the world know.

## Become an FOI warrior

You now know how to research the law, find records, ask for them in different ways and overcome denials. You are prepared to write about FOI and foster the responsible use of government documents. With practice you are going to get what you want without having to sue.

Now we ask one more thing of you: Champion FOI.

### Educate the public

Few citizens routinely work with FOI laws as much as you do. Most people have never filed a public records request with their city. You have seen the value of access, so let others know.

The American Society of News Editors and other groups have promoted FOI through national Sunshine Week, usually held in mid-March. Each year hundreds of news organizations promote the value of FOI through editorials, stories explaining useful records and how to get them, public forums and high school essay contests.

Around January start planning what you will do for Sunshine Week (get ideas at www.sunshineweek.org), but you don't have to relegate access information to just one week of the year.

Let readers know where they can get public records that can help them. Conduct FOI audits in your community to assess the level of transparency in your local governments. Tell people where you got the information, even if it's just a simple attribution in a story.

### Make better law

Sometimes agencies can get away with denials because the law allows them to, or because the law doesn't address the issue. In that case, work to change the law.

Many journalists avoid getting directly involved in advocating for better laws, but talk with your state press association or state coalition for open government to get the momentum going.

If you talk to legislators about the need for change, make sure you know the people you are talking to. Know the issues that are important to them and how access can help them with their issue. Don't worry if they are liberal or conservative—access tends to be a bipartisan issue that has supporters and detractors on both sides of the political spectrum.

Get real anecdotes of how the information helps the public, and conduct a state FOI audit to empirically show how the information is kept secret. Compare your state's law to other states to show that it is one of the worst in the country. That will move legislators to action.

Also, make sure to get broad support for legislative change so it is not perceived as just a "media bill." Legislators aren't opposed to the media, but they are opposed to individual groups or institutions trying to get through "special interest" legislation. Show that this isn't being pushed by one interested party. Find citizens who have been stonewalled, perhaps by looking at the FOI request logs at agencies, and then invite them to help make government more transparent.

Betsy Z. Russell, *Spokesman-Review* bureau chief in Boise, Idaho, found that working with the state attorney general and the associations for cities and counties helped to get the Idaho Legislature to adopt improvements to the state open meeting law. As president of Idahoans for Openness in Government she found she could effectively work with officials without compromising her journalistic independence.

"I have to be careful because I cover the Legislature—I can't lobby and I can't talk to them about it," Russell said. "But I don't think, and my newspaper does not think, that it's a conflict of interest to stand up for what I need to do my job, and for the public's right to access government."

## Apply it daily

Make access a daily part of your life, as a journalist and a citizen. After all, this isn't about bylines or gotcha stories. It isn't about lofty principles, or even the "right to know." It's about acquiring the public information we need to make good decisions and help our democracy function.

We encourage you to join the ranks of FOI warriors, true "citizen journalists" who live up to the expectations of early American patriots—stalwarts against tyranny and the abuse of power. Freedom of information is fundamental to democracy, and without exercising our rights we will gradually, and without noticing, slide into a dark, ill-informed society.

Master and apply the skills from this book. Learn to navigate the bureaucratic maze with ease. Strengthen your document state of mind. Become a master in the art of access.

**Exercises and ideas for journalists, newsrooms and classrooms to improve your skills and foster FOI in your community.**

### 1. Build a doc spreadsheet

Open an Excel spreadsheet and create a file that will enable you to keep track of disparate pieces of information from documents for a story, perhaps one you are working on now. If you are a student, set up a spreadsheet for a term paper. Set up the columns ("fields") into different categories that make sense for what you are working with. You might consider these fields (fields go across the top, but we'll list them running down to fit in the book):

- ☑ Document number (you give a special individual number for each document)
- ☑ Name of document
- ☑ Date it was created
- ☑ Agency
- ☑ When you received it
- ☑ Who gave it to you
- ☑ Size (pages or megabytes)
- ☑ Key fact for story (long memo field or reference to a page number)
- ☑ Key people mentioned in the record
- ☑ Other documents mentioned in the record

## 2. Visit the people's court

Go to your city or county courthouse and look up a half-dozen divorce court files. Find a bulky, contentious file. As you read through the file, substitute your name for the husband or wife and read it as if it is your divorce (don't mark on actual court records, but feel free to mark up copies!). Read through the details, including allegations between spouses. Look at the personal details included in the files, including any home addresses, personal possessions they own or claims of alcoholism or abuse. Ask yourself these questions:

- ☑ What information should be posted online for everyone to read?
- ☑ What information should be redacted and not posted? Why?
- ☑ If one of the people in the file were the mayor or a movie star would that change what you would post online?
- ☑ Balance the privacy concerns of the individual with the benefit to the public. If you published this document online, what would you say to the husband or wife if they called? Does it matter that anyone, such as you, could look up the file at the courthouse?

## 3. Get real with relatives

At your next family gathering, ask your relatives what they think about press and citizen access to government records. Ask them a series of questions:

- ☑ What do you think of the public's right to access government documents?
- ☑ Have you ever requested a document from a government agency?
- ☑ Do you think the media and public should have access to bridge inspection records?
- ☑ Do you think the media and public should have access to public officials' annual salaries?
- ☑ Do you think the media and public should have access to divorce court files?
- ☑ Do you think the media and public should have access to property tax records?
- ☑ Why or why not?

Listen to what they say, without arguing or trying to explain the importance of these records. Note why they support or don't support those records being open. What are the underlying reasons for their support or opposition? Fear? Concern for people included in the records (victims, or themselves)? What sense do you have of their views toward how the media would use the records? Jot down what you heard and your thoughts, then keep that paper handy for when you request sensitive documents or data. Think about how readers will react to your decision to publish information from records or post raw data online. Weigh the public interest vs. the potential harm, and the potential backlash that could lead to closure of the records. What would you have to explain to people to justify publication of the information?

### 4. Find a quote machine

Identify an expert or two in your state who you can call to get a good quote for a story when you are denied public records. See the list on pages 193–194 for ideas, including your press association director, a media law professor or the SPJ sunshine chair. Get to know the expert and see if he or she will provide home contact information for after-hours interviews. To be fair, make sure to find experts in municipal government who can provide other perspectives. Possible sources include your state's association of cities or counties, or an assistant attorney general.

### 5. Spread sunshine in your community

As journalists we have an ethical duty to protect freedom of information. In fact, it's in the SPJ Code of Ethics: "Recognize a special obligation to ensure that the public's business is conducted in the open and that government records are open to inspection." To ensure openness, the public has to buy in, so build support for open government through a variety of projects, either as a newsroom, class or SPJ chapter, perhaps timed to national Sunshine Week in mid-March:

- ☑ Create a video for DVD and online that shows the importance of open government. Distribute to schools in the area.
- ☑ Develop catchy logos for posters or T-shirts promoting open government. Provide to groups and sell at journalism and library conferences.

☑ Develop FOI guides for citizens, explaining 100 public records they can access to help them with their lives and describing how to ask for records.

☑ Hold an FOI training day for high school journalists.

☑ Sponsor a high school FOI essay contest.

☑ Organize a running team and hit all the local 10k runs or charity walks in your community, with everyone wearing the same FOI shirt with a catchy FOI slogan.

**Suggested links**

**Access audit toolkit**   www.spj.org/foitoolkit.asp
Find out how to conduct an FOI audit in your community by checking out this FOI Audit Toolkit, provided by the Society of Professional Journalists (and written by one of this book's authors).

**FOI experts in your state**   www.spj.org/foi.asp
Find an FOI expert in your state to put in your story about a records denial. SPJ provides online the contact information for several experts for each state.

**More *Art of Access***   www.theartofaccess.com
Check out the authors' blog for this book, *The Art of Access,* to find more story ideas, tips, classroom activities for teaching FOI and Web links.

**National Sunshine Week**   www.sunshineweek.org
Sponsored by the American Society of News Editors, this Web site provides a wealth of ideas for FOI promotions, including editorials, stories, contests and other projects produced by news organizations.

# Appendix A
# The Record Album

Here is a sampling of some public records, A to Z, that you can tap into for stories or to find out more about your neighborhood. Go to the authors' blog for this book, at www.theartofaccess.com, to find hundreds more records. Individual records may be closed in some states and open in others—to find out consult an expert or the Open Government Guide for your state at www.rcfp.org/ogg, and find dozens of experts on the blog for *The Art of Access.*

**Abandoned buildings.** Identify trends in deteriorating neighborhoods. Cities often track reports of vacant or abandoned buildings, as well as junk cars and other neighborhood nuisances.

**Agricultural trends.** Find trends in important agricultural commodities in your county or state through agricultural census statistics, updated every five years by the U.S. Department of Agriculture's National Agricultural Statistics Service (www.agcensus.usda.gov). To find descriptions of markets and export strategy by crop, check out the USDA's Foreign Agricultural Service's export strategy reports.

**Airplanes.** Identify airplane crash trends and find pilots and plane owners. The Federal Aviation Administration's accident and incident reports are available at www.faa.gov/data_statistics. Also, the FAA Aircraft Registry includes owner name and pilot information at www.landings.com.

**Airport noise.** Ask to see airport noise maps and flight pattern maps. Airports track noise complaints from neighbors when jets fly low or are particularly noisy.

**Air quality.** Check with your county or state environmental agency about air quality. Big polluters are fined by county and state air quality departments.

**Arrest reports.** Verify the arrest of a specific person in connection with a specific event. Arrest reports are available at local law enforcement offices, usually from a public information officer or officer in charge. In most states if the case is still under investigation (someone's still on the loose or police haven't forwarded the information to the prosecutor yet for potential charges), then police might be able to keep some of the information secret if they can demonstrate it would harm the investigation.

**Arrest warrants.** Ensure fairness in the arrest of suspects and get a lead on potential big busts. An arrest warrant is signed by a judge authorizing the arrest of someone for probable cause. Often warrants have a lot of information because police are trying to justify to a judge the need to arrest a person. These are similar to search warrants, which also require justification and approval by a judge. Warrants are usually made public once the person is served (arrested or searched), or when it appears the person won't be able to be served (he or she has skipped the country).

**Audits.** Monitor problems in government agencies, particularly financial woes. Look carefully to find any irregularities—often clouded by vague terms and wishy-washy language. Ask to get more details.

**Autopsy reports.** Confirm the cause of death or circumstances of a person's death and evaluate the quality of medical examiners. States vary on whether they allow these records to be open. Also, they could be closed in connection with pending criminal investigations or to protect personal privacy.

**Bankruptcy files.** Identify trends in bankruptcies, spot fraud and find people with unfortunate financial pasts. Chapter 7 is a straight bankruptcy and Chapter 11 is a reorganization that usually allows the business to stay open. Businesses in bankruptcy lose a fair amount of privacy as the files list assets, how they got into trouble and what they intend to do to get back on their feet. Check the U.S. Bankruptcy Court in your area.

**Birth certificates.** Verify the identity, birth date and birthplace of a person. Birth certificates are closed in some states.

**Boating accidents.** Analyze boating accident trends. States maintain this information, usually by parks agencies. Also, the U.S. Coast Guard maintains the same information nationwide.

**Boat registration.** Find trends in boating and owners of watercraft. Check with your state department of parks and recreation, natural resources or boating, or with another similar agency.

**Bridge inspections.** Assess the safety of bridges in the community. Inspection records are maintained by states and the Federal Highway Administration (www.fhwa.dot.gov/bridge/britab.htm; click on "Download NBI ASCII files").

**Broadcaster files.** Check out broadcaster files at the station. The Federal Communications Commission requires broadcasters to keep records available to the public, including educational programming they are required to air.

**Budgets.** Obtain budgets from the agency's budget officer to see what departments are getting more money over time and what areas are getting less funding. Detailed budgets are available before and after approval.

**Calendars.** Find out how top officials are spending their time. Look at their calendars, or day schedules, to see who they are meeting with and the extent of their workload. You should also be able to get travel expenses. Request from the office you are interested in, such as the mayor's office if you want to see the mayor's calendar.

**Campus crime.** Find serious incidents happening on crime. This data must be released by campus police because of the federal Clery Act. Get police logs and incident reports at the campus police department. You also can get statistics online for all universities and compare nationally at http://ope.ed.gov/security. Note that studies have shown universities to underreport their violent crimes.

**Census.** Use demographic data—available down to the block group level—to analyze shifts in community demographics, including in migration, income, race, education, gender and age. It's challenging to burrow through the Census Web site (www.census.gov), but it's all there.

**Charities.** Find out whether someone asking for money is registered with the state. Check with your state attorney general's office or secretary of state (also see Nonprofits).

**Child care complaints.** Assess how well daycare is handled in your community and how well the government monitors child care. Often handled by your city, and some state agencies monitor this as well.

**Civil lawsuits.** Make sure civil cases are handled equitably and disputes resolved fairly. Examples of civil cases include malpractice, child support, divorce, libel, paternity, property rights, restraining orders and breach of contract. In most states the Superior Court handles big cases and municipal courts (small claims) handle the little things (like you see on "Judge Judy").

**Claims.** If someone feels a government agency owes them compensation for damages (slipping on a sidewalk, hit by police car, etc.), they often file a claim before filing a lawsuit. Check with the risk management officer or attorney for the agency.

**Code enforcement.** Examine trends and fairness in applying local nuisance laws. Code enforcement records detail noise violations, illegal businesses in residential zones, illegal dumping, huge signs and other problems.

**Concealed weapon permits.** See who is packing heat in secret. The idea is it is a privilege to carry a hidden gun because it gives you an advantage over other people who don't know you have it, so we entrust the government to make sure qualified people are carrying concealed weapons. However, in many states these permits are secret.

**Contracts.** Contact an agency's business office to find out who is benefiting from government projects. Should include the amount agreed upon, the amount paid (often more), who the money went to, etc.

**Coroners' reports.** Inspect to see the cause of an unusual death. Most are open to the public.

**Corporate records.** Spot connections between public companies and identify key officers. The federal Securities and Exchange Commission provides a wealth of information on public companies online, including initial public offering files (Form S-1), quarterly reports (Form 10-Q), annual reports (Form 10-K) and top officer information (Form DEF 14A). You can search the clunky Web site www.sec .gov, or also search EDGAR (www.sec.gov/edgar/searchedgar/web users.htm) and enforcement records. Or you can check state business licenses at your secretary of state's office, corporate commission or similar agency.

**Court records.** Find if someone has a criminal background or has been sued in civil court. Also monitor trends in a variety of criminal justice issues, including crime, sentencing, racial profiling (speeding tickets) and judge performance. In general, court records are public unless they have been sealed by a judge for a specific reason.

**Crime log.** Analyze for trends in calls and response times. Also sometimes called a "police blotter," this is a barebones list of incidents, usually including address, time/date, one-word description and disposition.

**Criminal records.** Find trends in crime, monitor the criminal justice system and find backgrounds of individuals. Compilations of criminal histories are closed in many states, but you can get court records from individual courthouses and piece together a history.

**Cruise ship inspections.** Check out the Centers for Disease Control's inspection reports and statistics of sickness outbreaks for cruise lines and individual ships at the Vessel Sanitation Program Web site, www.cdc.gov/nceh/vsp.

**Death certificates.** Examine to find causes of death. However, they are closed in some states.

**Development.** Identify development trends and potential building that could impact the community or a neighborhood. Find out what permits for development have been submitted and approved for an area. Go to the city or county planning and development department to see the plans.

**Divorce cases.** See if men and women are treated equally in divorces and examine backgrounds of prominent individuals. Available at the courthouse.

**Driving records.** Examine the safety records of individuals or a group of drivers, such as cabbies or bus drivers. While personal driver's license information is generally not public (except for special access through contracts with commercial companies), it is usually possible to find driving violations, such as speeding.

**Drug houses.** Find locations of homes that were once used as meth labs or other clandestine drug labs. Identify trends in drug houses. You can also see if any homes in your neighborhood (or a house you're thinking of buying) had drug problems. Provided by the U.S. Drug Enforcement Administration (www.dea.gov/seizures).

**Educational records.** Find budgets, criminal incidents, grade inflation and other problems in schools. Records regarding grades of specific identified students are secret because of FERPA, except for directory information, including name, year, home address, phone number, date of birth, etc. (unless the parent or adult student wishes the information to not be disclosed). See www.ed.gov/policy/gen/guid/fpco/ferpa/index.html. Serious criminal incidents are public, per the Clery Act.

**Elections.** See who is funding candidates and campaigns. Counties typically keep records on local candidates, and state elections offices keep information on state candidates. Federal records are kept by the Federal Elections Commission.

**E-mail.** Monitor government functions and make sure business that should be conducted in public isn't being handled secretly via e-mail.

**Employees.** Identify cronyism and find former employees. You can request records of employee names, titles and salaries. Employee home addresses and home phone numbers, however, are generally not public in most states (even though you can find that information for most people in the phone book, through www.pipl.com, many types of public licensing records or a commercial information provider).

**Environment.** Examine toxic release inventory information to learn what bad stuff different companies and industry release in your community. A good site to find that EPA information is at the Right to Know Web site: http://data.rtknet.org/tri. Government also monitors other environmental hazards, such as leaking underground gas tanks.

**Expense reports.** Monitor government spending and see if government employees are cheating the system. Check with the business office of an agency. You can ask for agency credit card logs as well.

**Fire incident reports.** Monitor fire departments and spot trends, such as arson, dangerous homes, public buildings that are hazards, etc. Check with the fire agency to examine incident reports.

**Foreclosures.** Spot trends in home foreclosures. You can identify areas that are hardest hit and types of people losing their homes. These are civil court files held at the county courthouse. Also, check out home mortgage lending trends (and whether minorities are denied home loans more often than whites, called "red lining") by examining Home Mortgage Disclosure Act data (www.ffiec.gov/hmda).

**Gas-pump inspections.** Make sure gas stations aren't ripping off consumers. Check your state's office of weights and measures.

**Graffiti.** Track decaying neighborhoods and hooliganism. Check with your city to find graffiti reports and other records.

**Hospitals.** Examine public hospitals' financial records (these are public, though a person's individual medical records usually are not). Non-profit hospitals file tax returns, which are public (see Nonprofits).

Also, you should be able to get records from public hospitals that do not identify individual patients, such as statistical data or files with names and other identifiers redacted.

**Income taxes.** Examine income tax returns for nonprofits. This is public material, though individual and corporate income tax returns are private (see Nonprofits). Also, when taxpayers want to challenge the IRS they do so in U.S. Tax Court, and those records are public.

**Incorporation records.** Find out who owns a business. Look up city business licenses at the finance department at City Hall. Find state incorporation records at your secretary of state's office.

**Jail records.** See who is jailed and who oversees jail operations. The jail log is a list of people booked in the jail, including name, time/date and charge. More detailed information can be found in the booking sheets. You also can get jail mugs (public in most states) and examine budgets, jail population statistics and overtime to monitor operations.

**Juvenile records.** Monitor the juvenile justice system to make sure it's working well.

**Lawyer discipline.** Find lawyers who have been disciplined and monitor the oversight of attorneys. Find these records (online and on paper) held by your state's commission on attorney conduct, or check with your state courts system or bar association.

**Legislative records.** Examine the voting records of legislators, bill wording and legislators' attendance. Find people who testify on issues. Many records held by legislatures are not subject to state public records laws—check in your state.

**Licensing.** Check your state licensing departments to see if a person is licensed or has had a license revoked. States monitor a variety of professionals, including barbers, beauticians, accountants, appraisers, chiropractors, nurses, realtors, etc.

**Liquor licenses.** Identify bars and restaurants that are nuisances (have a lot of bar fights and problems for neighbors) and not following liquor laws. Check with your state liquor board.

**Lottery winners.** Make sure the lottery is being handled fairly (and that the employees' friends and families aren't winning). Also see how sales are affecting different parts of a community. Often you can get the winner's name, date, amount and the retail outlet where the ticket was sold. You should be able to get lottery ticket sales and payouts by retail outlet as well. Check with your state lottery commission.

**Marriage licenses.** Monitor marriage statistics and find current and ex-spouses. Not open in some states, although marriage license applications are usually public.

**Medical devices.** Identify medical devices that have failed, how they failed and the manufacturer. The "MAUDE" database is maintained by the U.S. Food and Drug Administration, which also maintains the Adverse Event Reporting system that flags safety issues regarding pharmaceutical drugs. Check out www.accessdata.fda.gov/scripts/cdrh/cfdocs/cfMAUDE/search.cfm.

**Medical records.** Check out disciplinary records against doctors held by your state medical board. While these are public, individual medical record information generally is not public information. State statutes and HIPAA make most medical information private.

**Meeting minutes.** Monitor city councils, school boards and other government bodies. Meeting notices, agendas and minutes are almost always public. Check with the clerk's office at the respective agency.

**Name change.** See if someone is hiding under a new identity. Records are held by the courthouse.

**911 logs.** Spot trends in crime, medical calls and response times by police officers and fire trucks. They typically list time/date, location, call type and responding units. Check with your local 911 center.

**Nonprofit 990 forms.** Make sure nonprofits are actually not out to make a profit and just using 501c(3) status to avoid paying taxes. You also can find a variety of information about nonprofits' income, expenses and officers through the 990 forms they file annually. To quickly see 990 forms, go to www.guidestar.com. You have to register, but most of the site is free. Go to the IRS for more information.

**Nursing home inspections.** Check your state department of health to identify unsafe nursing homes. You can get comparisons nationally by Medicare at www.medicare.gov/NHCompare.

**Odor complaints.** Identify odor complaints in different neighborhoods. Most municipal sewage treatment plants track complaints of their sewage stink, which enables people to identify trends and know where not to buy a house.

**Parking tickets.** Identify parking scofflaws, trends and fairness in ticketing (any special persons get their tickets waived?).

**Personnel records.** Confirm whether someone is a public employee and identify bad workers through disciplinary records. These are not always public in all states, so they can be difficult to get—for example, disciplinary actions against teachers. It depends on the state. Getting personnel records for high-ranking officials is easier because of greater public interest. Performance evaluations are public in some states.

**Pet licenses.** Examine trends in pet ownership and dog bites. Pet licenses include information about licensed animals (name, breed, last rabies shot, etc.), as well as name of owner, address and phone number. A good database to start with for learning computer-assisted reporting.

**Price-scanning inspections.** Assess which stores might be ripping off consumers. Find this information at your state office of weights and measures.

**Probate.** Make sure possessions are disbursed fairly and find family members of the deceased. When someone dies and leaves property and doesn't have a will, the property goes through probate—the government has to figure out how to fairly divvy up the goods. Check the courthouse.

**Product recalls.** Monitor the safety of consumer products, including food and medicine (FDA), consumer products (CPSC), meat (USDA), cars (NHTSA), pesticides (EPA) and boating safety (Coast Guard). Check out recalled products for all these agencies at www.recalls.gov/search.html.

**Property taxes.** Assess whether everyone is paying their fair share of property taxes and also find out who is buying what in the community. Property tax records are public at county courthouses. You can find out how much homes in your neighborhood are worth and what they sold for, along with details such as the homes' square footage and number of bedrooms. Find this information at your county assessor's office.

**Public records requests.** Find what public records are being requested by businesses, citizens, government employees and journalists. Request from the public records officer copies of the public records request and any log used to track requests.

**Restaurant inspections.** Make sure the public is protected from unsanitary conditions at restaurants and other venues (e.g., public pools, school cafeterias, hotels). Check with your city or county. Some states collect the records as well, or monitor the local agencies. Find out if regulations or state law require restaurants to be inspected every six months and then check to see if it's happening.

**Retention schedules.** Find out what records an agency keeps and when it purges them. Most public agencies have established retention schedules to determine how long they will keep different records and when they can get rid of them. Check with the individual agency to find its retention schedule, usually held by a clerk or records officer. Your state archives office will likely have a retention schedule for state records.

**Salaries.** Find cronyism and disparity in pay. Names, titles and salaries of public employees are almost always available. Also, get overtime pay and actual pay (not just budgeted salary) to find janitors who make more money than the mayor. This is a good way to find former employees (great sources!) by looking at lists from prior years.

**School test scores.** Check with individual schools, school districts or your state department of education to identify poorly performing schools. Often the statistics are all online.

**Sex offenders.** Find if sex offenders live close to vulnerable populations. Note that a variety of studies have found registries to be relatively inaccurate, so the person may or may not actually live where the registry says the person lives. Check with your state police department, which will likely have a searchable Web site, or request the whole list as an Excel file.

**Stolen vehicles.** Identify trends in vehicle theft. Request from your police stolen vehicle data to analyze popular makes, models and locations of car thieves.

**Street maintenance.** Examine trends in bad streets, who gets them fixed and who doesn't. Check with your local street department.

**Taxi inspections.** Assess the safety of taxis, often regulated by cities. Also check to see if they regulate other public vehicle operators (horse-drawn carriages, valet parking, etc.).

**Tax refunds.** Find whether someone is scamming the system by setting up dummy corporations to get bogus property tax refunds. *The Washington Post* analyzed Washington, D.C., tax refunds in 2007 to find that nearly $32 million had been refunded illegally to government employees and their friends, including to a fictitious company it established called "Bilkemor LLC" (www.washingtonpost .com/wp-dyn/content/article/2007/11/13/AR2007111302394.html? referrer%3Demailarticle&sub=AR).

**Telephone records.** Identify corruption and questionable connections of public employees. Telephone records of their work phones, including cell phone records, can provide this information by listing who the employee talked to along with the time and date. In some states, such as Texas, courts are ruling that messages regarding work topics of public officials are open, even when sent on personal cell phones and Blackberry devices.

**Traffic accident reports.** Find dangerous intersections and stretches of roads. Also, you can analyze the federal Fatality Analysis Reporting System data for every fatal accident in the nation going back to 1975 (www-fars.nhtsa.dot.gov/Main/index.aspx).

**Train wreck data.** Identify the most dangerous train-road intersection in the community and other trends. The Federal Railroad Administration provides train wreck data back to 1975 online for downloading and analysis (http://safetydata.fra.dot.gov/officeofsafety). Click on "Accident Data on Demand," then choose "Highway Rail Accidents." Choose a year, your state and a format (Excel).

**Tribal records.** American Indian tribes are considered sovereign nations and not subject to FOIA or state public records laws. If a federal agency holds tribal documents, those should be public if you request them from the federal agency that has them (per U.S. Supreme Court case *Dept. of Interior v. Klamath*). For more information about access to tribal information, see the Reporter's Guide to American Indian Law by the Reporters Committee for Freedom of the Press (www.rcfp.org/americanindian/index.html).

**Truck accidents.** Identify trouble spots in the community where semitrucks tend to crash and burn (particularly on interstate highways). The U.S. Department of Transportation collects accident reports involving commercial trucks weighing over 10,000 pounds. The agency now keeps secret hazardous waste information, citing national security reasons, so we don't know what stuff is traveling on our freeways or how dangerous it is if the trucks crash. Get federal data from the U.S. Department of Transportation Federal Highway Administration.

**Unclaimed property.** See what property and funds are owed to citizens by the government (and have gone unclaimed). Request records from the state Department of Revenue.

**Uniform Commercial Code.** Find what loans someone has for property, yachts, etc.

**University records.** Find student records. Educational records are secret (per FERPA), but operational records and statistical information about students is public. Student directory information and criminal records are public.

**Use of force.** Look at how police use—or overuse—force during arrests. Each time an officer uses a choke hold, gun, taser, police dog, baton or other use of force a form is filled out. Get them from the police department.

**Utility bills.** Personal use of electricity, water and other utilities generally isn't public, even though it might be of public interest to know the big users of public water. Individuals' usage might be available from public utilities in some states.

**Voter registration.** See whether people, particularly candidates, have voted or lived in a community. Also help prevent voter fraud (check to see if dead people are voting). Voter registration records include name, address, year of birth, party affiliation and whether a person voted in the previous election (but not how they voted). Check with your county or city.

**Weather.** Examine trends in climate change in the community and compare weather conditions in one neighborhood to another (weather can vary among different parts of town because of elevation, topography and pavement effects). The National Climatic Data Center provides tons of data summarizing temperatures, rain, wind and other conditions for each individual monitoring station going back more than 100 years. The agency also has a database of storms, including tornadoes, hurricanes, snowstorms, flash floods and drought. See www.ncdc.noaa.gov/oa/ncdc.html.

**Worker safety.** Identify dangerous workplaces and trends in workplace accidents. State and federal agencies track injuries at companies. Look at federal Occupational Safety and Health Administration records at www.osha.gov/oshstats/index.html.

**Zoning.** Analyze growth planning and find who is benefiting by development. Find out how land is zoned and what development is possible. Also look at comprehensive plans, which map out the general future of a community. Go to the city planning and development department to find zoning maps, comprehensive plans and development plans. Check with your city planning or zoning department.

# Appendix B
# FOI resources

1. Request letters
2. Laws
3. Allies and help
4. Blogs and news
5. Document story ideas
6. Electronic records
7. Document repositories
8. Groups
9. Contests
10. Online interactive FOI fun
11. Books

## 1. Request letters
**Federal appeal forms**   www.rcfp.org/fogg/index.php
>   Reporters Committee for Freedom of the Press online appeal form
**Federal FOIA letter**   www.rcfp.org/foialetter/index.php
>   Reporters Committee for Freedom of the Press neutral letter (also state)
**State request letter**   www.splc.org/foiletter.asp
>   Student Press Law Center letter generator (more legalistic)
**Tips for effective letters**   www.rcfp.org/fogg/index.php?i=pt1#b
>   Reporters Committee for Freedom of the Press tips for effective letters

## 2. Laws
**Campus crime records**   www.securityoncampus.org
>   Nonprofit provides information on the Clery Act and crime records

**Educational records**   www.splc.org/legalresearch.asp?maincat=2
   Student Press Law Center guide to educational records and the
   Family Educational Rights and Privacy Act (FERPA)
**FOIA-able agencies**   www.usdoj.gov/oip/foiacontacts.htm
   U.S. Justice Department list of federal agencies subject to FOIA
**FOIA guide**   www.rcfp.org/fogg
   Reporters Committee for Freedom of the Press federal FOIA
   guide
**Guide to HIPAA**   www.rcfp.org/hipaa/index.html
   Reporters Committee for Freedom of the Press guide to the
   Health Insurance Portability and Accountability Act (HIPAA)
**International FOI**   www.freedominfo.org
   Rundown of FOI laws by country
**Legal information**   www.law.cornell.edu
   Provides free access to statutes and court opinions
**Open Government Guide**   www.rcfp.org/ogg
   Reporters Committee for Freedom of the Press state public
   record/meeting law summaries with statute

## 3. Allies and help

**Access audit toolkit**   www.spj.org/foitoolkit.asp
   Society of Professional Journalists tips for conducting FOI audits
**FOIA ombudsman**   www.archives.gov/ogis
   Director of the Office of Government Information Services
**Learn about mediation**   www.nfoic.org/white_papers
   "Mediation without Litigation," by Harry Hammitt
**Legal help for students**   www.splc.org
   Student Press Law Center free legal assistance to student
   journalists
**National Sunshine Week**   www.sunshineweek.org
   American Society of News Editors resources for promoting FOI
**Newsroom FOI training**   www.spj.org/bbtraining.asp
   Society of Professional Journalists newsroom training program
**Reporters legal hotline**   www.rcfp.org/about.html#hotline
   Reporters Committee for Freedom of the Press legal hotline for
   journalists

State coalitions   www.nfoic.org/nfoicmembers
> National Freedom of Information Coalition list of coalitions

State FOI experts   www.spj.org/foi.asp
> Society of Professional Journalists Sunshine Network

Watchdog training   www.ire.org/training
> Investigative Reporters and Editors watchdog training sessions

## 4. Blogs and news

FOI Advocate   www.foiadvocate.blogspot.com
> National Freedom of Information Coalition blog

FOI on Alltop   http://freedom-of-information.alltop.com
> A compilation of all FOI blog posts, all in one place

FOI FYI blog   www.blogs.spjnetwork.org/foi
> Society of Professional Journalists FOI blog

FOI in the UK   http://foia.blogspot.com/index.html
> FOI in the United Kingdom (also www.bbc.co.uk/blogs/opensecrets)

Free government info   www.freegovinfo.info
> A wide variety of groups interested in open government

News Media Update   www.rcfp.org
> Reporters Committee for Freedom of the Press media news Web site

State Sunshine   http://openrecords.wordpress.com
> A wiki-type blog by all sorts of folks, with good links to other FOI blogs

## 5. Document story ideas

Extra! Extra!   www.ire.org/extraextra
> Investigative Reporters and Editors daily investigative reports

FOIA files   www.sunshineingovernment.org/index.php?cat=33
> The Sunshine in Government Initiative's database of record stories

FOI ideas A to Z   www.spj.org/opendoors.asp
> Society of Professional Journalists Open Doors publication guide

Idiganswers   www.idiganswers.com
> Document ideas from Joe Adams, an editorial writer from Florida

## 6. Electronic records

**Access by state**   www.rcfp.org/ecourt/index.html
>  Reporters Committee summary of access to data by state

**Beat Page**   www.ire.org/resourcecenter/initial-search-beat.html
>  Links to online records and resources ordered by beat

**Database journalism help**   http://data.nicar.org
>  The National Institute for Computer-Assisted Reporting

**Drew Sullivan's databases**   www.drewsullivan.com/database.html
>  List of free downloadable and searchable databases on the Internet

**Power reporting**   www.powerreporting.com
>  Bill Dedman's links to great sites, although he is relinquishing the site

## 7. Document repositories

**Everyblock.com**   www.everyblock.com
>  Look through the wealth of data posted online by city

**Federal records**   www.gpo.gov/fdsys
>  The Government Printing Office's Federal Digital System (FDsys)

**The Government's Attic**   www.governmentattic.org
>  This Web site posts a variety of federal documents, including FOI logs

**The National Security Archive**   www.nsarchive.org
>  This nonprofit group requests and posts online federal records

**Online collectors**   www.pipl.com
>  An Internet information gleaner, Pipl provides a sense of what's available

**Uploaded documents**   www.governmentdocs.org
>  Citizens for Responsibility and Ethics in Washington allows doc uploads

## 8. Groups

**American Society of Access Professionals (ASAP)**   www.accesspro.org

**Collaboration on Government Secrecy**   http://www.wcl.american.edu/lawandgov/cgs

**Investigative Reporters and Editors (IRE)**   www.ire.org/foi
>  IRE's FOI page

National Freedom of Information Coalition (NFOIC)   www.nfoic.org
   Coordinates state coalitions (look under "Members" link for your
   state)
The National Security Archive   www.nsarchive.org
   Nonprofit group at George Washington University that gathers
   records
OMB Watch   www.ombwatch.org
   Nonprofit group that advocates for transparency and other issues
OpenTheGovernment.org   www.openthegovernment.org
   Advocates for openness at the federal level
Reporters Committee for Freedom of the Press (RCFP)   www.rcfp
.org
Society of Environmental Journalists   www.sej.org/foia/index.htm
Society of Professional Journalists (SPJ)   www.spj.org/foi.asp
   SPJ's FOI page
Student Press Law Center (SPLC)   www.splc.org
   Assists high school and college journalists
Sunshine in Government Initiative   www.sunshineingovernment
.org
WikiFOIA   www.wikifoia.pbwiki.com
   Information added by folks from all walks of life

## 9. Contests
   Investigative Reporters and Editors FOI Award   www.ire.org/
   resourcecenter/contest/index.html
   Open Gov Hall of Fame   www.nfoic.org
      National Freedom of Information Coalition and SPJ's Heroes of
      the States
   Society of Professional Journalists' Sunshine Award   www.spj.org/
   a-sunshine.asp

## 10. Online interactive FOI fun
   Are we safer in the dark?
         OpenTheGovernment.org (2006)
         http://inthedark.openthegovernment.org

(Classified) clip about (classified)
>The Onion (2007)
>www.theonion.com/content/video/proposed_classified_bill_will

**Democracy in jeopardy!**
>OpenTheGovernment.org (2007)
>http://democracy.openthegovernment.org

**Do you suffer from Congressional Data Frustration (CVF)? Try Sunlightalinazinosec!**
>Sunlight Foundation (September 2007)
>www.youtube.com/watch?v=xEO7yglGfd8

**Save the e-mail records from deletion!**
>Missouri Democratic Party (2007)
>www.bluntdocumentdestroyer.com

## 11. Books

Alterman, E. *When Presidents Lie: A History of Official Deception and Its Consequences.* New York: Penguin, 2004.

Bok, S. *Lying: Moral Choice in Public and Private Life.* New York: Pantheon, 1999.

_____. *Secrets: On the Ethics of Concealment and Revelation.* New York: Pantheon, 1982.

Brin, D. *The Transparent Society: Will Technology Force Us to Choose Between Privacy and Freedom?* New York: Perseus, 1999.

Brucker, H. *Freedom of Information.* New York: Macmillan Co., 1949.

Chapman, R. A., and M. Hunt. *Open Government in a Theoretical and Practical Context.* Burlington, Vt.: Ashgate, 2006.

Cross, H. *The People's Right to Know.* New York: Columbia, 1953.

Davis, C. N., and S. L. Splichal. *Access Denied: Freedom of Information in the Information Age.* Ames: Iowa State University Press, 2000.

Demac, D. A. *Liberty Denied: The Current Rise of Censorship.* New Brunswick: Rutgers University Press, 1988.

Devolpi, A., et al. *Born Secret: The H-Bomb, the Progressive Case and National Security.* New York: Pergamon, 1981.

Florini, A. *The Right to Know: Transparency for an Open World.* New York: Columbia University Press, 2007.

Foerstel, H. N. *Freedom of Information and the Right to Know: The Origins and Applications of the Freedom of Information Act.* Westport, Conn.: Greenwood Press, 1999.

Franck, T. M., and E. Weisband. *Secrecy and Foreign Policy.* New York: Oxford University Press, 1986.

Fung, A., M. Graham and D. Weil. *Full Disclosure: The Perils and Promise of Transparency.* New York: Cambridge University Press, 2007.

Gup, T. *Nation of Secrets: The Threat to Democracy and the American Way of Life.* New York: Doubleday, 2007.

Halprin, M., and D. Hoffman. *Freedom vs. National Security: Secrecy and Surveillance.* New York: Chelsea House, 1977.

Hoffman, D. *Governmental Secrecy and the Founding Fathers: A Study in Constitutional Controls.* Westport, Conn.: Greenwood Press, 1981.

Hood, C., and D. Heald. *Transparency: The Key to Better Governance?* New York: Oxford University Press, 2006.

Kimball, P. *The File.* San Diego: Harcourt Brace Jovanovich, 1983.

Lord, K. M. *The Perils and Promise of Global Transparency: Why the Information Revolution May Not Lead to Security, Democracy or Peace.* Albany: State University of New York Press, 2006.

Marchetti, V. *CIA and the Cult of Intelligence.* New York: Dell, 1974.

McDermott, P. *Who Needs to Know? The State of Public Access to Federal Government Information.* Lanham, Md.: Bernan Press, 2007.

Moynihan, D. P. *Secrecy: The American Experience.* New Haven: Yale University Press, 1999.

Piotrowski, S. J. *Governmental Transparency in the Path of Administrative Reform.* Albany: State University of New York Press, 2007.

Roberts, A. *Blacked Out: Government Secrecy in the Information Age.* New York: Cambridge University Press, 2006.

Shawcross, W. *Sideshow: Kissinger, Nixon and the Destruction of Cambodia.* New York: Simon and Schuster, 1979.

Snepp, F. *Decent Interval: An Insider's Account of Saigon's Indecent End Told by the CIA's Chief Strategy Analyst in Vietnam.* New York: Random House, 1977.

_____. *Irreparable Harm: A Firsthand Account of How One Agent Took on the CIA in an Epic Battle over Free Speech.* New York: Random House, 2001.

Stone, G. R. *Perilous Times: Free Speech in Wartime.* New York: Norton, 2004.

_____. *Top Secret: When Our Government Keeps Us in the Dark.* Lanham, Md.: Rowman and Littlefield, 2007.

_____. *War and Liberty: An American Dilemma, 1790 to the Present.* New York: Norton, 2007.

Ungar, S. J. *The Papers and the Papers: An Account of the Legal and Political Battle over the Pentagon Papers.* New York: E. P. Dutton, 1972.

Wiener, J. *Gimme Some Truth: The John Lennon FBI Files.* Berkeley: University of California Press, 1999.

Wiggins, J. R. *Freedom or Secrecy.* New York: Oxford University Press, 1964.

# Notes

## Preface

1. For a great rundown of the facts on increasing secrecy, see OpenTheGovernment.org's annual "Secrecy Report Card" (www.openthegovernment.org/otg/SecrecyRC_2009.pdf). Other reports documenting increased secrecy include the Obama Administration Secrecy/Transparency Scorecard by the Collaboration on Government Secrecy (2010), http://www.wcl.american.edu/lawandgov/cgs/about.cfm; "Homefront Confidential" (2005), by the Reporters Committee for Freedom of the Press (www.rcfp.org/homefront-confidential); "Government Secrecy: Decisions without Democracy" (2007), by David Banisar (www.openthegovernment.org/otg/govtsecrecy.pdf); "Secrecy in the Bush Administration" (2004), by Rep. Henry A. Waxman (www.fas.org/sgp/library/waxman.pdf); and "The Lost Stories" (2003), by Jennifer LaFleur for the Reporters Committee for Freedom of the Press (www.rcfp.org/loststories).
2. Based on an analysis by David Cuillier of 32 state public records audits conducted nationally from 1992 through 2004, presented at the national Society of Professional Journalists conference, September 10, 2004, New York.

## Chapter 1. Records that matter

1. Michael J. Sniffen, "Study Questions Deportation Effort; Few People Were Targeted on Charges Related to Terrorism," Associated Press article in *Houston Chronicle*, May 28, 2007, A8.
2. Sara Kehaulani Goo, "Airport Finds That More Screeners Are Questionable," *Washington Post*, June 12, 2003, A3.
3. Ibid.
4. Laura Meckler, "Air-Security Fines Under Scrutiny—Analysis of Data Finds Wide Disparities in TSA's Penalties for Travelers Carrying Banned Items," *Wall Street Journal*, June 28, 2005, D1.
5. Colleen O'Connor, "Katrina, Then Culture Shock," *Denver Post*, September 25, 2005, L1.
6. "Files prove Pentagon is profiling reporters," *Stars and Stripes*, August 27, 2009, www.stripes.com/article.asp?section=104&article=64401.

7. Justin Mayo and Glenn Leshner, "Assessing the Credibility of Computer-Assisted Reporting," *Newspaper Research Journal* 21 (Fall 2000): 68–82.

## Chapter 2. Develop a document state of mind

1. See the Pulitzer Prize–winning coverage in Nigel Jacquiss, "The 30-Year Secret," *Willamette Week,* May 12, 2004, http://wweek.com/editorial/3028/5091.
2. Harold L. Cross, *The People's Right to Know* (New York: Columbia University Press, 1953), xiii.
3. John Adams, A *Dissertation on the Canon and Feudal Law* (1765), www.ashbrook.org/library/18/adams/canonlaw.html.
4. See the 2006 study by the Coalition of Journalists for Open Government, www.spj.org/rrr.asp?ref=31&t=foia, and the study by the Heritage Foundation, www.heritage.org/Press/MediaCenter/FOIA.cfm.
5. J. G. Randall, *Constitutional Problems under Lincoln* (New York: D. Appleton and Company, 1926).
6. Stephen Lamble, "Freedom of Information, a Finnish Clergyman's Gift to Democracy," *Freedom of Information Review* 97 (February 2002): 2–8; available online at http://members.optusnet.com.au/~slamble/freedom_of_information.html#_ednref27. Also, find more information at the Anders Chydenius Foundation Web site: www.chydenius.net.
7. Ibid.
8. See the state of right to know laws around the world at www.freedominfo.org.
9. Scott Reinardy, "Beyond Satisfaction: Journalists Doubt Career Intentions as Organizational Support Diminishes and Job Satisfaction Declines," *Atlantic Journal of Communication* 17 (July 2009): 126–139.

## Chapter 3. Become an access law expert

1. Allan R. Adler, "Litigation under the Federal Freedom of Information Act and Privacy Act, 1990" (Washington, D.C.: American Civil Liberties Union, June 1990).
2. "Freedom of Information Act Guide" (Washington, D.C.: U.S. Department of Justice, Office of Information Policy, March 2007).
3. Wendell Cochran, "You Have the Right to Remain Silent: FOIA in the Bush Administration," presentation at the Investigative Reporters and Editors national conference, June 2007, Phoenix, Ariz.

## Chapter 4. The hunt

1. Eric Nalder, "In Seattle, Old Warrants Never Die," *Seattle Times,* October 27, 1997, http://community.seattletimes.nwsource.com/archive/?date=19971027&slug=2568710.

2. Alexandra Berzon, "Construction Deaths," *Las Vegas Sun,* March 30, 2008. See story compilation at www.lasvegassun.com/news/topics/construction-deaths.

3. Debbie Cenziper, Oscar Corral and Larry Lebowitz, "House of Lies: Miami's Crisis," *Miami Herald,* June 3, 2007. See the "How it was done" explanation at www.miamiherald.com/multimedia/news/houseoflies2/facts.html.

4. Debbie Cenziper and Sara Cohen, "Forced Out: The Cost of D.C.'s Condo Boom," *Washington Post,* March 8, 2008, www.washingtonpost.com/wp-srv/metro/forcedout/index.html.

## Chapter 5. Strategies for effective requests

1. For a good description of access to places, records and meetings on tribal reservations, see Reporters Committee for Freedom of the Press, "Reporter's Guide to American Indian Law," www.rcfp.org/americanindian/index.html.

2. Roger Fisher and William Ury, *Getting to Yes: Negotiating Agreement without Giving In* (New York: Penguin Books, 1991); also check out Ury's other books, including *Getting Past No: Negotiating with Difficult People* (New York: Bantam, 1991).

3. Robert B. Cialdini, *Influence: Science and Practice* (Needham Heights, Mass.: Allyn and Bacon, 2001).

## Chapter 6. How to overcome denials

1. For a great rundown on increasing secrecy, see OpenTheGovernment. org's annual "Secrecy Report Card" (www.openthegovernment.org/otg/SecrecyRC_2009.pdf). Other reports documenting increased secrecy include "Homefront Confidential" (2005), by the Reporters Committee for Freedom of the Press (www.rcfp.org/homefrontconfidential); "Government Secrecy: Decisions without Democracy" (2007), by David Banisar (www.openthegovernment.org/otg/govtsecrecy.pdf); "Secrecy in the Bush Administration" (2004), by Rep. Henry A. Waxman (www.fas.org/sgp/library/waxman.pdf) and "The Lost Stories" (2003), by Jennifer LaFleur for the Reporters Committee for Freedom of the Press (www.rcfp.org/loststories).

2. Study conducted by one of the book's authors, David Cuillier, in 2004 on behalf of AccessNorthwest at Washington State University.

3. Wendell Cochran and Jonathan Katz, "FOIA Requests Increasingly Denied for Privacy, Not Security, Grounds," *IRE Journal* (July 2003); also, new data presented by Cochran at the Investigative Reporters and Editors national conference in 2007 in Phoenix.

4. See "40 Years of FOIA, 20 Years of Delay" (2007), by The National Security Archive (www.gwu.edu/~nsarchiv/NSAEBB/NSAEBB224/index.htm), which follows up on a similar study, "Outstanding Freedom of Information Requests Date to 1980s" (2003), also by The National Security Archive (www.gwu.edu/~nsarchiv/NSAEBB/NSAEBB102/press.htm).

5. David Cuillier, "Access Attitudes: Importance of Community Engagement in Support for Press Access to Government Records," *Journalism and Mass Communication Quarterly* (Winter 2008): 95; David Cuillier, "The Public's Concern for Privacy Invasion and Its Relationship to Support for Press Access to Government Records," *Newspaper Research Journal* (Fall 2004): 95–103; Paul D. Driscoll, Sigmund L. Splichal, Michael B. Salwen and Bruce Garrison, "Public Support for Access to Government Records: A National Survey," in Charles N. Davis and Sigmund L. Splichal, eds., *Access Denied: Freedom of Information in the Information Age* (Ames: Iowa State University Press, 2000), 23–36; Suzanne J. Piotrowski and Gregg G. Van Ryzin, "Citizen Attitudes Toward Transparency in Local Government," *The American Review of Public Administration* 37, no. 3 (2007): 306–323.
6. Presented by Wendell Cochran at the Investigative Reporters and Editors conference, June 2007, Phoenix.
7. Harry Hammitt, "Mediation without Litigation" (2007), National Freedom of Information Coalition (www.nfoic.org/hammitt_mediation_without_litigation). Also see Daxton Stewart, "Managing Conflict over Access: A Typology of Sunshine Law Dispute Resolution Systems," *Journal of Media Law and Ethics* 1, nos. 1/2 (Winter/Spring 2009): 49–82.
8. Scott Shane, "A.C.L.U. Lawyers Mine Documents for Truth," *New York Times*, August 29, 2009, A4.

## Chapter 7. Going digital

1. Randy Ludlow and Jill Riepenhoff, "Fit to Drive?" *Columbus Dispatch*, February 11, 2007, A1.
2. Gavin Off, "Crime on Campus," *Tulsa World*, April 5, 2009, A1.
3. Andy Hall and Phil Brinkman, "From Dog Track to Their Doom," *Wisconsin State Journal*, May 14, 2000, 1A.
4. For a state-by-state guide to obtaining government data, see Reporters Committee for Freedom of the Press, "Access to Electronic Records" (2003), www.rcfp.org/elecaccess; also Reporters Committee for Freedom of the Press, "Electronic Access to Court Records" (2007), www.rcfp.org/ecourt/index.html.
5. Melisma Cox, "The Development of Computer-Assisted Reporting," paper presented to the Newspaper Division of the Association for Education in Journalism and Mass Communication Southeast Colloquium, March 17–18, 2000, University of North Carolina at Chapel Hill.
6. Bruce Garrison, "Computer-Assisted Reporting Near Complete Adoption," *Newspaper Research Journal* (Winter 2001): 65–79.
7. Scott R. Maier, "Digital Diffusion in Newsrooms: The Uneven Advance of Computer-Assisted Reporting," *Newspaper Research Journal* (Spring 2000): 95–110.

## Chapter 8. Understand how public officials think

1. Michael G. Powell, "The Emergence and Institutionalization of Regimes of Transparency and Anti-Corruption in Poland," Ph.D. dissertation for Rice University, 2006, UMI Number 3216763.
2. Michele Bush Kimball, "Law Enforcement Records Custodians' Decision-Making Behaviors in Response to Florida's Public Records Law," *Communication Law and Policy* 8 (2003): 313–360.
3. Suzanne J. Piotrowski, *Governmental Transparency in the Path of Administrative Reform* (Albany: State University of New York Press, 2007).
4. Thomas Susman, "Delay and the Freedom of Information Act: Senator Cornyn's Legislative Prescriptions," *Open Government* 1, no. 2 (2005): www.opengovjournal.org/article/viewArticle/326.
5. Piotrowski, *Governmental Transparency in the Path of Administrative Reform.*
6. Alasdair Roberts, "Spin Control and Freedom of Information: Lessons for the United Kingdom from Canada," *Public Administration* 83, no. 1 (2005): 1–25. Also see Alasdair Roberts, "Administrative Discretion and the Access to Information Act: An 'Internal Law' on Open Government," *Canadian Public Administration* 45, no. 3 (2002): 175–194.
7. Kimball, "Law Enforcement Records Custodians' Decision-Making Behaviors in Response to Florida's Public Records Law," 346.
8. "States Failing FOI Responsiveness," Columbia, Miss.: National Freedom of Information Coalition and Better Government Association, 2007, www.nfoic.org/bga.
9. Yunjuan Luo and Anthony L. Fargo, "Measuring Attitudes about the Indiana Public Access Counselor's Office: An Empirical Study," 2008, available at the Indiana Coalition for Open Government Web site, http://indianacog.org/files/PAC_final2.pdf.
10. Stephanie Warsmith, "Akron Swamped with Public Record Requests," *Akron Beacon Journal,* April 7, 2009, http://www.ohio.com/news/42570696.html.

## Chapter 9. Putting it together

1. David Weaver and Leanne Daniels, "Public Opinion on Investigative Reporting in the 1980s," *Journalism Quarterly* (Spring 1992): 146–155.
2. Justin Mayo and Glenn Leshner, "Assessing the Credibility of Computer-Assisted Reporting," *Newspaper Research Journal* (Fall 2000): 68–82.
3. Ryan Gabrielson and Paul Giblin, "Reasonable Doubt," *East Valley Tribune,* five-part series, starting July 9, 2008, www.eastvalleytribune.com/page/reasonable_doubt.
4. Roy Peter Clark, e-mail to David Cuillier, April 24, 2009.

5. Shanto Iyengar and Donald R. Kinder, "Vivid Cases and Lead Stories," in *News That Matters: Television and American Opinion* (Chicago: University of Chicago Press, 1987), 34–46.

6. Tom Kennedy and Paul McEnroe, "The Informant," *The Star Tribune*, April 23, 2009, www.startribune.com/local/43226777.html.

7. "Larry Craig Investigation," *The Idaho Statesman*, www.idahostatesman .com/larrycraig.

8. Society of Professional Journalists Code of Ethics, first written in 1973 and last updated in 1996, www.spj.org/ethicscode.asp.

9. "Leaks Spark Debate among Journalists, Legislative Staff," Reporters Committee for Freedom of the Press, March 19, 2002, www.rcfp.org/news/ 2002/0319leaks.html.

10. "Federal Government Still Viewed as Secretive; President's FOI Orders Get High Marks," survey results available at the national Sunshine Week Web site, March 13, 2009, www.sunshineweek.org/sunshineweek/secrecy_poll_09.

11. David Cuillier, "The Public's Concern for Privacy Invasion and Its Relationship to Support for Press Access to Government Records," *Newspaper Research Journal* (Fall 2004): 95–103.

12. Random-digit dial phone survey conducted March 2006. See David Cuillier, "Access Attitudes: A Social Learning Approach to Examining Community Engagement and Support for Press Access to Government Records," *Journalism and Mass Communication Quarterly* (Fall 2008): 549–576.

13. Cuillier, "The Public's Concern for Privacy Invasion."

14. Cuillier, "Access Attitudes"; David Cuillier and Suzanne J. Piotrowski, "Internet Information Seeking and Its Relation to Support for Access to Government Records," *Government Information Quarterly* (July 2009): 441–449.

15. David Cuillier, Blythe Duell and Jeff Joireman, "FOI Friction: The Thought of Death, National Security Values and Polarization of Attitudes toward Freedom of Information," *Open Government* (Winter 2009): www.opengov journal.org.

# Index